Who Gets Sick

"This is the best book of its kind....It is beautifully written, entertaining, and richly informative. It would be useful not only to intelligent laymen but to physicians as well."

—Stewart Wolf, M.D., past president,
American Psychosomatic Society

"Highly readable. This book is unprecedented in its depth and simple usefulness."

—*Brain/Mind Bulletin*

"A very significant work! I wish every pastor and theologian would read it."

—Rev. Robert H. Schuller, D.D.,
author of *The Be Happy Attitudes*

"Timely and excellent....a remarkable encyclopedic compilation. It should be kept handy as a desk reference."

—American Association for the
Advancement of Science

"*Who Gets Sick* is great! A 'must' on the 'read' list for almost anyone who has wondered, 'How come I'm sick?'...It helps us feel like active participants in life rather than victims."

—Leslie B. Kadis, Clinical Professor of Psychiatry,
Stanford School of Medicine

Who Gets Sick

How Beliefs, Moods, and Thoughts Affect Your Health

Blair Justice, Ph.D.

JEREMY P. TARCHER, INC.
Los Angeles
In cooperation with Peak Press, Houston

Copyright acknowledgments appear on page 381.

Library of Congress Cataloging-in-Publication Data

Justice, Blair.
  Who gets sick / Blair Justice.
    p.   cm.
  Bibliography
  Includes index.
  ISBN 0-87477-507-8 (pbk)
    1. Medicine and psychology.   2. Sick—Psychology.   I. Title.
  R726.5.J87 1988
  616',001'9 — dc19   87-18172
                                                                       CIP

Copyright ©1987 by Blair Justice
Originally published by Houston: Peak Press, 1987.

Jeremy P. Tarcher, Inc.
5858 Wilshire Blvd., Suite 200
Los Angeles, CA 90036

Manufactured in the United States of America
10 9 8 7 6 5 4 3

Book design by Joan Stoliar

To Rita,
for her love and support
during the eight years it
took to do this book.

Contents

Introduction: The Heady Revolution

We're in the midst of as dramatic a transformation as has ever occurred in science.[1]

This book is about the heady revolution that is going on around us—how the new knowledge about the brain is transforming our understanding of why we get sick and what we can do about it. The book is about how something as seemingly intangible as the way we think can be converted into something as tangible as disease. It is for people who want to know what the evidence is that our attitudes, beliefs and ways of reacting to life affect whether we get sick. It is for those who realize that illness is something other than "a matter of random chance, not to be averted."[2]

No one factor determines who gets sick and who does not. Whether we are talking about heart attacks, cancer or AIDS, "cofactors"—not single causes—are responsible.[3] And a key cofactor, now intensely researched as part of the new science of biological and molecular psychology, is the cognitive—how our heads affect our health. Since it is now known that the brain has power to regulate all bodily functions, disregulation of the central nervous system is increasingly being implicated as a contributing factor in disease.[4] What goes on in our heads, then, has far-reaching influence on not only our nervous system but also the immune system, the hormone system and our health.

Most health professionals, as well as patients, concede that the mind has something to do with physical illness, but few know how the two affect each other or what the evidence is that they are related. Even fewer can keep up with the mushrooming research, from the molecular to the behavioral, that generates new findings almost daily on the profound effect of the brain on the body.

Connecting Mind and Body

For our beliefs to influence our physical functions, there must not only be pathways and channels connecting head to toe but also some system of messengers for the brain to issue directives to the body. An explosion of knowledge in the neurosciences has uncovered dozens of chemical messengers that the brain uses for its far-ranging influence in the body and communication between cells. Among these potent compounds are stress hormones and fast-acting neurotransmitters that vary in magnitude or kind depending—at least, in part—on our attitudes, moods and ways of reacting to problems. How we experience something—how we define our situations—has effects on the very molecules that act as cell receptors for the neurochemicals, and this kind of remarkable influence is a concrete example of how the mind/body barrier has evaporated.[5]

But if mental states—thoughts, attitudes, moods—do, in fact, cause neural events—changes in brain cells and their activity—how does this effect occur? The answer seems to lie at the fascinating intersection between the new physics and neuroscience, where the intangible (thinking) is now seen as perfectly capable of affecting the tangible (nerve endings that release chemical transmitters), somewhat as the electric field around physical bodies is a nonmaterial force that produces material consequences.[6]

Our Changing Brains

The heady revolution has overthrown a number of myths about the brain. Contrary to the long-held belief that the structure of the adult brain does not change, mounting evidence from animal studies shows that the cerebral cortex can actually grow in response to stimulating environments and activity.[7] Rather than losing brain cells as we grow older, we can actually extend our neural connections—just as old rats become smarter and run mazes better. Both brain chemistry and structure are affected by the way we experience and perceive the environment.

As neurons change their signals in the brain and to the body as they respond to our perceptions, they seem to make switches in the communication molecules they use to transmit messages. Our brains, then, are distinguished by their dynamic plasticity, making them highly responsive to the environment and our interpretation of it.[8]

Unravelling some of the chemistry of thinking is helping to build the foundation of an exciting new field of molecular psychology, which is devoted to probing the interaction between chemical molecules in the brain and our cognitions and behavior. And what is being found is that just as brain chemicals can change thoughts, so too can thoughts change the chemicals—and how well we feel and function.

"Breakthrough" is a word used with caution in science, but the strides made in understanding the chemical machinery of our cognitions—our thoughts, feelings, perceptions and experiences—are dramatic. Sir John Eccles, a Nobel laureate in neurophysiology, calls "extraordinary" the new knowledge of how the mental can affect the physical at the most basic level. Even color-coded pictures of some of the effects of the mental on the physical are increasingly common.

Brain scanning is permitting us for the first time to picture what is going on in our heads as we worry, anticipate and change our thoughts and moods—or as we get sick and recover. For instance, positron emission tomography (PET) is providing a "window into the brain" as the brain functions or falters from a deficiency or excess of the chemical messengers that largely regulate our mental and physical health.[9] Brain scanners, which are a boon to medical diagnosis and science, have also been described as promising "to do for human psychology what the telescope did for astronomy and the microscope for biology."[10]

Those Who Still Doubt

Despite this growing evidence, there are still doubters who do not believe that what goes on in our heads profoundly affects the health of our bodies. Some people do not want to believe, because if the brain has such power over what happens in our bodies, then we might have to watch our attitudes if we wish to be healthy. Others gladly accept such responsibility in return for the control it bestows on each of us in contributing to our own physical destinies.

Still others, who continue to believe simplistically in single causes (viruses, genes, etc.) as sufficient to explain disease, angrily charge that anyone who suggests that our attitudes and moods contribute to whether we get sick is "blaming the victim" and implying the person "caused" his own illness.[11] This is not true. Recognizing that mind and body are one—with the evidence clearly showing that each constantly affects the other—is not blaming the victim but acknowledging that disease is multidetermined, and the mind cannot be ignored as an influence. How important the influence is will vary with the disease or the stage of illness.

Many professionals, as well as people in general, have been reluctant to accept the role of the mind in health and disease because they simply could not understand how having certain attitudes or moods could make any difference one way or the other in whether a person gets sick. How could being cynical or pessimistic or believing everything is beyond control possibly do damage to the body? How could our thinking style affect our immune system? The biological mechanisms seemed all too mysterious.

The How of Illness

A primary purpose of this book is to present what has been demonstrated about the part that our heads play in why, when and *how* we get sick. One of the reasons the cognitive has been neglected is that the evidence was lacking on the ways, the mechanisms, by which psychological factors affect physical processes.

To show the physical impact, for instance, of what happens when people perceive no control in their lives awaited development of instrumentation and techniques that could measure fluctuations in hormone and immune responses in the course of daily activity. Detecting the degree to which a person's hostile attitude correlates with blockage of his coronary arteries required the bringing together of angiography and psychological inventories.

Determining the effect of poor coping on the natural killer cells that help defend us against cancer has come only after the discovery that such cells exist and can be compromised by stress chemicals. The development of monoclonal antibodies has made it more possible to identify and quantify specific subunits of the immune system, like helper and suppressor T-cells, which are affected by our stressful appraisals or ways of viewing things.

The ability to use saliva, instead of blood samples, to detect and measure our stress hormones has facilitated research on how our attitudes and coping styles influence our physical health. It is now possible to demonstrate the differences that such feelings as love, intimacy and affiliation—as opposed to the need for power and domination—have on certain antibody levels.[12]

Resistance to the Revolution

Physicians and scientists who doubt that there is any physical impact of thoughts and feelings have resisted the findings of mind-body research. A distinguished psychologist at Harvard sought out a Nobel Prize-winning scientist to consult about the ways that thoughts and motives can affect the immune system.[13] He was promptly told that there are no psychological effects on the immune system. When the psychologist noted that receptor sites for stress hormones have been found on a variety of immune system cells, the noted scientist admitted that was true but denied that our heads have anything to do with the state of our immunity against illness.

Even Eccles, speaking before a packed house at the annual meeting of the Society for Neuroscience in 1985, became the target of heated rebuttal when he presented "the first statement" on how neural events—such as thoughts—could affect the probability of neurotransmitter release, using quantum mechanics as a model.[6] As Candace Pert, whose landmark work on receptors helped spark the neuroscience explosion, has observed:

> Scientific revolutions are very interesting. The way they happen is that most people deny them and resist them. And then there's more and more of an explosion, and there's a paradigm shift.[14]

Emotions in the Body?

The emerging new scientific model provides for the influence of the mind on the brain and body, of the nonmaterial on the material. Says Pert, who is chief of the section on brain biochemistry at the National Institute of Mental Health: "I'm no longer interested in studying merely the brain. I'm ready now to study the mind. And I think it's now possible to do."[15]

Pert sees the "body as the outward manifestation of the mind" and body and brain as inseparable.[16] Evidence of that inseparability comes from the discovery that a number of the chemical messengers in the body are the same as the ones in the brain. Among these "communication molecules" are neuropeptides that regulate our moods and emotions. Because some can be found in the intestines as well as in the limbic system—our "feeling brain"—Pert says, "the emotions are not just in the brain, they're in the body." Having a "gut feeling" about something, then, is more than just a figure of speech.

Effects on Molecular Level

Out of the new knowledge the heady revolution has generated comes the recognition that the brain, nervous system, immune system and endocrine system may be so closely linked that they constitute a single regulatory network in the body.[17] How we view something in our environment and the way we react trigger activity in the hypothalamus and limbic area of the brain, leading to the release of hormones, which then influence the white blood cells of our immune systems and affect our vulnerability to disease. White cells, as well as brain cells and nerve fibers, may release stress chemicals when we view something as a threat.[18] And, because the body seems regulated by a single interlinking network, the immune system influences the nervous system just as the nervous system affects the immune system.

Direct effects on even the molecular level may occur if we chronically cope poorly and are highly distressed. Recent research suggests that in addition to impairment of our immune system, another important defense against cancer—our DNA repair—may be compromised.[19]

But most of medicine continues to pretend that mind and body are separate and that the pathways by which attitudes and moods physically affect our organs and tissue are really imaginary. We are told that too much is being made of the psyche's influence on health and that simple "physical" explanations will be found to account for the major disorders, as if mind and brain have no physical reality.[11]

"Medical Marvels" and Crisis

Although much of the evidence on disease mechanisms is new, studies linking psychological factors to physiological effects have been accumulating for several decades. Yet the heady revolution has made little difference in the practice of medicine and the treatment of patients. Medical practice largely remains wedded to a mind-less concept of disease that is clearly limited, and in many cases, unhelpful.

Much of the armamentarium of medicine is increasingly irrelevant to the disorders that afflict people today. Medicine's record in controlling heart disease, strokes, cancer, arthritis, mental illness and other chronic diseases is not impressive. The "medical marvels" that physicians can bring to bear on disease apply to perhaps 20 percent of those who get sick—victims of trauma, some acute illness but not chronic disease.[20] Medicine's crisis has to do with the 80 percent that need doctors who have a good understanding of the mind as well as the body and who appreciate the interaction between the two.

Many of our current maladies are strongly influenced, both in onset and duration, by the way we think and behave—demanding no frustrations, seeing problems as overwhelming, looking for the worst, alienating ourselves and others, smoking, overdrinking, overeating, not exercising. But medicine considers psychosocial factors peripherally, if at all, and continues to emphasize pathogenic germs and other agents as "the cause" of illness and drugs as "the cure." Most of the leading health problems are due to a disregulation or imbalance of bodily functions, stemming, for example, from a deficiency or excess of neurochemicals. To speak of "the cause" of disease today, as if some virus will be found solely responsible, is anachronistic.

Despite these limitations, medicine is still the beacon to which people flock for health care. Although some of its researchers are leaders of the heady revolution in science, most of its practitioners are not prepared to prevent or effectively treat the major health problems we face.

Thrust Toward Cancer Prevention

Cancer is an example. Although claims are made yearly that the cure rate is steadily improving, people with the leading kinds of cancer are no more likely to survive than they were a generation ago.[21] Deaths from cancer continue to rise yearly in the United States, even though we have spent about $18.5 billion on research since the national Cancer Act of 1971 was passed and "the war on cancer" declared. By comparison, it cost about $10 billion to develop and launch the first space shuttle.[22]

Even with all the powerful anticancer drugs, new forms of radiation therapy and surgical approaches, little progress has been made in the last 25 years on the biggest cancer killers—cancer of the lung, the breast, the colon, and the prostate. Since many tumors metastasize quite easily, researchers have recognized that radiation therapy and surgery will never be "the answer," and no magic bullet is likely to be found.

Despite the lack of major therapeutic advances, there is now "high confidence" among biomedical researchers about making a significant impact on cancer.[23] A better understanding of the disease is emerging from fundamental research on how cancer develops. As a result, "cancer finally has the look of a soluble problem."[24] Basic molecular discoveries and the "astonishing technology" of recombinant DNA have turned cancer research into "something like a running hunt. The fox is not yet within sight, but it is at least known that there is indeed a fox, and this is a great change from the sense of things 20 years ago."[23] Exciting new insights are thus being gained on what cancer is, how it arises from genes we all have and need for life, and how most of us have defenses that protect us when tumor cells try to develop.

A second reason for optimism comes from the recognition that the majority of cancers seem to be initiated or promoted by factors we can control. "Diet and nutrition appear to be related to the largest number of human cancers, tobacco smoking is related to about 30 to 40 percent. . . ."[25] Other known risk factors include alcohol, chemicals and drugs.

Our moods seem to be a strong influence in what foods we choose to eat, and the more people perceive uncontrollable stress in their lives, the more they may turn to diets that place them at greater risk of cancer as well as heart disease.[26] What we can do mentally and behaviorally —such as watching more carefully what we eat—is an emerging new theme in cancer prevention efforts. Psychosocial factors are strongly suspected of promoting the growth and spread of tumors by suppressing the immune system, which apparently plays a big part in keeping incipient cancer cells from developing.[27]

That our attitudes and coping reactions may contribute to whether we get cancer is an idea now supported by evidence beyond anecdotal and retrospective studies. When the prestigious *Science* magazine published a review of the subject, the title given the report was "Cancer and the Mind: How Are They Connected?" not "Are They Connected?"[28]

Overselling Germs and Stress

Just as we have been oversold on the notion that we are helpless victims in a world full of germs and other malevolent forces, the popular wisdom in recent years has also told us that stress is making us sick. Stress is depicted as another one of those powerful external agents that victimize us, so it is not that different from its kissing cousin, germ theory.

The evidence disputing both these ideas comes out of a larger concept of disease that shifts the focus from the stresses of life and the ubiquitous bugs of the world to how we respond to them. It turns out that how we react is more important than is the fact that life can be hard or fraught with peril.

This book is for users of health services as well as practicing and aspiring health professionals who would like to know what the evidence is for this larger concept of who gets sick. It starts with the new understanding of why germs do not explain disease, of the difference between people who get exposed to microorganisms and remain healthy and those who become ill. We then look at why stress also is not the cause of our ill health. The reasons tell us something about the profound shift that is taking place in traditional views of disease etiology.

In *Who Gets Sick: How Beliefs, Moods, and Thoughts Affect Your Health,* we explore the key role of recently discovered neurotransmitters, brain hormones and other chemical messengers in the functioning of the body and some of the ways by which these powerful molecules play a part in illness and disease. How the chemical messengers of the body are affected by our attitudes and reactions to stress is examined. We trace the pioneering work on "giving up" as a major factor that precipitates illness and look at how people postpone their deaths until after some special occasion. We end with the growing new evidence suggesting that positive attitudes and beliefs can protect and restore our health by turning on self-healing systems.

PART 1
Germs and Stress

1. It Takes More Than Germs

It's very hard to give tuberculosis, a cold, or infectious hepatitis to someone.[1]

Even . . . carcinogens, which are various chemicals that produce cancerous changes in cells, are not sufficient to produce disease.[2]

A new understanding of why some people get sick when exposed to germs while others remain healthy is radically revising the popular concept of what causes illness. How resistant we are to the microbes in our lives is a function of how well we are coping, which in turn depends largely on how we look at problems—our "cognitive appraisal"—and the chemical changes that our thoughts produce in our brains and bodies.

Growing knowledge about the influence of people's attitudes and appraisals on their physiological functions is forging a heady revolution in health sciences. Recent research has demonstrated, for instance, how our immunity is affected by what goes on in our heads, by hormonal changes that are brought on from poor coping or by direct effects of our central nervous systems.[3]

Our cognitions (thoughts, beliefs, attitudes) and the social support we perceive in our lives can alter the levels of our hormones and neurotransmitters, the chemical messengers that carry on communication between our cells and largely govern the activity of many of our physical processes (see Chapter 4).[4]

An expanded explanation of disease is emerging that is "bio-psycho-social," meaning that a person's mind, body and environment together determine whether he gets sick.[5] Disease is not so much the effect of noxious, external forces—the "bugs," both literal and figurative, in our lives—as it is the faulty efforts of our minds and bodies to deal with them.[6] Most of the "bugs," the literal kind, already reside in our bodies.[6] When our responses to problems in life are excessive or deficient, the central nervous system and hormones act on our immune defenses in such a way that the microbes aid and abet disease.[7] The balance is upset between us and our resident pathogens.

Only If We Are Vulnerable

The term "pathogen" or germ, then, does not mean something that invariably "causes" illness or disease. Pathogens refer to bacteria, viruses or other microorganisms that have the *potential* to induce disease.[8] Physician Andrew Weil, research associate in ethnopharmacology at Harvard and author of *Health and Healing*, reminds us:

> . . . this point must be stressed: external, material objects are never causes of disease, merely agents waiting to cause specific symptoms in susceptible hosts. . . .Rather than warring on disease agents with the hope (vain, I suspect) of eliminating them, we ought to worry more about strengthening resistance to them and learning to live in balance with them more of the time.[9]

If we have poor coping skills, deficient social support and high stress, then the internal balance of our bodies may be easily upset and our resistance lowered. Weil adds: "At a time of impending breakdown of equilibrium, an agent of disease might find fertile ground in which to develop or might act as the straw that breaks the camel's back."[9]

Illness or disease, then, occurs more from our vulnerability than from external agents that are "the cause" of our health problems. The more vulnerable we are, the more risk we run of getting sick. The factors that place us at risk range from our attitudes and appraisals in coping with stress to the kind of food we eat and the genes we inherit.

Our mind and behavior, our environment and our genetic predispositions are the common contributors to disease.[2] The relative importance of each of these three spheres varies with the disease in question. A few diseases, like cystic fibrosis, are almost entirely genetic and require very little "push" from psychological or environmental influences to develop. On the other hand, the most prevalent diseases today are significantly affected by our coping styles (including our thinking) and our environment. Carcinogens in the environment or our diets may produce cancerous changes in our cells, but the evidence suggests that malignancy will not occur unless other risk factors are present and our immune systems are depressed.[2]

No Single "Cause" or "Cure"

Risk factors—anything in our thinking, behavior, body or environment that increases the likelihood of illness—are opposed by "resistance resources" we possess. These may include an optimistic way of looking at life, a good social support system, and a strong set of genes. The balance between risk factors and resistance resources largely determines whether we get sick or stay healthy.[10]

How much risk a factor may contribute to our getting sick has been established for various diseases. For instance, cigarette smoking doubles our risk of developing coronary heart disease.[11] High serum cholesterol, hypertension and Type A behavior have each been found to contribute about the same amount of risk for CHD as does smoking. When two of these factors are present, the risk is four times greater; when we have three risk factors, the risk is eightfold higher.[11]

Although heart disease and all other leading causes of death and disability today require the presence of multiple risk factors, there is still "mounting pressure to explain the appearance of most chronic diseases on the basis of such single variables as cigarette smoking, alcohol consumption or exposure to other hazardous substances. . . ."[12] Smoking, drinking and hazardous substances by themselves do not "cause" disease, although "this assumption is widely held despite the fact that the majority of those thus exposed do not succumb prematurely to the disorder in question."[12]

Fund-raising campaigns urge the public to "fight disease" with dollars so that "the cause" and "cure" can be found for everything from cancer to chronic ileitis. Internist Caroline Thomas of Johns Hopkins observes that medicine's "notable success in eradicating specific infectious diseases by means of specific agents has led to the general belief that chronic disease can be similarly abolished when the single 'cause' for each disorder is found." But she notes:

> Thirty years of intensive research . . . have so far failed to discover the single "cause" of cancer, heart attack, or mental illness. The time has now come to consider another concept of disease etiology. . . .[12]

Normal Processes Gone Awry

The biopsychosocial risk-factor concept of disease is a marked departure from germ theory, which has been the cornerstone of the medical model. Although medicine no longer attempts to explain all illness in terms of a specific microorganism for every disease, its model still suggests that pathology is largely caused by foreign forces that invade our bodies and damage our organs.[13]

Under the newer concept of disease, tissue damage is seen as more the result of normal bodily processes gone awry or disrupted than it is the dirty work of microbes or other external culprits. These processes include the activity of the neurotransmitters in our brain cells, the stress hormones of our endocrine glands and nervous systems, and the helper and suppressor cells of our immune functioning. When imbalances occur in these processes, pathology often results.

For example, excessive stress hormones—cortisol and catecholamines—can lead to artery damage, cholesterol buildup and heart disease.[14] As we will see, chronic high levels of these chemicals can diminish the activity of antibodies and natural killer cells that protect us against foreign invaders and tumors.[15] Deficient suppressor cells may permit overreaction of the immune system to the point that the body starts attacking itself, as in rheumatoid arthritis.[16] Imbalances between the sympathetic nervous system, which mostly accelerates functions of our bodies, and the parasympathetic system, which usually slows them down, may trigger cardiac arrest or arrhythmia.[17]

Disease as "A Way of Life"

What is becoming increasingly clear is that all these mechanisms of disease are connected with the brain and may be profoundly influenced by our mental processes. The meaning and interpretation we give to frustrations and problems of life can markedly affect whether our bodily processes are "too much or too little."[7] We need high levels of adrenaline (epinephrine), elevated blood sugar and other strong biochemical responses when we are physically threatened and we must literally fight or flee. But when we inappropriately and chronically evoke these reactions, the excesses can turn against us. By the way we define situations, we can call forth inappropriate chemical and nervous system reactions. When we habitually act as if a frustration, disappointment or loss is a matter of life and death and we "can't stand it," then we are calling forth correspondingly strong bodily responses that can make us vulnerable to disease.

If we see life, as many coronary-prone individuals do, as requiring us constantly to dominate people and things, such an attitude contributes to a "chronic disarray" of internal processes: excessive outpourings of cholesterol, triglycerides, norepinephrine, ACTH (adrenocorticotrophic hormone) and insulin, on the one hand, and a deficient circulating level of pituitary growth hormone, on the other.[18]

Evidence suggests that people who define their situations as hopeless may elicit an excessive conservation of oxygen, as if they were trying to hold their breath or "play dead" until hope returns. The vagal nerve reaction that is triggered can slow the heart to the point of cardiac arrest and sudden death.[19] Disease, even death, then, can come from our evoking reaction patterns that are meant to protect us when we are physically threatened but are destructive when used inappropriately to fight symbolic battles.

Stewart Wolf, a longtime clinical researcher in medicine and physiology now affiliated with Temple University in Philadelphia, has suggested that "disease is a way of life," the end result of a way that people react to life's problems.[20]

Poor Coping and Illness

The way we react to the daily hassles of life or to specific stressful events can mean the difference between "coming down with" an infection or remaining symptom-free. Since most of the microbes that afflict humans are already in our bodies, they play a part in disease only when other risk factors lower our immunity or otherwise increase our susceptibility.[6] As we have indicated, a risk factor is any characteristic, condition or behavior we have that increases our chances of getting sick. Smoking is a risk factor; so is a persistent perception of life as hopeless or uncontrollable.

Scientific recognition that germs cannot explain disease has grown as researchers began to pay attention to the uneven distribution of illness in groups of people exposed to the same conditions or environments. Lawrence Hinkle and his colleagues at Cornell Medical College in New York studied the illness patterns of more than 3,500 people over a 20-year period.[21] Included were five groups of workers and students who shared the same work environments or living conditions. Those in each group had approximately the same exposure to potential pathogenic microbes and other external agents identified with disease. But the amount of illness experienced by individuals in each group was far from equal. About one-fourth of the individuals experienced more than half of all the illnesses and over two-thirds of the total days of disability (see also Chapter 3).

For instance, one group was made up of 1,297 telephone operators, some of whom were frequently ill and others seldom sick. When women with a high absentee rate were compared with those who had a low rate, the researchers found that the frequently sick operators experienced illness "clusters" when they saw themselves as having great difficulty in coping with situations at work or home. Those who were more dissatisfied and discontented in general had more numerous illnesses.[22]

In all the groups studied, illness clusters were found. Although the researchers did not rule out the possiblity that constitutional differences might contribute to some people being more vulnerable to illness than others were, they noted that genetic variability could not explain why the illness episodes came in clusters. The clusters were associated with periods when the person was having trouble adapting to a situation perceived as stressful.

Illness clusters occurred around conflicts with parents, siblings and spouses, threats to status, loss of support and excessive demands from others. How the people defined such difficulties and reacted to them seemed to play an important part in whether illness occurred. On the role of germs and other external influences, Hinkle and his co-workers concluded:

> So far as we have been able to determine, physical hardship, geographic and climatic change, and changing exposures to toxic or infectious agents, are not the signifi-

cant variables. Only occasionally does it appear that the development of an isolated illness, or a cluster of illnesses, is simply the result of some fortuitous encounter with bacteria, trauma, or other influences arising from the physical environment.[23]

Another important finding in these pioneering studies was that a wide variety of illnesses and diseases was experienced by the workers and students. No special category of disease, such as peptic ulcer, asthma or arthritis, predominated. Later research has confirmed that the onset or course of virtually all disease is influenced by the physiological effects of the way people appraise troublesome situations and attempt to adapt to them. The Cornell investigators were among the first to object to the term "psychosomatic disorder," because it has been interpreted to mean that only a special group of diseases (like peptic ulcers) are subject to psychosocial influences.[21]

Hinkle and his group also followed for one year the illness episodes of 139 managerial employees in a corporation.[24] The managers were alike in age, sex, occupation, income, social and economic status, diet and hereditary backgrounds. Again, the researchers found that some of the employees had a large number of illnesses during the years and others had little sickness. Those in the frequent-illness group were high school graduates who had been made managers without having gone to college. Those in the low-illness group were college graduates. The first group perceived more threats and challenges in their lives than did the second group and had a greater number of physiological and psychological reactions.

Although physiological reactions are a function of the way we define difficulties in our lives and try to handle them, disease is the complex consequence of many factors acting in combination or in a certain sequence. A simple cause-and-effect relationship no more exists between cognitive appraisal and illness than between germs and disease. For instance, in the case of the managers, those with the more frequent illnesses not only perceived more threats but also smoked more. Smoking can serve as a person's attempt to relieve stress generated by perceiving frequent threats. Tissue damage may occur directly from our behavior—smoking or drinking—or indirectly from our excessive appraisals of threat, leading to heightened physiological reactions. In many instances, pathology is a result of a combination of both direct and indirect factors.

The same uneven distribution of illness that Hinkle observed was also found in a three-year study of air traffic controllers by psychiatrist Robert Rose and his coworkers at Boston University School of Medicine.[25] Twenty percent of the 416 controllers averaged more than five episodes a year of mild to moderate illness, mostly upper respiratory infections, asthma, viral disorders and gastrointestinal upsets. Another 20 percent had fewer than one episode per year. The frequently-sick men had lower morale (which was determined in advance of their illnesses) and greater job dissatisfaction. They also perceived more events in their lives away from work as stressful.

"Peaceful Coexistence" the Rule

For the American population at large, the majority of all acute cases of illness in any given year are upper respiratory infections. What evidence do we have that "bugs"—viruses and bacteria—are not "the cause" of our coughs, colds, congestion and sore throats? For decades, biological scientists have observed that most microbes are "ubiquitous in the environment" and "persist in the body without causing obvious harm under ordinary circumstances."[26] Endocrinologist John Mason, a pioneer stress researcher now at Yale Medical School, points out:

It is common, in fact, for many pathogenic microorganisms to be harbored within hosts without producing disease or illness. There is a complex assemblage of intervening "host resistance" machinery which has a major role in determining whether infection will progress into illness or not.[27]

If we get sick, then, chances are we did not suddenly "catch a bug" that caused our illness, but we probably did something to lower our immunity. Although the relationship is not simple between our thinking and behavior and our immune defenses, a connection does exist and psychosocial factors can pave the way for disease to occur.

Peaceful coexistence between microorganisms—such as streptococci, for example—and their human hosts is "the rule, while disease is the exception."[28] The question is: What determines which of us will develop an illness and which will not?

Infected But Not Ill

To investigate the question of who gets sick, pediatricians Roger Meyer and Robert Haggerty of Harvard Medical School did extensive examinations of 16 families, consisting of 100 persons, at periodic intervals for a year.[29] They made throat cultures on all family members every three weeks and did various laboratory and clinical tests for signs of streptococcal illness. More than 52 percent of the streptococcal acquisitions by family members were not associated with illness. In other words, tests established that for most of the infections that family members acquired, illness did not result.

All families had approximately the same potential contact with streptococci, as judged by their number of school-age children, degree of neighborhood crowding and other kinds of contacts, including the fathers' working environments. Throughout the study year, families commented on the connection between acute family crises and the onset of illness. The researchers determined that both streptococcal illnesses and other respiratory diseases were about four times more frequent after episodes the families defined as stressful.

Families with high levels of chronic stress had significantly more streptococcal illness as well as more acquisition of microorganisms. In 11 of the 16 families, parents were able to predict accurately which child in the family was more likely to become ill. For instance, in one family the parents and all four children were exposed to streptococci on the same day but only one child got sick. This was a daughter who was under increasing pressure during the week to learn her catechism for confirmation on Sunday.

Contrary to popular beliefs about respiratory infections being "caused" by cold drafts, changes in temperature, dampness and the like, the study found that family members who were exposed to wet and cold rarely became ill unless they were also tired. Besides fatigue, another physical condition known to lower resistance to illness is poor nutrition, although this factor was not directly tested in the 16-family study.

As we will see, viruses as well as bacteria usually require the contribution of other factors—such as inadequate coping or low moods—to produce illness. For example, herpes viruses seem to remain latent in the body until the immune system is "unbalanced" by negative moods or poor coping (see Chapter 8). Some diseases that have unclear or unknown etiology, such as systemic lupus erythematosis (SLE), may depend on a virus that becomes active only when a susceptible person is having trouble coping or feels chronically distressed.[30] Cognitive and emotional factors, then, are implicated in both the activation of viruses as well as the body's ability to resist and contain such agents.

Age as a Mediator

Other "mediators" that can contribute to our risk of getting sick include our genetic traits, our age, our prior experience with stress and whether we coped successfully, the context of the situation and how much support we perceive we have from others.[31] Mediators are anything that affects our perceptions of situations and our reactions to them.[32]

Age can be an influence in more than one way. Not only may our immune defenses diminish as we get older but also the meaning we give to stressful events differs depending on our age. For example, younger women seem to take a death in their families harder than do older women, perhaps because the older we get the more we anticipate death or learn to adjust to loss.[33] A young child, to whom learning her catechism and being confirmed are very important, may react much more intensely to a Sunday deadline that would an adult undergoing the same experience.

But regardless of age, if we are exposed to pathogenic agents such as streptococci when we are already having to contend with other stressors, our vulnerability will almost certainly be greater. If we are not dealing with other problems when we are faced with a stressor and if we see ourselves as being supported by family or friends, our susceptibility will likely be less. However, in the case of some physical stressors, such as powerful toxins or radiation, they may be so overwhelming that they make the influence of psychosocial mediators irrelevant.

"Weak" and Hyperreactive Body Parts

Although our perceptions of both the situation and our capacity to handle it are important to our health, genetic or constitutional traits often determine which parts of our bodies are most vulnerable to dysfunction or disease. Findings

39

indicate "there is always one system that, according to external influences or hereditary, is the weakest. It is the weak system that is first affected by stressors."[34]

Some people seem to be "vascular responders"—meaning their blood vessel systems are hyperreactive and are most likely to be the target of disease or distress.[35] Others are "cardiac responders" with the heart most likely to be affected. Still others may have gastrointestinal tracts that overreact or are "nasal and respiratory responders." People who get tension headaches often are "muscle responders." A biological sensitivity, then, that combines with psychosocial factors must be considered in explaining both the presence of a disorder and the target organ.

Army recruits who developed peptic ulcers under the pressure of basic training not only perceived greater stress and had high dependency needs but also had elevated levels of gastric stomach acid by reason of their constitutional makeup.[36] Their digestive tracts were predisposed to be the distressed organ. Similarly, people who have trouble coping and develop rheumatoid arthritis are likely to have raised levels of "rheumatoid factor"—an autoimmune antibody—already in their bloodstreams. As long as their coping is adequate, the rheumatoid factor does not seem to give rise to symptoms of arthritis.[35]

Given that we all are exposed to germs and that we all have organs and parts that may be weak or hypersensitive, is stress then the deciding factor in who gets sick and who stays well? The answer, as we will see in the next chapter, is no.

2. The Future That Failed to Shock

Ask most people what they think about stress—the bugaboo of the '80s—and they're certain to tell you something bad. . . . It wrecks the immune system, gives people heart attacks, raises the risk of cancer. . . . the antistress scare makes it seem that nothing short of retiring to rural Vermont could keep people healthy.[1]

The conclusion that the stress of life today is making us sick, that we have become victims of accelerated change in society and impossible demands in our personal lives, has collapsed under the weight of better evidence.[2] The theory that stress causes disease, mental illness, human distress and disturbance of all kinds has failed to withstand the light of closer scientific scrutiny. Persuasive findings have emerged that severely challenge the popular notion that living under stress and staying healthy are a contradiction in terms.[2]

In 1970 Alvin Toffler, in a widely read book promoted as "the best study of our times," warned us of consequences of "future shock"—the physical and psychological impact of too much change too fast. He identified a "pathology that pervades the air" from uncontrolled technological, scientific and social change.[3] Relentless change was seen as causing a nationwide stress reaction that exceeded our limits of adaptation. Coronaries, crime, alienation, apathy, suicides could be expected to multiply.

The future that Toffler was worried about is with us now, but the consequences of the shock are not those he predicted. For example, for the decade ending in 1979, age-adjusted death rates for cardiovascular disease declined 25 percent.[4] Deaths from heart disease of all kinds dropped below 1 million for the first time since 1967. For the 10-year period ending in 1981, mortality from strokes, the second leading killer, went down 42 percent. In nearly all categories of major diseases, deaths declined. In addition, motor vehicle fatalities went down 4 percent. Homicides increased, but only 0.5 percent, and suicides went up even less, 0.2 percent. Juvenile crime rates have dropped each year since 1975, except for a slight rise in 1978. First-time admissions to state and county mental hospitals dropped 18 percent from 1965 to 1975.[5] Thirty years ago, mental illness was found in one widely reported study to impair some 23 percent of the population.[6] Today, the figure is 19 percent, based on a National Institute of Mental Health survey.[7]

Other evidence contradicting the theory that present-day stress is doing us in comes from midtown Manhattan. In 1974, when a follow-up study was done of residents there who had been interviewed 20 years earlier, researchers were surprised that more people (32.5 percent) had improved in their mental health than had experienced declines (26.6 percent).[8] The researchers had explained the mental illness found in their initial, 1954, study as the consequence of stress and strain in a high-pressure urban environment. No one could argue that life in New York was more tranquil 20 years later when less illness was found or that the city was less noisy and congested or safer and cleaner. If two decades had not brought less stress and strain, why was the mental health of Manhattan residents improving, not deteriorating?

For the nation at large, if a pervasive pathology from the rampant stress of relentless change is overtaking us, it should be reflected in an increase, not decrease, in illness, accidents and the many other expressions of human distress and maladaptive behavior.

The Meaning, Not the Stress, of Change

Whether rapid change, the pressures of life or all the personal crises we may face damage our mental or physical health is not just a question of how much stress and strain are involved. Far more important is the meaning of the situation to us and how we react to the problem. When the Irish were transplanted by the thousands to the eastern seaboard of America in the last century, deaths from tubercu-

43

losis soared.[9] Although they were better housed and fed, the TB death rate was 100 percent higher than what it was at the same time in Dublin, where living conditions were much worse. Many did not want to migrate and were not prepared for the discrimination they faced. No matter what starvation they might have escaped, a number of the immigrants viewed their new home with distress.

After American Indians were forced off the plains, they had better sanitation and a higher standard of living on reservations not many miles away. Yet deaths from tuberculosis shot up.[10] The meaning of the move to them was that they were being uprooted from the land of their forebears, and they simply gave up in the face of being powerless. The same disease killed hundreds of Bantu natives who were moved from the countryside into Johannesburg. Many of the dying were allowed to go back to their kraals. Although the TB bacillus was then spread to the villages, the natives there suffered no significant increase in the disease.[11]

An early study of urban "removal" looked at mortality rates in a poverty population that was relocated from an "unhealthy area" to a city housing development. Deaths went up.[12] It was not the stress of the change that killed the people as much as it was the feeling of having no control over their lives. The same sense of powerlessness was found among the Bedouins and other nomadic Arabs who were caught up in the urbanization of Kuwait City. Ulcerative colitis became widespread.[13]

Yet many people migrate and move from country to city without ill effects. Portuguese men immigrating to Canada, and convinced that their move meant new jobs and a new future, actually improved in health.[14] Their wives, who viewed the migration as a disruption of strong family ties in Portugal, experienced an increase in symptoms. Chinese and Hungarian refugees, who overcame political upheaval and revolution to reach the United States, viewed their new lives as a challenge and an opportunity and maintained good health despite multiple changes and obstacles.[15]

But "casualties of change" are what we more often hear about—victims of population dislocations, industrialization, urbanization, migration and technological and social revolutions.[16] Hippocrates, some 2,400 years ago, diagnosed all human ills as being the consequence of change. The father of western medicine argued:

> It is changes that are chiefly responsible for diseases, especially the greatest changes, the violent alterations both in the seasons and in other things.[17]

Hippocrates also noted that "those things which one has been accustomed to for a long time, although worse than things which one is not accustomed to, usually give less disturbance."[17] Although clinicians since the time of the early Greek physicians have observed that abrupt changes are often associated with our getting sick, Adolf Meyer was the first doctor in this century to make systematic correlations between the two. He emphasized that mental illness, for example, is a reaction to life events. In 1910, Meyer developed what he called a patient's "life chart," on which he would enter "the period of disorders of the various organs" and the changes the patient had recently experienced in life.[18]

The Making of a Myth

The tradition gradually grew, then, of equating stress and change with death and illness. "Stress" had the same cause-and-effect simplicity that marked germ theory, which held a "bug" responsible for every illness. The evidence is now clear that neither stress nor germs are "the cause" of disease.

The work of Hans Selye, the endocrinologist who popularized "stress" and its relationship to disease, was interpreted to mean that any change or demand can act as a stressor.[19] Selye discovered that the body attempts to adapt by making hormonal and neurochemical adjustments, but if the demand or stressor continues, the adaptive capacity of the body may be exceeded and disease may result.[20] But what Selye failed to measure was the effect of appraisal— how the physiological impact of any demand will vary with how we interpret the situation and our ability to do something about it.[21]

To test the idea more broadly that illness is linked with change of all kinds, psychiatrists Thomas Holmes and Richard Rahe of the University of Washington developed a simple scale for measuring life events.[22] From about 5,000 life charts of medical patients, the doctors culled a list of events that had occurred to the people at the time of their getting sick. Holmes and Rahe boiled the list down to 43 common events, both positive (such as a promotion) and negative (death of a spouse), and assigned weights to each. The bigger score a person had, the more adjustment he presumably had to make and the greater likelihood he would get sick.

The simplicity of the scale and its accompanying checklist, called the Schedule of Recent Experience, made it possible for large numbers of people to be tested by scores of researchers. The researchers proceeded to find stress (change) playing a causal role in an evergrowing list of human maladies: heart attacks, accidents, athletic injuries, tuberculosis, leukemia, multiple sclerosis, diabetes, depression and other psychiatric problems, poor teacher performance and low college grade point average.[23]

Development of the Holmes-Rahe scale in 1967 was "greeted with enthusiasm because it offered a parsimonious explanatory scheme and a simple, operational measure."[24] It seemed to confirm what everyone had believed all along— that stress causes sickness.

Stress Causes Death?

Stress has also been indicted as a cause of death. Numerous examples have been cited of people being overwhelmed by stressful events and suddenly dying.[25] For instance, Pope Innocent IV died suddenly after the overthrow of his army; Emperor Nerva died from the insults of a senator who offended him; King Philip V dropped dead when he learned the Spaniards had been defeated; the doorkeeper of the Continental Congress presumably was killed by the joyful news that Lord Cornwallis had been defeated.

More recently, the 27-year-old Army captain who had commanded the ceremonial troops at President John F. Kennedy's funeral died suddenly 10 days later. The wife of the owner of the motel where Martin Luther King was assassinated collapsed the same day and died the next. At 51, the newly appointed president of CBS dropped dead as he was on his way to the funeral of his father, who had died the day before. Lyndon Johnson—who had said that when the Great Society died, he would die—succumbed to a heart attack the day after the Nixon administration announced a complete dismantling of the former president's programs.

In all these examples, the stressful event, rather than how the person viewed it, came to be identified as the critical factor, leaving the erroneous impression that what happens to us is more important than how we take it.

The Treadmill and Rat Race

Historical figures in medicine had spoken out on stress long before Selye gave the subject scientific respectability and the Holmes-Rahe scale provided readers of popular magazines with a quick measure of their risk of illness from change. More than a century ago, Daniel Tuke, author of a landmark study on *Insanity in Ancient and Modern Life*, linked the accelerated tempo and changes of city life with mental strain and physical disease.[26] Even earlier, the noted French physician J.E. Esquirol had deplored the stressful effects of changing values toward authority and the changing roles of women, noting that "we shall no longer . . . have a right to complain if nervous disorders, and particularly insanity, multiply. . . ."[27]

In 1910, the famous British physician Sir William Osler devoted his Lumleian Lectures on angina pectoris to "stress and strain." Merchants and physicians alike, he said, were particularly susceptible to heart trouble because of the "incessant treadmill" they were on.[28] At midcentury a Scottish physician, James Halliday, looked at changes that had swept across Britain in the last 70 years and arrived at a diagnosis of a "sick society."[29] Causing the pathology, he said, were new and "unnatural" by-the-book methods of child rearing, increasing standardization of education, growing urbanization, frustration from traffic, the collapse of rigid societal roles and the loss of aim and direction in life.

In the United States, anthropologists fretted about differential rates of cultural change—some parts of our culture changing faster than other parts. William Ogburn called it "cultural lag" and pointed to the blurring roles of women as an example.[30] While the prevailing ideology required that the woman's "place was in the home," technology was making it possible for more and more women to work outside the home as well as in it. Cultural lag, Ogburn said, produced maladjustments in the form of mental and physical illness.

Meanwhile, competitive struggles in urban life had grown to the point that anthropologist Jules Henry feared our culture was "out of control," with its "spiraling desire for an ever higher standard of living."[31] The "rat race" became the cliché to explain pathology from competitive pressures. By 1970, Toffler had decided that we all were not only being pressured by the rat race but faced even more trouble from a future that would exceed our capacities to adjust.

From Job Stress to Crime in the Streets

Although Osler singled out medicine and the mercantile business as the two occupations producing stress hazards, by the 1960s hardly any job had escaped being listed as over-demanding, understimulating, too repetitious, unpredictable, dehumanizing, impersonal or in some other way stressful.

On the occupational stress list were accountants facing income tax deadlines and experiencing high cholesterol, invoice clerks shifted to piece work wages and excreting excessive adrenaline, assembly line workers suffering from sexual impotence and decreased fertility, executives with too many decisions and somatic symptoms, workers rotating shifts and experiencing hormonal disturbances and peptic ulcers, office clerks required to put in overtime and manifesting higher heart rates and more irritability at home, telephone workers complaining of poor working conditions and too much noise and responding by drinking and drug use, medical students with rapid pulse rates and elevated levels of epinephrine, lawyers feeling unprepared to meet the demands on them, air traffic traffic controllers with high rates of hypertension, nurses, policemen, members of the armed forces, space flight personnel—all with disorders attributed to stress.[32] The list is still lengthening.

By 1968, U.S. Department of the Interior Secretary Stewart Udall, worried that we were all on the verge of a collective breakdown, was calling for the country to stop emphasizing the Gross National Product as its "holy grail" and to start developing a "tranquillity index."[33]

A decade before Toffler, Kenneth Kenniston, a

49

leading educator, was saying that we could not cope with the accelerating rate of change, that technological and social innovation was outstripping our physiological and psychological equipment.[34] Zoologist Desmond Morris compared conditions in cities to those in overcrowded zoos and found that "behavior in both environments took forms almost unknown in wild habitats."[35] Cities were depicted as so stressful that they were "behavioral sinks."[36] In 1973, psychologist James C. Coleman saw stress and change as responsible for increased crime, suicide, alcoholism, drug abuse, coronary heart disease, alienation, aimlessness and apathy.[37] Finally, as Paul Rosch, the physician who heads the American Institute of Stress, has observed:

> It is difficult to pick up a newspaper, magazine, or medical journal today without reading about the role of stress in causing hypertension, heart disease, ulcer, cancer, emotional illness. . . .We are told that "stress has surpassed the common cold as the most prevalent health problem in America" and that "stress-related conditions" are responsible for $10 to $20 billion annually in loss of industrial productivity.[38]

The 20th Century Scapegoat

So the stress-and-sickness legend has continued to grow. It has grown to the point that stress has become the 20th century scapegoat for our problems. A former official in Washington was found innocent by a federal grand jury of failing to answer a congressional subpoena after she testified that she had been under extreme stress.[39] A district court in Texas awarded $30,000 in workmen's compensation to a university employee who claimed that job stress resulted in physiological disorders.[40] In California, a jury awarded $32.2 million in damages to the family of a man who died after trying to rescue his daughter from the Hare Krishna religious cult. He suffered a stroke allegedly brought on by stress.[41]

Stress provides a simple explanation for why we are sick, depressed, bored, alcoholic or assaultive. It also provides a way to blame all our troubles on external sources. It is, as we have suggested, the modern-day counterpart to germ theory, which says outside forces make us unhealthy. Stress is a disease that is presumably "slowly killing us all." Psychologist Rex Julian Beaber, who teaches family medicine at UCLA Medical School, comments:

> How remarkable it is that this illness was unknown several hundred years ago. During the 18th century, when disease and war wiped out hordes, when people toiled long hours under poor conditions, when there was no modern medicine, no unemployment insurance, stress somehow slipped the minds of medical thinkers. Now, when people merely need to worry about the few hardships that have survived progress, we are suddenly dying of stress.[42]

Stress, as a possible precipitating factor in disease, cannot be dismissed as unimportant. But neither can it be cited as the cause of all our pathology. The oversimplified message we have been given is that stress from trying events, from technological and social change, from the incessant pace of modern life and the disorientation of "future shock"— that the demands and adjustments from all these are making us sick. This is the conclusion that has now collapsed.

Enter the Brain

Who Gets Sick is only partly about the mounting evidence that shows many people stay healthy under both everyday stress and extreme circumstances. Mostly this book is about the heady revolution (see Introduction), the scientific advances confirming the link between what goes on in our heads and what happens in our bodies. It is concerned with the critical part the mind and brain play in health and disease. Whether stress does us in depends largely on how we view our troubles and what chemical messages we trigger in our brains.

The connections between mental and bodily processes are real and anatomical. To say "it's only in your head" or "it's just your imagination," as a way of dismissing pain or illness, is to deny physical fact. Head and body are one inseparable unit. As microbiologist René Dubos reminded us, even Greek medicine, as reflected in the Hippocratic Corpus, recognized them as one: "Whatever happens in the mind influences the body and vice versa. In fact, mind and body cannot be considered independently one from the other."[43] For instance, the hypothalamus control center of the brain is directly "wired" to the immune system. If a portion of the hypothalamus is electrically stimulated, antibodies increase. If it is cut, immune activity is depressed.[44]

Thoughts, beliefs, imaginations are not ephemeral abstractions but electrochemical events with physiological consequences. Sophisticated instrumentation such as PET-scanning now permits us to see the brain in action as thinking occurs and to map blood flow in the cerebral hemispheres as thoughts and feelings change. Advances in radioimmunoassay techniques make it possible to pick up hormonal changes as a function of different appraisals of stressful situations.[45]

Recent findings have repeatedly affirmed the link between mind and health. A sense of control can keep our stress chemicals from reaching damaging levels while we are under pressure.[46] An openness to change and an attitude of involvement can increase our resistance to illness.[47] On the other hand, a sense of helplessness can depress our immune system and decrease our resistance.[48] A belief that we must have power and dominance can also affect our immunity when we are under stress.[49] A giving-up reaction to life stresses can increase our risk of sudden death or cancer.[50] A chronically hostile, cynical or distrusting attitude can contribute to our risk of atherosclerosis and heart disease.[51]

How the Brain Directs the Body

All these examples of how our beliefs, attitudes and appraisals affect our bodies are no longer impressions based on clinical anecdotes but empirical facts anchored in physiological findings. "Proof" of the mind's influence on the body has grown rapidly in the last few decades. But as recently as the 1950s, skeptics were arguing that there were no nerves connecting the brain to our anterior pituitary, and thus there was no way a stressful thought or appraisal could trigger release of powerful stress hormones from the adrenal cortex.[52] The connection was confirmed, however, when it was shown that a rich network of blood vessels link the hypothalamus to our "master gland." Simple brain peptides—small molecules of amino acids—travel down the vessels and stimulate the pituitary, which in turn activates release of adrenal cortical hormones.[53]

In 1977 Roger Guillemin and Andrew Schally received the Nobel Prize in physiology or medicine after demonstrating how the brain "gives orders" to the body, using these chemical messengers. Working independently these two scientists, originally from Hans Selye's stress research laboratory, isolated a series of tiny molecules that are made in the brain's hypothalamus and travel to the body's "master gland," the pituitary, where they then affect the functioning of our thyroids, adrenals, gonads and the very course of our somatic growth.[54]

It took Guillemin, then in Houston, 10 years and 300,000 hypothalami from sheep to isolate 1 milligram of the molecule by which the brain is able to direct the thyroid gland. Schally, at the Veterans Administration Hospital in

New Orleans, used 100,000 pig hypothalami to isolate 2.8 milligrams of TRF (thyroid-releasing factor).[55] It was the first of some eight hormones and chemicals—each a transmitter of messages from the brain—that were isolated from the hypothalamus. So tiny are these potent chemical messengers that they had eluded identification for years in laboratories around the world.

"Chemistry of Thought"

A second milestone came in 1973 when a doctoral student named Candace Pert and neuroscientist Solomon Snyder, a young faculty member at Johns Hopkins in whose laboratory she worked, succeeded in locating and labeling receptors the brain uses in communication among cells.[56] That discovery nailed down the theory that messages sent by brain cells in the form of neurotransmitters and hormones are "heard" by receiving cells that have "buttons" (receptors) all over their surface membranes. Depending on the button that is "pushed," different reactions occur in the brain or body— an emotion, a constriction of blood vessels, the release of gastric acid.[57] Our very thoughts and perceptions can push the buttons by releasing various neurochemicals.

As we mentioned in the Introduction, the way we define our experiences can affect cell receptors. For instance, glucocorticoids—including stress hormones we generate from an overly negative view of problems—can produce changes in cell receptors for serotonin, a neurotransmitter that plays an important role in modifying psychic and physical pain.[58]

Pert, now chief of the brain biochemistry section at the National Institute of Mental Health in Bethesda, Maryland, has noted that "a major conceptual shift in neuroscience" has resulted from the recognition that scores of neuropeptides—the kind of chemicals Guillemin and Schally isolated—and their receptors constitute a "psychosomatic network" in our brains and bodies.[59] Because they communicate directly with our glands and immune systems, they cannot help but profoundly affect our health. And because these internal "informational substances" are so sensitive to the way we define our difficulties and react to what troubles us, our thinking cannot help but affect our health. Some observers are convinced that "the chemistry of thought" and "the new science of molecular psychology" are now at hand.[60]

The brain, then, uses neuroactive chemicals and their receptors, as well as electrical impulses, to establish its far-reaching influence over our bodies and our health.[61] These chemicals behave according to the changes we perceive in our personal well-being as we deal with the people and situations in our lives. Every change we appraise gives rise to a host of questions: Can I handle it? What's in jeopardy if I can't? What responses are possible?[62] Such thoughts produce, through the brain's neurotransmitters and neuro-regulators, "coordinated metabolic and cardiovascular alterations" that prepare us for action or retreat.[52]

Thus how we look at a stressful situation, the attitudes and beliefs we bring to the problem, influences what chemical messages the brain sends the body. If we see things as hopeless and decide to give up, that decision is dutifully conveyed by the brain to the body, which proceeds to carry out the order.

Choosing the Wrong Reaction

Selye, who spent 50 years doing stress research, came to the conclusion that it is not what stresses us that counts, it is the way we react.[13] What "causes" distress or disease, then, takes on a different meaning and shifts the focus from what confronts us to how we cope. Selye liked to tell the story of what happens if you pass a helpless drunk who showers you with insults. If you pass on by, ignoring the drunk, you are not likely to experience any physiological consequences of significance. However, if you choose to fight back, verbally or otherwise, "you will discharge adrenalines that increase blood pressure and pulse rate, while your whole nervous system becomes alarmed and tense in anticipation of combat. If you happen to be a coronary candidate, the result may be a fatal heart accident." Selye would then ask: What caused your death? The drunk? His insults? No, "death was caused by choosing the wrong reaction."[63]

This is a book about the reactions that we choose and their effects on our bodies.

3. Those Who Stay Healthy

Now . . . there is a more hopeful way of looking at stress—one that's closer to reality . . . you don't have to accept a victim's fate. There are ways to change from helpless to hardy.[1]

When a team of University of Chicago behavioral scientists decided to test the popular theory that high stress means high risk of illness, they did something different. Instead of seeing if they could find people who seemed to get sick from exposure to excessive stress, the researchers looked for persons who had few symptoms after high stress in their lives.

Led by psychologists Suzanne Kobasa and Salvatore Maddi, the group identified 200 business executives at Illinois Bell Telephone Company who had experienced an especially large number of stressful events during the AT&T divestiture. One hundred of the managers and officers reported numerous symptoms, but the other 100 had few signs of diagnosable illness.[2] If excessive stress makes people sick, how could half of the high-stress executives escape illness? Clearly the amount of stress was not the key to whether the person got ill or not.

What Kobasa and her colleagues found was that the executives who stayed healthy had a different way of looking at, and dealing with, stressful events than did the managers who became sick. For instance, the healthy managers considered change, good or bad, as an inevitable part of life and an opportunity for growth and new experience rather than as a threat to security. They took the sting out of setbacks and losses by how they looked at bad events—as not the end of the world or beyond solution. They made practical use of an "optimistic cognitive appraisal."[3] Thus they had a sense that they could control things—they could control the impact of problems if not the problems themselves.

Hardy Personality Protects

The up-and-coming business executive has so often been identified with stress and a heart attack by age 50 that corporate headquarters in the Chicago study had even installed a cardiac unit. The message that has been given to the business world is the same as the one the general public has bought: Stress kills and should be avoided if at all possible. When it cannot be avoided, then tranquilizers, alcohol, exercise or a triple bypass may help. But the new evidence is that stress is not the problem; it is our response that largely determines health or sickness.

Those who stay healthy under stress, Kobasa found, have in addition to a sense of control and challenge a commitment to life. They are deeply involved in their work and families, and this commitment gives them a sense of meaning, direction and excitement. They have acquired "hardy" personalities, which helps to protect them against illness.

The Kobasa research team also studied lawyers.[4] Focusing on a group of 157 attorneys in general practice, the psychologists found that many had experienced frequent changes at work, such as hiring and firing of staff and salary adjustments. Some reported severe stresses off the job—deaths in their families, separations and divorces. But no correlation of any significance could be found between the lawyers' stressful life events and their physical health.

When the researchers looked at the attorneys' "strain symptoms"—such as headaches, nervousness, trouble sleeping—they again discovered a powerful role being played by certain attitudes and beliefs. The lawyers who believed in the importance and value of what they were doing and had a sense of purpose experienced the fewest symptoms. The way the attorneys reacted to stress at work and at home was also strongly related to the strain they reported. The more they got angry, became indifferent, withdrew, smoked or drank, the more symptoms they ended up with.

Different Attitude toward Stress

Kobasa, who joined the graduate faculty at City University of New York after leaving the University of Chicago, wanted to study lawyers because of their image as people who thrive on stress. The rigors of law school apparently teach many of them to work at a strenuous pace. Stories are told, Kobasa noted, about how lawyers perform best under a great deal of pressure, never get sick and live long lives.[5] She concluded that many attorneys may have developed responses to stress that keep them healthy because they believe lawyers are expected to thrive under pressure.

Our attitudes, then, toward the very subject of stress can influence our reactions when we are in trying situations. Our physiological responses will be considerably less intense if we see stress as an inevitable part of life and a challenge rather than something that is awful and must be avoided.

Women and the 3 Cs

Since both the study of the executives and the one of the lawyers included only men, the psychologists wanted to determine if their findings would also apply to women.[6] They tested a total of 100 gynecology outpatients, the majority being white, 25 to 35 years old, and middle class. This time, the researchers decided to see if high stress meant more emotional distress. Forty of the 100 women had undergone a large number of stressful experiences recently but had few psychiatric symptoms. The other 60 scored high on both stress and symptoms. Women in the first group were distinguished by a greater sense of control, more commitment to work, family and self, and a stronger sense of challenge.

Belief in control, commitment and challenge is the key to "psychological hardiness"—something Kobasa and her collaborators are convinced that people can be taught to increase resistance to illness.[7] After these initial studies, the Chicago Stress Project tested the effects of psychological hardiness by tracking the illnesses of 259 executives over five years.[8] For this prospective study, the researchers determined which of the managers were high in control, commitment and challenge and which were low. During later periods of increased stress, those high in hardiness continued in good health while those who had low hardiness had significantly poorer health. In their research, Kobasa and Maddi checked medical records of executives to confirm the amount and severity of illness reported. Under equally high stress, the managers with hardy personalities had half the illness of those with little hardiness.[9]

Acquiring a Sense of Control

The psychological hardiness studies helped to confirm a basic proposition: The sense of control that is crucial to coping effectively and staying healthy is largely a belief, which we can either adopt or reject. Some psychologists have come to define control, in fact, as "a belief that one has at one's disposal a response that can influence the aversiveness of an event. . . ."[10] How aversive or damaging an event is depends on how we choose to take it—which means that we can control its effects on our bodies and health by our attitudes and beliefs (see Chapter 7). Acquiring a sense of control can thus come from recognizing that we can have a powerful impact on our bodily processes by what we do in our heads.

A sense of control does *not* mean that we must control everything around us—other people, our environment, all situations and circumstances, both good and bad. People who try this are at a higher risk of illness, not a reduced risk.[11] Negative realities—bad happenings by anyone's definition—are inevitable in life, and many cannot be controlled. Some people are subjected to harsher circumstances than others are, such as through war, racism, poverty, unemployment or age. But, as we will see, even under extreme conditions, it is possible not only to survive but to retain some sense of health and well-being. One key is through what we do cognitively and how we appraise the bad things around us. We often cannot control the objective reality, but we can learn to control how we react to it. Such inner control seems to come easier for those who have a strong faith—a faith in their own coping skills or in God—or some special place from which they draw strength or people they love and trust.

Regardless of what underlies inner control and the ability to view life less pessimistically, the evidence strongly suggests that we are healthier for them. Such a sense of control is one component of what medical sociologist Aaron Antonovsky (see Chapter 6) calls a "sense of coherence," which he has found characteristic of people who stay healthy.[12] This inner control may also be enhanced by what Thomas Boyce of the department of pediatrics at the University of Arizona School of Medicine has described as a "sense of permanence and continuity," which comes from a belief in certain central, valued and enduring elements of life experience.[13] Boyce has found such a sense to reduce the risk of certain disorders and to be related to psychological well-being.

What Cognitive Control Is

The most powerful control, then, as Kobasa and her colleagues confirmed, is cognitive, which means appraising a bad situation in such a way as to reduce its stress.[14] Cognitive control stems from the belief that we can affect the hurtful impact—both the psychological and physiological impact—of a situation by how we look at the problem. It means that by choosing to regard losses, hurts, frustrations and stressful life changes with less gloom and doom and not as the end of the world, we control their power to do us damage.

The executives who were high in hardiness and low in illness used "transformational coping" to deal with problems. Transformational coping involves "altering the events so they are less stressful. To do this, you must interact with the events, and, by thinking about them optimistically and acting toward them decisively, change them in a less stressful direction."[15] On the other hand, the managers who were low in hardiness and high in illness mostly used "regressive coping." This style involves thinking about the events pessimistically and acting "evasively to avoid contact with them."[16]

Thus effective coping, which means the ability to increase our resistance to both mental and physical illness, consists of (1) viewing problems with less pessimism and reducing the intensity of their psychological and physiological impact; (2) taking some action to change the external problem, if change is possible, and (3) palliating the physical and mental effects of the problem by exercise, relaxation training or some other healthy behavior.[17]

Although many people may do (2) or (3) but not (1), the evidence strongly suggests that the critical starting point to stress resistance is "optimistic appraisal." It is the cornerstone of ego strength, the capacity to cope with both external and internal stress adaptively. Ego strength, like psychological hardiness, correlates with staying healthy under stress. For instance, a study at Vanderbilt University showed that ego strength was the most powerful predictor of whether a person experienced acute illness and for how long.[18]

Failure to Adapt

Our beliefs, attitudes and basic positions toward life all shape the way we react when we face a threat or are required to make adjustments and changes. The way we react is expressed in our central nervous system (brain and spinal cord) and a variety of hormones and other compounds in the body. These, in turn, affect target organs—heart, stomach, brain—and influence our immune system. Our reaction is determined not only by our basic beliefs and perceptions but also by our genes, the nature of the stress, our coping resources, our past experiences and the context of the situation we are confronted with.[19] Disease or dysfunction is the body's way of saying that we have failed to adapt, adjust or change to meet the situation or that we have done so at the price of physical or mental disturbance.[20]

What is new about the powerful role that mental processes play in our health is the growing number of studies, from diverse disciplines, that have confirmed the strong link between mind and body. On the cellular level, studies in psychoneuroimmunology show that the ability of our lymphocytes and antibodies, our resistance to infection, can be affected by how we appraise stressful events and react to them.[21] On the behavioral level, the constant drive to dominate has been correlated with a higher risk of heart disease.[22] Regardless of which level researchers investigate, the brain orchestrates and directs the complex reactions. The very feature of the brain that distinguishes us from other living creatures—our capacity to form beliefs and make inferences—can be used either to promote or impair our health.

Good Attitude and Low Illness

According to stress-strain theory, people undergoing rapid changes, upheavals and dislocations in their lives are likely "victims" of illness. But as we have suggested, this theory fails to explain how many people undergo high stress and multiple changes without getting sick. Lawrence Hinkle and his collaborators in the departments of medicine and psychiatry at New York Hospital-Cornell Medical Center (see

Chapter 1) were among the first to identify what distinguishes those who stay well from those who get sick. Based on studies of several populations over 20 years, the researchers concluded that a "good attitude and ability to get along with other people" characterized those with a low frequency of illness.[23]

Among those Hinkle and his colleagues studied were 100 Chinese immigrants who were stranded in the United States by political upheaval in their homeland.[24] Many had been exposed to rapid changes in both Chinese and American culture, and a number had personal experience with wars and revolutions as well as new customs. All were having to adapt to an uncertain future in this country, not knowing what their occupations would be or what the fate of their family and friends in China was. Yet a considerable percent of the group remained healthy.

The healthy were distinguished by the way they looked upon their past and present difficulties, viewing their lives as interesting, varied and relatively satisfying. By contrast, those who had frequent illnesses looked at their situation as threatening, demanding and frustrating.

The Cornell researchers also did in-depth testing of 76 Hungarian refugees who fled the Communist revolution in their homeland.[25] Many had experienced loss of fortune, family and social status, and some had suffered rape and imprisonment. Now they were having to adjust to a new language and different customs. As with the Chinese, 25 percent experienced approximately 50 percent of the total number of illness episodes recorded for the group as a whole. Another 25 percent had less than 10 percent of the illnesses. Again, more benign attitudes toward adversity distinguished the refugees who had few illnesses from those who were frequently sick.

The studies by Hinkle and his coworkers demonstrated that it is also possible for someone to reduce his risk of illness if he insulates himself emotionally and invests little in life.[26] By viewing everything as if nothing matters, we can keep our physiological processes from becoming aroused and stress hormones from doing damage, but our social health will suffer and our relations with others will have no depth. Emotional insulation is the opposite of the commitment and challenge that Kobasa and the University of Chicago psychologists found in the lives of healthy men and women who used optimistic attitudes to deal with setbacks and negative realities.

No Greater Illness from Stress

Because of the many changes and adjustments that people experience when they migrate from one country to another, immigration was long considered as "pathogenic" in terms of producing mental and physical illness. As we saw, men migrating to Montreal from Portugal were motivated by economic opportunities in Canada. The meaning of the migration to them was a better life materially. Despite a high life-change score, their health was unaffected by the move.[27] In fact, some of them appeared to thrive on the many life changes involved and had even better health. Portuguese women, however, did report numerous illness in the wake of the move. As we noted, the meaning they seemed to attach to migrating was that it disrupted a satisfying personal and family life. They valued relationships more than economic improvement.

Other evidence that high stress cannot be equated with high risk of illness comes from the Honolulu Heart Program.[28] Epidemiologists tested for the effects of "chronic stress" on health by looking at such factors as moving up or down in occupational status, living with an inconsistency between one's educational status and occupation, changing religion, being different in background, education and customs from one's spouse and having few initimate ties with relatives. Contrary to stress-strain theory, the study found no significant impact on health.

The researchers noted that social strains such as status incongruity cannot be considered inherently stressful. The effect is more likely to depend on people's perception of their situation, their personality, prior experience and coping style.

Different Appraisals, Different Outcomes

The meaning we give events and the satisfaction we find, then, profoundly influence the stressful effects of changes we make in our lives. Psychiatrist David Hamburg, past president of the National Academy of Sciences' Institute of Medicine and a pioneer in coping research, cites this common experience:

> . . . a recently married couple will move to a city where both are strangers—a circumstance inherently somewhat stressful. But, the meaning of the experience may be quite different for the two. He may be immersed in fascinating new work. . . . she may be largely isolated with a new baby. Or conversely, he may be under harsh competitive pressures in a nonsupportive work environment, while she is welcomed into a friendly, respectful neighborhood group. . . . the same experience . . . can have very different meanings for different people, even people as close as husband and wife. And the different meanings can elicit very different emotional responses and hence very different physiological responses.[29]

The meaning we give to situations is embedded in the kind of cognitive appraisal we make. As we have seen, our appraisal begins with looking at what we are faced with and asking ourselves: "Am I okay or in trouble?" If the answer is, "in trouble," then a second question quickly follows: "What can I do about it?"[30] Our physiological reactions are related to how much trouble we perceive and how much control, if any, we believe we have over the situation. When we perceive our trouble as being more threatening than challenging or our capacity to cope as more hopeless than promising, the physiological changes that ensue may lead to illness.

The critical importance of appraisal in producing physiological distress was being noted decades ago, but little attention was given to the finding. In 1949, for example, Stewart Wolf, a physician physiologist who later became president of the American Psychosomatic Society, underlined the key role of "the attitude of the patient, i.e., his interpretation of the significance of the stimulus situation."[31] But such observations were overshadowed by the growing attention that stress per se—that is, the "stimulus situation"—was beginning to receive both inside and outside of medicine. As we suggested in Chapter 2, the tireless efforts of one man, Hans Selye, were largely responsible for putting "stress" into the world's vocabulary.

Stress Without Distress

Hans Selye's theory that stress causes disease is based on the idea that excessive demands in a person's life produce high levels of hormones from the adrenal glands, specifically the outer shell or cover (the cortex) of the adrenals. These hormones, in turn, lead to a lowering of bodily resistance, to organ damage and disease.[32] Such hormonal activity, when pronounced and prolonged, does seem to have such an effect, but the question is whether the stress that someone experiences invariably triggers the excessive hormonal response. In other words, does stress automatically cause distress?

Two psychiatrists, an endocrinologist and a cancer specialist in New York teamed up to determine what hormonal stress reactions were present in a truly life-threatening situation.[33] They studied 30 women with breast tumors at Montefiore Hospital and Medical Center. The women were in the hospital to undergo biopsies. As an index of "distress," the physicians focused on the daily amount of hydrocortisone (an adrenal hormone) each patient excreted for three days before undergoing biopsy.

Contrary to stress-strain theory, the adrenal reaction of the women fell within normal range. What psychiatrist Jack Katz and his research group concluded was that the psychological defenses of the women—their outlooks, beliefs and coping styles—were the critical factor in how much (or how little) distress they experienced. It was not the crisis of possibly having breast cancer that determined the stress reaction. Biopsies confirmed that 22 of the 30 women had malignancies. No relationship was found between amount of hydrocortisone excreted prior to biopsy and the presence or absence of malignancy.

The lowest adrenal reaction came from a 45-year-old woman who used faith and prayer to deal with stressful life events. The next lowest was from a 54-year-old woman who had a philosophical acceptance of adversity. Overall, women who used either faith or acceptance showed less stressful reactions.

The link between people's attitudes toward a stressful situation and their physiological reaction was also demonstrated in studies by Richard Rahe and his colleagues. Rahe was codeveloper of the Social Readjustment Rating Scale, the checklist that has been so widely used to measure stress (see Chapter 2). He came to recognize that neither the number nor the magnitude of stressful events could account for whether an individual gets sick. Again, the crucial factor is the meaning that the person attaches to the events.

At the Naval Health Research Center in San Diego, Captain Rahe examined the physiological reactions of Navy recruits undergoing severe training stresses.[34] When the men viewed their training as burdensome, depressing and likely to end in failure, their cholesterol levels rose sharply. When they perceived the training as challenging, although somewhat frightening, no such cholesterol reaction occurred.

Surviving War and Captivity

Rahe has noted that even in situations of the severest stress, such as being a prisoner of war, not everyone breaks down physically or emotionally.[34] In examinations, for example, of Air Force personnel released by North Viet Nam after an average of six years of captivity, researchers from the School of Aerospace Medicine found none had gone crazy and the majority showed considerable resiliency in terms of surviving without lasting psychic damage.[35] Psychologist Margaret Singer of the University of California commented: " . . . there is an apocryphal expectancy that severe trauma and stress per se 'drive people out of their minds.'"[36] The evidence from the repatriated POWs cast doubt on such shibboleths, "imbedded in both the lay and professional folklore about responses to stress."[36]

The devastating effects of the Nazi concentration camps have been discussed for decades, but not much attention was given for a long time to the question, "how did anyone keep going and survive such stress?" Psychiatrist Joel Dimsdale, then at Stanford University School of Medicine, located 19 survivors in the San Francisco area who were in relatively good health. He said that it was not surprising they had not been studied before, "since the concept of coping, which essentially focuses on how a person responds to stress, is relatively new."[37]

Dimsdale identified the survivors' beliefs and appraisals as the source of their successful coping methods. For instance, a number of the survivors learned to "focus on the good." Dimsdale explained that "a person at all times has a choice as to what to focus on—foreground or background, good or bad."[38] Focusing on the good meant being thankful for getting through the food line without a beating or appreciating the sunset against the distant fields.

The former captives also benefited from focusing on a purpose for survival. Some survived to be reunited with their families, others to bear witness to the world of the atrocities, still others to seek revenge. A number kept from being defeated by retaining a sense of mastery or autonomy over some corner of their lives. They persisted in observing Yom Kippur in the face of all odds. They learned to congratulate themselves on just staying alive in a place whose very purpose was to kill everyone.

In Israel, sociologist Antonovsky headed a research team that compared 77 women who had been in a Nazi concentration camp with 210 who had not.[39] The researchers identified a "not-inconsiderable number" among the camp survivors who were "well-adapted, despite the extreme trauma."[40] One of the reasons for their health, the social scientists concluded, was the ability to view current stresses with some equanimity.

Physical and emotional illness "caused" by war has been cited as evidence supporting stress-strain theory. When England, for instance, entered the war with Germany in 1939, British hospitals reported a sharp increase in admissions of people with peptic ulcers.[41] A year later, when the heavy bombing raids over London started, another significant increase in persons with perforated ulcers occurred.

But later studies showed that no simple assumption could be made that the hardship of war meant more illness. In Holland, a Dutch physician named J.J. Gröen entered a concentration camp with a group of Amsterdam merchants and professionals he had treated before the outbreak of war for peptic ulcers.[42] During the confinement he noticed that despite indignities, deprivations and threats to survival, most members of the group lost their ulcer symptoms. They were no longer concerned with striving and getting ahead in careers; now they were preoccupied with survival. After being released and restored to the customs and competition of civilian life, many again developed manifestations of peptic ulcers.[42]

In Denmark, the number of people entering mental hospitals decreased at the start of the German occupation.[43] In London, the suicide rate dropped during the blitz.[44] Both findings suggested that people may respond to threatening conditions with a sense of purpose or resolve that deflects the effects of stress. Among American troops in Europe, it was not uncommon for levels of sickness and disability to be higher at base camps and in rear areas than in forward areas where the threat of military action was greater.[45]

Coping with the Stress of Combat

Even in combat, then, which has long been identified with breakdowns under stress, more recent evidence has challenged the theory that given enough pressure, everyone cracks up. As we have seen, our reactions to stress are largely a function of how much control we perceive or give ourselves. In the Korean War, a comparison was made between an "attacking company" actively initiating a battle and a "defending company," which was on the fighting line but not engaged in the offensive.[46] It took the men in the attacking company about six days to recover physiologically from their stress (in terms of hormone levels and other indices), compared with an average of 13 days for the defending company. A major difference between the two units was that "while the 'attacking company' was engaged in an offensive attack, initiated by them and generally under their control, the 'defending company' played a predominantly passive role. . . ."[47]

One way a sense of control may develop is through feeling prepared. This point was illustrated by a study in Viet Nam combat of the physiological reactions of a Special Forces unit expecting an enemy attack.[48] Peter Bourne, then an Army psychiatrist, lived in the camp with the combat team and took adrenal hormone measurements for an 18-day period. The soldiers' levels of 17-hydroxycorticosteroid (a hormone from the adrenal cortex) did not indicate any significant stress reaction. Their levels of anxiety and depression, as measured by a standardized checklist, were even lower than those of basic recruits entering training. The men coped with the threat of impending battle by engaging in a "furor of activity," building defenses and maintaining equipment. The only men in the unit who showed elevated hormonal activity were the two officers and the radio operator, each of whom had to stay in constant contact with a distant command post that issued orders they could not control.

Bourne and his coresearchers, Robert Rose and John Mason, also investigated the effects of chronic stress on helicopter medics in Viet Nam.[49] They found that individual perception and interpretation of the stressful environment were more important than any "objective" measure of the danger involved. Although risk increased for the medics on flying days, as compared with days on the ground, the men did not differ in their daily corticosteroid reactions. Their anxiety levels went up slightly on mission days, but even these were lower than those of basic trainees. One possible reason for the medics' lack of distress was that they looked upon their job as a life-saving mission, for which they could expect recognition and prestige.

All these studies suggest that hardship, difficulty, even danger cannot be equated with distress and increased risk of illness. The adversity we face does not determine our physical or psychological arousal, our health or disease. How we interpret the situation and cope with it is what counts.

How We Cope Affects Our Immunity

Our resistance to infectious diseases, allergies and other disorders, including probably cancer, largely depends on our immune systems. Does high stress impair our immune defenses? Again, the evidence indicates that the amount of stress we face is not as important as how we react to it and cope with it. For example, when 124 people were inoculated with swine flu vaccine, it was found that the amount of protection they received, as measured by a rise in antibody titer after vaccination, was not correlated with how much stress they had experienced over the last month or year from life changes.[50] On the other hand, in a related study of 108 undergraduates immunized for swine flu, researchers found that those who coped poorly with stress had significantly impaired immune response, as measured by diminished activity of natural killer (NK) cells, a special type of leukocyte or white blood cell that destroys viruses and cancer cells without having encountered them previously.[51] Just as important was the finding that students with high stress but good coping ability had the highest level of NK cell activity.

A similar finding came from a later study of 117 college students by psychiatrist Steven Locke of Harvard and his research team.[52] In the face of high stress, "good copers" had significantly greater NK cell activity than did "poor copers." When anxiety and depression were high, activity of natural killer cells was low, suggesting that such reactions may adversely affect immunity.

From studies done by Janice Kiecolt-Glaser, a psychologist at Ohio State University College of Medicine in Columbus, and her colleagues, it seems that the most hazardous health effects of anxiety, distress, anger or depression may occur in people who already have lowered immune function (see also Chapters 6 and 8).[53] Among those particularly vulnerable would be the elderly and those who may have pre-existing infections or other illnesses. The Ohio

State scientists have found that in acute distress, such as experienced by many medical students during final examinations, there is suppression of not only natural killer cells but also interferon, an important protein produced in the body that stimulates NK cell activity and inhibits multiplication of viruses.

Effect on Antibodies

Antibodies, which help protect us from infections, can also be impaired by how we cope. For example, people with high needs to dominate and make an impression on others have been found to experience a reduction in an important antibody, salivary IgA, when faced with performance stresses.[54] Salivary IgA antibodies are part of our firstline defenses against upper respiratory disease. Harvard researchers reported a higher incidence of upper respiratory illness and lower levels of s-IgA among the people with high needs to control and impress.[54]

The evidence indicates that when we chronically generate stress hormones—whether by having undue needs to dominate every situation or by viewing setbacks as catastrophes—we run the risk of compromising our body's ability to fight illness. T-cells—cells derived from the thymus gland—as well as NK cells can be depressed when we cope poorly or constantly feel the need to dominate every situation. Unhampered T-lymphocytes, which are the key actors in cellular immunity, wipe out invading organisms if they have been exposed to them before whereas NK cells kill on first contact. Our B-cells—which constitute our humoral immunity—and the antibodies they produce can be similarly suppressed by faulty reactions to stress.

Helper Cells Help or Hurt

Production of antibodies is stimulated by helper T-cells, which are lymphocytes that give the immune system an added boost. The more we perceive ourselves as being chronically hassled or experience negative moods, the more likely we will have lower levels of helper T-cells and greater susceptibility to some illnesses.[55] Suppressor T-cells, which inhibit helper cell action and dampen our immune responses, also are affected by perceptions of stress—a point that is important to people who have certain allergies due to too few suppressor T-cells and an overactive immune system.

Stressful perceptions resulting in *acute* anxiety may significantly increase helper T-cells. Tests on entering medical students during their first week have shown sharp rises in helper T-cells, compared with the levels of less anxious second-year students.[56] The fact that we may have excessive helper T-cells could partly explain why some of us come down with bouts of rheumatoid arthritis under acute stress, since this disorder seems to involve overactive immune defenses mistaking the body's own joint tissue as foreign and attacking it.

Links between Brain and Immune System

Immunologists have suspected for years that stress hormones affect people's immunity. Robert Good, former president and director of Memorial Sloan-Kettering Cancer Hospital in New York, was one of the first authorities in the field to recognize also that "a positive attitude" and "a constructive frame of mind," as well as depression, can alter our ability to resist "infections, allergies, autoimmunities or even cancer."[57] However, he could not explain the processes and mechanisms by which such effects occurred.

Just how our reactions to stress and our ability to cope affect our resistance to disease is the focus of intensive research. Much remains to be clarified, but it is known that the immune system is directly influenced by nerve impulses from the brain as well as by hormones that are increased by stress reactions.[58] The brain's hypothalamus, through the sympathetic and parasympathetic nervous systems, can affect both the thymus gland, which lies behind the upper part of the breastbone, and the spleen, located near the stomach or intestines. These two organs manufacture lymphocytes, the white blood cells that protect us against bacteria, viruses and other intruders, including incipient cancers.

The direct links that the brain has with the immune system can be demonstrated by experiments in which lesions in the hypothalamus—the all-important pea-sized structure near the center of the brain—produce decreases in a variety of immune functions.[59] Lesions in the amygdala or hippocampus—other powerful parts of the limbic system in the midbrain—lead to increases in immune activity.

Higher centers of the brain also connect with the immune system. When a portion of the left cerebral hemisphere is removed, researchers have found that the number of T-cells drops. This is the side of the brain where language functions and reasoning seem to be focused for most people. French researchers have shown in mice that the immune system's response to foreign materials diminishes after removal of the left neocortex but increases if the right neocortex is removed.[60] They have suggested that the left hemisphere appears to govern the immune system although the right brain has some influence.

That stress hormones have the capacity to diminish our immune defenses was demonstrated in animal experiments at M.D. Anderson Hospital and Tumor Institute of the University of Texas Cancer Center in Houston. Researchers showed that norepinephrine completely blocked the ability of macrophages—scavenger cells that help give us innate resistance against disease—to kill tumor cells.[61] Other stress-related neuropeptides and neurohormones had similar effects.

Cardiovascular Damage

Another important bodily system affected by how we view life and react to stressful situations is the heart and our arteries. People who are cynical or have hostile attitudes or suppressed anger have been found to have more atherosclerosis and blockage of coronary arteries.[62] And they are more likely to experience heart attacks. In a study over 25 years of 255 physicians who took a battery of psychological tests while they were still students at the University of North Carolina Medical School, those with higher hostility scores had four times greater incidence of heart disease and six times the mortality.[63]

Individuals who are in a chronic struggle to exert domination and control—Type A personalities—may also be "coronary prone," particularly if they are hostile.[64] Chronic activation of the fight-flight response means that the neurotransmitter norepinephrine is liberated in increased amounts from the ends of sympathetic nervous system fibers, acting upon blood vessels, the heart and other organs. Excessive norepinephrine has been also associated with hostile attitudes.[65] In excessive amounts it may do damage to the lining of coronary arteries, provide a chemical insult to the heart muscle, promote high blood pressure and disturb platelets and red blood cells—all of which can contribute to the increased risk of a myocardial infarction or some other form of serious heart disease. The constant turning on of fight-flight responses can also trigger a coronary artery spasm, which may result in a heart attack.[66]

Overreactions to stress may stir up other biochemical

changes that can threaten our cardiac health. Cholesterol levels rise and uric acid goes up, and each of these has been associated with coronary heart disease.[67]

Diminished DNA Repair

Just as our cardiovascular and immune systems can be compromised by perceptions of chronic stress, another line of defense—on the molecular level—may also be affected. Researchers at Ohio State University College of Medicine and Comprehensive Cancer Center have reported impaired DNA repair in people who are highly distressed and have continued difficulty with coping.[68] The investigators found differences in DNA repair between psychiatric patients with high and low levels of distress.

The DNA repair system is a basic line of defense against development of cancer. When cells receive damage to genes from chemicals or radiation in our diets or environment, the DNA repair system—if it is not compromised—can keep mutations from occurring and tumors developing.

Damage to Brain Cells

Still another site of damage from high levels of certain stress hormones is the brain itself. Researchers at the Salk Institute for Biological Studies, San Diego, have found that glucocorticoids—steroid hormones produced by the outer parts of the adrenal glands during sustained stress—can damage brain cells, particularly in the hippocampus.[69] This part of the brain is critical for memory and damage to it can produce an inability to store new memories.

One of the effects of the corticoids during stress is that they block the entry of glucose into many types of cells, thus preserving the fuel for muscle movements and physical action. Brain cells use only glucose for energy and when deprived of "sugar," they have no other source of fuel and die.

The stress of such events as a cardiac arrest, stroke or Alzheimer's disease can cause glucocorticoids to flood into the bloodstream. In each of these disorders, brain cells already suffer from reduced oxygen, and the wave of stress hormones only adds to the threat of damage since they cut the cells off from glucose.

Regardless, then, of whether the stress we experience comes from our own perceptions or from physical events, powerful chemicals are released that can have far-reaching effects on the brain and body. From the nucleus of cells right up to the level of our immune defenses and cardiovascular system, what we do in our heads, as well as our behavior, emerges as a critical influence in whether we stay well or get sick. The brain plays a leading role either way.

PART 2
Neurotransmitters

4. Brain Messengers and What They Mean to Health

It's not just in your mind; it's in your brain.[1]

The human brain is designed to run the human body.[2]

Stated at its simplest, our health is controlled by our brain.[3]

The new knowledge of how our brains profoundly affect the functioning and malfunctioning of our internal organs has far-ranging implications for our health. Of key importance is the way the brain and body use a variety of chemical messengers to carry on proper communication among our 100 trillion cells.

The discovery that our very attitudes, beliefs and moods influence the action of the messengers has greatly expanded knowledge of how we can get sick—or, conversely, protect our health.[4] For instance, when we are chronically hostile, excessive secretion of one of these neurochemicals—norepinephrine—contributes to our risk of hypertension, arteriosclerosis or a heart attack.[5] When we believe our problems are beyond control, another hormone—cortisol—increases and can impair our immune system, making us more vulnerable to infections and some cancer.[6] When we think we cannot cope effectively, still another chemical messenger—dopamine, which is related to our sense of reward and pleasure—diminishes.[7] On the other hand, when we have a sense of being able to cope, when we have a sense of control or self-efficacy, our stress hormones—cortisol, norepinephrine and epinephrine—decline.[8]

These chemical transmitters and regulators come in a variety of molecular sizes and shapes with different critical functions. They can either stimulate or depress activity in the brain and body—in neurons, muscles and glands. To reach their target sites and organs, they use either nerve fibers or the bloodstream.

Neural transmitters bring fast action and excite or inhibit the cells they contact. Hormonal messengers, travelling in the blood, work slower (a matter of minutes or hours) and speed up or slow down target cells' metabolism and activity. A third group of messenger molecules are those that induce cells to grow in size and number and to differentiate. The activity of many of these "cell-growth factors" is modulated or influenced by neurotransmitters.[9] In fact, one of the features of various neurotransmitters and peptide messengers, including the endorphins, is the ability to enhance or diminish the activity of other messengers. Neurotransmitters may switch on genes in cells and thus influence the production of proteins, including receptors and new transmitters.[10]

Some neurotransmitters—such as glutamate—are excitatory while others (GABA, for instance) are inhibitory. If there are excessive amounts of a messenger or its receptor, there may be overstimulation of the receiving cells and an impairment of their function. If there is a deficiency of a messenger, there may be too little excitement or activity. However, dysfunction of neurotransmitter systems is more than simply an excess or deficiency of the messenger molecules. The problem may be a disregulation due, for instance, to lack of responsiveness by receiving cells or to too many or too few receptors on those cells.[11]

Whatever the disturbance, it can now be pictured in color-coded images produced by the advanced technology of positron emission tomography. Throughout the body, the systems most important to our health—the brain, the glands and the immune system—connect up and communicate, then, by way of "informational substances," messenger molecules that are exquisitely sensitive to our thoughts and reactions.[12] They can do "spectacular things," observed one molecular psychologist, working on the effect of stress and serotonin on learning and memory.[13] And, he added, "probably we have discovered only 5 percent of the messenger molecules in the body."

Keys and Combinations

Neurotransmitters and other informational substances are so important that their imbalances and abnormalities are now being tracked with the same intensity that was given in past generations of medical science to looking at tissue structure under a microscope.[14]

Our all-important chemical transmitters carry on their intercellular communication like so many keys opening the locks of countless doors. Since some messenger molecules promote or retard the activity of other transmitters, which then influence bodily functions, a "combination lock" metaphor may be more appropriate.[9]

Their presence and amount are affected by both environment and genetics, by our appraisals of what the world is doing to us and by how strong or weak our neural systems constitutionally are. Their action, then, can be jammed, shut down, overdone or inhibited by the interference of a variety of influences: drugs, viruses, bacteria, faulty nutrition, defective genes, aging—or stressful perceptions and beliefs.

The various effects that occur in our brains and bodies as a result of informational substances are also often a function of "second messengers" released inside our cells. When many neurotransmitters and hormones bind to the receptor sites on cells they are contacting, a special enzyme is generated that carries the message of the informational substances into the cells' interior, acting, then, as a second messenger.[15]

Kinds of Brain Messengers

The first generation of neurotransmitters to be identified were amines—having nitrogen components—and include norepinephrine, dopamine, serotonin and acetylcholine, the most common chemical messenger in our brains. But important as these are, they provide signals for only a small percent of the brain's circuitry. The monoamines, as these transmitters are called, are substances that nerve cells synthesize by making small changes in an amino acid.

Somewhat surprisingly, the same substances that go into the production of proteins in the body have been found to make up many of the transmitters in the brain. These are amino acids, which when linked together form peptides. One example of peptide messengers that have been discovered is the endorphins, the brain's natural opiates. However, individual amino acids—like glutamate, aspartate and GABA—also act as informational substances for the brain and body and carry on more communication among neurons than do brain peptides. (See Chapter 5 for how our moods and mental functioning can be influenced by the amino acids in the food we eat).

There are more than 20 different amino acids, and these can be strung together in various combinations like beads of different colors to form peptide necklaces or chains. Peptide messengers, although they are in lower concentrations in the brain, continue to be discovered and have sparked great excitement in neuroscience. As we noted in the Introduction, some of these communication molecules—which go into the regulation of our moods and emotions—are found in the intestines as well as the brain, suggesting why our "gut feelings" have such real meaning. Examples are vasoactive intestinal polypeptide (VIP), insulin, and cholecystokinin (CCK).

The Importance of Balance

Several of our informational substances act as both neurotransmitters and hormones. Norepinephrine, one of the biogenic amines, is an example. It increases when we are angry or exercise vigorously. As a neurotransmitter, it is secreted by cells in our brains and by our sympathetic nerve fibers. As a stress hormone, it is released by gland cells in the medulla (middle) of our adrenals. At excessive levels over time, it may damage the lining of our coronary arteries and our heart muscle as well as play a part in increasing our blood pressure and cholesterol.[4] If it is deficient, norepinephrine is implicated in our feeling depressed.[16]

A related chemical, ephinephrine or adrenaline, is another messenger that acts as both a neurotransmitter and a hormone. It increases when we are anxious or face unpredictable situations and sense a loss of control. Like the stress hormone cortisol, in excessive amounts it can interfere with the cells in our immune system.[5] Also related chemically to norepinephrine are the monoamines dopamine and serotonin, which play an important part in healthy mental functioning. As we will see, excessive dopamine seems to be involved in schizophrenia and deficient serotonin in depression.

Since 1975, when the brain's endogenous analgesics—the enkephalins and endorphins—were discovered, there has been an explosive increase in our knowledge about what the various messengers and regulators do, how widespread their action is in the body and the problems that develop when they are excessive or deficient. However, as we noted, when our brains and bodies malfunction, the explanation is not likely to be simple excesses or deficiencies of chemical messengers. An imbalance between neurotransmitters or other informational substances, as well as a disregulation, may be involved.[15] Our chemical messengers often work in coordination with each other, and one may require another—a partner—to function properly. For instance, a peptide messenger may make a cell more or less sensitive to its amino acid or monoamine partner.

Just as the interaction and balance among informational substances are important, so is recognition that nerve cells may communicate—or miscommunicate—in ways other than by neurotransmitters. The "branches" or dendrites of each of our 100 billion neurons have been found to generate tiny electric currents, which may constitute multiple networks of microcircuits in the brain and body and serve as another way that cells can make contact and carry on their influence.[15]

In any event, the internal communication in brain and body is sensitive to both the way we act and the way we think. How we look at problems and what we do about them, then, is critical to healthy functioning of cells and organs, starting at the basic molecular level.

A Man-made Chemical to Block Stress?

When we perceive a situation as stressful or threatening, the powerful changes that then occur in our bodies are orchestrated by a chemical called CRF (corticotropin releasing factor).[17] CRF belongs to a neuropeptide class of messengers, which are composed of longer strings of amino acids but are still not large enough to be called proteins; they are more protein fragments (proteins have thousands of amino acids, while peptides range from two amino acids to chains of 200). CRF was isolated and purified in 1981 at the Salk Institute in San Diego after 10 years of effort. It is produced by a cluster of cells in a part of the hypothalamus ("the brain's brain") called the paraventricular nucleus.

As a substance that largely controls the biochemical stress response, CRF travels from the hypothalamus to the pituitary gland (the body's master gland at the base of the brain), telling it to arouse the body for emergency action. The pituitary, in turn, sends a messenger —the ACTH peptide—to the cortex of the adrenal glands, where a cluster of steroids is released into the bloodstream and sent throughout the body, instructing organs and systems to perform to meet the demands.

At the same time, back in the brain, CRF also goes

to centers regulating mood and behavior. When given CRF, experimental animals become highly active but if they are placed in a strange environment, they go into a defensive posture and are less mobile and curious than untreated animals.[18] This "freeze" response is similar to what is seen in animals in stressful situations. CRF may increase the intensity of the stress we experience by having an "anti-Valium" effect.[19]

Another effect of CRF comes from its action on the control centers of the autonomic nervous system, which activates internal organs and systems with neural impulses.[18] Immediate effects are a rise in blood pressure and blood sugar, increased heart rate and a secretion of epinephrine from the adrenal medulla.

The discovery of CRF's structure has made it possible to prepare synthetic versions of the peptide messenger. Under Wylie Vale in the Peptide Biology Laboratory of the Salk Institute, scientists are now exploring ways to chemically prevent or treat stress responses so as to keep physiological damage from occurring. By modifying the CRF structure, a synthetic analogue of the brain peptide can block or inhibit action of the native hormone.[18]

For instance, chemical "keys" can be fashioned to fit receptor locks but not turn the nerve cells on. By occupying the cell receptor, the chemical prevents other transmitters or regulators from binding to the target molecule and activating it. An example of such action is provided by the narcotic "antagonist" naloxone, which binds to opiate receptors in the brain and keeps morphine or heroin from having an effect.

Reducing Stress Hormones

The Salk scientists have succeeded in creating a new molecule, a blocking agent, that reduces the release of stress hormones in laboratory animals that were administered CRF at the same time.[20] It may have considerable clinical promise in humans for reducing damage done by excessive or frequent release of stress hormones.

In addition, the CRF blocking agent may be useful in treating depression. High levels of CRF and stress hormones have been found in patients with major depressions. A third use may be in alcoholism. Chronic drinkers have high levels of the stress hormone cortisol (from the adrenal cortex), which produces heavy deposits of fat on the face and body and contributes to high blood pressure. CRF seems to be responsible and the new blocking agents may alleviate the problem.

Part of the Mechanism of Disease

Identifying the role of neurotransmitters, neuropeptides and hormones in the regulation of the body has led to a better understanding of how disease may occur. As we have seen, when we secrete excessive epinephrine and norepinephrine from, for example, a chronic struggle to dominate, the mechanism for cardiovascular disease and heart attacks may be triggered. When we overstimulate the adrenal cortex from a prolonged sense of no control in life, the hormonal build-up may impair the immune system and leave us vulnerable to viral and bacterial infections.[5] When we feel depressed and helpless for extended periods, the released chemicals may suppress the ability of our immune surveillance system to screen out renegade cells that lead to cancer.[21]

Neurotransmitters, which are particularly sensitive to whether we have a sense of control, may affect our immunity directly or indirectly. Through nerve fibers linking brain and body, they can influence by keying into receptors on the surface of lymphocytes. Or the transmitters may act through stimulating glands and hormones, which in turn affect immune function.

Communication Errors

With the discovery that cells "talk" to each other through chemical messengers, errors in communication, then, have been found to be the common mechanism for a number of diseases.[22] Because the brain and nervous systems control so many functions of the body, communication problems between neurons and among nerve cells that "talk" to muscles and glands can be particularly troublesome. Each neurotransmitter is made in the terminals of nerve cells and depends on various "raw materials," such as amino acids, for its manufacture. Many disorders seem to be due to deficiencies or excesses in these precursor "building blocks" or to mechanisms controlling the release of the neurotransmitter from its cell terminal or to its "re-uptake" (see Chapter 5 on "precursor treatment"). All these factors can influence how much or how little of the neurotransmitter reaches adjacent cells that it is trying to communicate with.

The communication errors may take the form not only of an excess or deficiency of the transmitters or messengers but also a defect in the cellular structures or receptors they contact. The "locks" that the messengers key into are molecules of various configurations on the membranes or surfaces of target cells. When they are defective or deficient, they jam the messengers or fail to "open" properly. For example, some types of diabetes—particularly Type II, the most common—now seem to be associated with deficient or defective receptors.[22] Glucose, from the digestion and absorption of carbohydrates or from release of supplies in the liver, builds up in the blood. It cannot gain entrance to our muscle and fat cells without insulin—a peptide messenger—"talking" to the receptors and getting them to provide a passageway.

Obesity seems to decrease the number of insulin receptors, thus keeping glucose out of cells, where it can be used for energy. When diabetes occurs with obesity, reducing the excess intake of calories appears to increase the number of insulin receptors and alleviates the problem. Regular exercise can also increase body cells' sensitivity to insulin and can lower blood sugar levels.

Identifying, then, the receptor "locks" as well as the neurochemical "keys" that fit them is central to understanding disease mechanisms and how to modify them. In 1984 the gene was isolated that carries the code of instructions for receptors on T-cells, which control and coordinate the immune system.[23] A few months later, scientists completed the "mapping" of the molecular structure of the protein receptor.[24] Both advances will help researchers understand how T-cells recognize foreign invaders, including cancer cells, in the body and latch onto them. Also, many diseases—such as rheumatoid arthritis and multiple sclerosis—involve disorders of T-cells, which may be more possible to correct now that the nature of the cell receptor is known.

Stress, Hypertension and Arthritis

Hypertension is another disorder whose treatment may depend on correcting an imbalance in neurotransmitters and their receptors. When our stress responses trigger sympathetic nervous system action, neurotransmitters are released that result in elevated blood pressure. But normally, tiny "thermostats" in the walls of blood vessels and the heart inform the brain of the elevation and instructions are given to stop firing sympathetic neurons and bring the blood pressure back within normal range.[25] Nerves from these "thermostats"—baroreceptors—terminate in the lower brainstem, where the amino acid L-glutamate is a major neurotransmitter. If this chemical messenger is interfered with or disrupted, an increased blood pressure brought on by our stress responses may continue and hypertension result.

Donald Reis, director of the Laboratory of Neurobiology at Cornell University Medical College in New York City, who is studying the role of glutamate and baroreceptors, notes that the connection between blood pressure and our thoughts and emotions involves the pathway between the forebrain, where we perceive and appraise the external environment, and a complex circuitry in the lower brainstem (the medulla oblongata), which is the blood pressure control center.[26] The pathway is part of the limbic system, the "feeling brain." The problem of high blood pressure, then, may be caused in part by the perceptions we make, the thoughts we have and the emotions we experience, as well as by the critical neurons at the base of the brain, which contain catecholamines and become unduly activated, interacting with other transmitters.

Rheumatoid arthritis, which flares up under stress, is also a common disorder that appears to involve excessive levels of a neuropeptide, in this case substance P.[27] This "short protein" or protein fragment, which is secreted from the ends of nerve fibers into joints, seems to contribute to joint damage. Arousal of the sympathetic nervous system by perceptions of stress may increase its activity. Importantly, substance P is also found in the immune system and may be the link between that system and the nervous system. Arthritis is believed to be an immune system disease in which people's cells attack their own joint tissue, which is mistaken as "foreign."

Another chemical messenger, prostaglandin, is also found in suspiciously high levels in the inflamed joints of people with arthritis. Prostaglandins, however, seem to be present wherever there is pain—from a headache, bruise, cut or burn. Excesses of the chemical are involved in pain, inflammation and fever.[28] At normal levels, prostaglandins—hormone-like substances that are made by almost every tissue in the body—are essential to kidney function, digestion, reproduction, nerve transmission and blood circulation. When prostaglandins are excessive and pain results, aspirin is useful. Aspirin seems to destroy an enzyme (cyclooxygenase) that cells use to manufacture prostaglandins.

Relief for Parkinson's Disease?

New treatment of Parkinson's disease may emerge from research on miscommunication by our chemical messengers. People with Parkinson's have trouble starting and sustaining voluntary movements and often have tremor, rigidity of the arms, legs and facial expression, and must walk with small, mincing steps. There is a loss of dopamine-containing neurons in a part of their midbrain known as the substantia nigra. Nerve fibers from this part extend to a higher section of the brain (the putamen) that regulates bodily movements, and the neurotransmitter dopamine is necessary for proper communication between the two areas.

Similar losses of dopamine cells may occur in old people in general, as may a decline in mental functioning. Deficient dopamine produced in an impaired substantia nigra also seems to affect another section of the brain to which fibers project—the caudate. The caudate is believed to be involved in cognitive functions.[29]

No one is certain what is responsible for the loss of dopamine neurons that gives rise to Parkinson's. A genetic predisposition may be involved, with some people from birth having smaller numbers of dopamine cells, which diminish even more as they approach old age.[30] Canadian researchers have reported a strong association between pesticide use and the disease, suggesting that environmental factors may possibly contribute to Parkinsonism. They note that the herbicide paraquat produces symptoms like those of Parkinson's disease in both humans and animals.[30]

As for treatment, the drug L-dopa relieves the condition in a number of cases but usually declines in effectiveness after a few years. L-dopa, unlike dopamine itself, can

95

pass from the bloodstream to the brain, where it is converted into the neurotransmitter. L (levo)-dopa is a naturally occurring amino acid that goes into the formation of dopamine. Another drug, bromocriptine, is also being tried in efforts to compensate for the dopamine deficiency in Parkinsonism. Bromocriptine is designed to stimulate dopamine receptors and relieve the rigidity and tremor characteristic of the disease.

In 1982 at the Karolinska Hospital in Stockholm, a piece of a man's adrenal medulla—taken from the adrenal glands over the kidneys—was grafted into his brain to trigger production of dopamine and to relieve the painful rigidity of Parkinson's disease. The medullary part or core of the adrenals contains dopamine cells, which can compensate for the destroyed or depleted ones in the brain. In 1985, two more patients received adrenal transplants in Sweden and were reported much improved in their movements.[31] But the positive effects have gradually disappeared. At the National Institute of Mental Health in this country, scientists have grafted adrenal medulla tissue into the damaged brains of rats and relieved Parkinsonism-like symptoms with restored dopamine production.[32] Yale researchers have reported success in transplanting adrenal gland cells into the brains of two monkeys.[31] But most people with Parkinson's disease are still given L-dopa, which their brains can use to help compensate temporarily for their loss of dopamine cells.

Inside the Brain with Living Color

Positron emission tomography, which provides a "window" into the actual functioning of the brain, has been used to visualize the disturbed chemistry involved in disorders such as Parkinson's disease. PET scanning involves injecting a radioactive sugar, for example, into a person and then using a ring of radiation detectors around the head to record the brain's activity as it uses the glucose for fuel.

Any number of compounds can be labeled with radioisotopes of natural elements in the body and then images obtained of the brain's use of the substances as they emit gamma rays. The images are produced on the scanner's computer screen and color-coded, with red, yellow and white indicating high activity in the brain area and blue, green and purple low activity. The images can be stored on a disc to be called up for comparison with later pictures of the same person's brain function.

When a person is in a depressed state, for example, a distinctly different image from normal is produced, showing reduced glucose utilization in key brain centers.[33] PET scans have shown increased activity in part of the frontal lobes of depressed patients who were given antidepressant drugs.[34] Such medication may have as much influence on the ability to concentrate and organize as on improving a person's depressed mood. In people with anxiety who are given antianxiety drugs, PET scans have pictured a "turned down" metabolic activity in the visual centers at the rear of the brain.[34]

Areas of the brain where receptors are low in concentration for certain transmitters—such as endorphins or dopamine—can be shown by PET. Images can also be obtained of the action of a drug like naloxone—which blocks the action of opiates—or chemicals that bind to dopamine receptors.[33] The new technology can "image" receptors for dopamine to show how they may decline or get blocked, preventing the neurotransmitter from communicating properly with target cells.[35]

Images of Disease

Even newer advances in positron tomography have permitted the use of radioactively labeled neurotransmitters to picture in still greater detail how the brain works and what happens in disease. Researchers at McMaster University

Center in Ontario have attached radioactive fluorine to dopa, the substance that converts to dopamine in the brain.[29] PET scans track its activity, showing little fluoradopamine along the damaged neural pathways of people with Parkinson's disease. One reason that such patients may be unable to respond to dopamine transmitters is an apparent decrease in dopamine receptors.

Scans have shown that dopamine receptors do, indeed, decline with age, and men experience sharper drops than women do.[36] Dopamine has not only been implicated in Parkinson's but also may be involved in schizophrenia, as we will see. In Parkinson's disease, Henry Wagner, director of nuclear medicine and radiation at Johns Hopkins, has shown that the density of dopamine neurons in the nigro-striatal pathway of the brain degenerates, while in schizophrenia an increase in dopamine receptors seems to occur.[35] It is now possible, with the development of receptor autoradiography, to make photographs of different types of receptors and the ways they respond to neurotransmitters.[37]

Restoring the Transmitter in Alzheimer's

Alzheimer's is another brain disorder that is being studied through the new scanning technology. It is a serious and not uncommon disease of middle and old age that is believed to involve destruction of nerve cells that synthesize acetylcholine, a neuropeptide that in other parts of the body triggers muscle action. As Alzheimer's progresses, a person becomes increasingly forgetful, undergoes personality changes and eventually may have to be fed, bathed and watched constantly.

Donald Gash of the University of Rochester and his colleagues have attempted to alleviate the condition experimentally by transplanting cells in the brain that produce acetylcholine.[38] The cells are from human tumors that have been deactivated by chemical treatment. A second approach has been to implant a pump designed to keep the area of the brain affected by Alzheimer's supplied with acetylcholine.[39]

Still another chemical messenger, vasopressin, which acts as both a peptide hormone and a neurotransmitter, may be associated with memory.[40] In Holland, researchers reported that a nasal spray of vasopressin seemed to enhance longterm memory.[10] Vasopressin is secreted during stress by cells in the hypothalamus, the brainstem, the limbic area and spinal cord. Fibers containing the compound also seem to extend to internal organs. The substance causes the kidneys to retain water, constricts certain arteries and raises blood pressure. Its role in memory is coordinated with action by norepinephrine. Increasing vasopressin in the brain may improve some people's ability to learn new information and, for certain victims of car accidents, may facilitate recovery from longterm amnesia.[41] Beneficial effects have also been noted in several tests to improve memory and attention in elderly persons.

During chronic or longterm stress, as we saw in Chapter 3, the surge of steroid hormones we experience is carried by the bloodstream to the hippocampus, a part of the limbic system in the brain that plays a critical role in memory and learning. In Alzheimer's, the loss of brain cells is aggravated by increased levels of glucocorticoids in the blood. Research on Alzheimer's may expand our knowledge of how memory and learning occur—and are lost.

What happens on the molecular level when we learn something, or hold on to it in our memory, is the subject of many experiments. One theory, based on animal research, is that brain cells sprout new dendrite branches and synaptic connections when learning occurs. Longterm memory of facts, faces, dates, numbers, etc., may leave cells in the cortex and hippocampus more sensitive to recall stimuli.[10] Adopting certain beliefs may result in certain neurons being more excitable and primed to fire.

Effect of Drugs on Messengers

Many of the early clues as to how the brain regulates our moods and behavior as well as our internal organs came from experiments with drugs given to people with various mental and physical disorders. In the 1950s, for instance, a drug derived from the plant rauwolfia was being used to treat hypertension. But it produced severe depression in some patients and was found to deplete the brain of three monoamines.[42] Two of these chemicals are close relatives of epinephrine, a neurotransmitter that excites cells and is generally associated with arousal and activity. It was found that rauwolfia—or reserpine—decreased the concentration in certain parts of the brain of norepinephrine, which was the first neurotransmitter conclusively shown to be involved in transmission of nerve impulses.[15]

Other evidence that the biogenic amines regulate mood came from a drug used to treat tuberculosis. Iproniazid produced euphoria in some TB patients and was found to increase monoamines in the brain. The increase occurred because iproniazid blocked the action of an enzyme (monoamine oxidase) that ordinarily breaks monoamines down and keeps them from accumulating.[42] For people who were taking reserpine for high blood pressure, depression could be prevented if iproniazid was given first.

Depression's Chemistry

Another drug discovered by accident was imipramine, an antidepressant currently in use. It jams the cell mechanism responsible for the re-uptake of three neurotransmitters important in depression—norepinephrine, dopamine and serotonin. These chemical messengers, secreted at the ends of certain brain cells to communicate with neighboring neurons, appear to become depleted in depression. Tricyclic drugs like imipramine and desipramine keep secreting cells from reabsorbing the three neurotransmitters, thus allowing the chemicals to build up in the synapse or gap between neurons. The substances cross the synapse to receptors on the membranes of adjacent cells, where they trigger electrical signals and nerve impulses.

Cocaine seems to have similar action, but—unlike the antidepressants—leads to addiction and depletion of the neurotransmitters.[43] People addicted to cocaine are now being treated with tricyclics, but some psychiatrists favor psychotherapy as the treatment of choice, reserving the antidepressants for severe cases.

The effectiveness of talk therapy in some cases of depression and cocaine addiction suggests that changes in neurotransmitters apparently occur in the brain as the patient changes the way he is looking at life and his problems (see also Chapter 12). When a person's customary way of dealing with difficulties is to consider them awful and beyond control, norepinephrine, dopamine and serotonin levels seem to decline. In experiments with rats subjected to unpredictable and uncontrollable shocks, alterations occurred in receptors for both norepinephrine and serotonin as the animals exhibited depressed behavior and apparently perceived their situation as hopeless.[44]

Paradoxically, in depression both an increase and decrease in catecholamines have been reported.[45] What seems clear is that there is a disregulation or disturbance of the neurotransmitter systems. The problem may lie in faulty synthesis of a neurotransmitter, too little or too much released, excesses not broken down or withdrawn, or it may be that receptors on receiving cells are not working right.

Depressive Effects of Our Hormones

Another possibility is that there is a disregulation of the hypothalamus-pituitary-adrenal system, since high levels of cortisol—a stress hormone from the adrenal cortex—have been found in depressed people. Studies have suggested that the trouble may start with excessive corticotropin-releasing factor or hormone produced by the hypothalamus.[46]

As we have noted, people who see stressful events as beyond control often secrete high levels of cortisol. Recently, researchers have uncovered clues on why high levels of cortisol may be associated with depression.[47] Animal studies suggest that a metabolite of cortisol may act like a barbiturate and depress nerve cell activity in the brain. Although other steroid hormones may excite nerve cells, the cortisol metabolite—THDOC—seems to mimic and enhance the effects of GABA, which, as we saw at the start of this chapter, is a neurotransmitter that inhibits cell activity. The inhibiting effect from the cortisol metabolite is like that of pentobarbital. If large numbers of brain cells are affected, depression of the central nervous system results.[47]

The mood changes, then, that come when we perceive excessive stress in our lives may stem from the effects that hormones, like cortisol, and their metabolites have on nerve cells in the brain.

Link with Endorphins

Improvement in cases of depression may also involve, through changes in serotonin receptors, the release of endorphins. Imipramine activates receptors in the limbic system—the "feeling" part of the brain—and triggers a metabolic reaction that lets the brain be more sensitive to its own serotonin. Serotonin is a transmitter that helps regulate our moods and, like endorphin, seems to relieve pain. An increase in serotonin apparently raises the activity of endorphins or enkephalins. A person who genetically has a weak endorphin system may have supersensitivity to psychological pain and, under stress, be particularly vulnerable to depression. As with other disorders, both genetic and environmental factors often combine to act on the brain and produce depression. As one author has observed:

> The brain doesn't care whether psychological pain is caused by a distant father or a misfiring endorphin system: its response will be the same.[48]

As we will see in Chapter 12, low levels of serotonin or its main metabolite, 5-HIAA, have been found both in persons who commit suicide and people who are alcoholic. Swedish researchers measured 5-HIAA levels in the cerebrospinal fluid of 119 suicidal or depressed patients and, on follow-up, found that 20 percent killed themselves within a year.[49] In this country, investigators at the National Institute of Mental Health have reported that alcoholics have low levels of serotonin.[50] Persons diagnosed as depressed who have a family history of alcoholism were found in another study to have significantly lower levels of 5-HIAA than was true of depressives with no alcoholism in their family history.[51] Whether deficient serotonin may, in part, be due to genetic factors and predispose some people to depression, alcoholism or suicidal behavior is a question under investigation.

Just as a sense of no control can change brain chemistry toward depression, other beliefs and perceptions may alter chemical processes in the opposite direction. For instance, aggression is associated with lower levels of GABA, which we noted is an inhibitory transmitter in the brain. Rats that have simply watched other animals be aggressive are then more violent themselves and have diminished levels of the inhibitor transmitter. One brain researcher in France has speculated that children who watch television violence are, in fact, more aggressive and that people generally are affected biologically by exposure to media violence.[44] In both people and animals, uncontrollable stress or violence may lead to changes in the brain that increase the risk of acting out and antisocial, aggressive behavior.

Evidence from Brain Surgery

In limited experiments with humans undergoing brain surgery, circumstantial evidence has pointed to the important effect biogenic amines have on a sense of well-being. When parts of the brain were electrically stimulated in surgery, patients reported an experience of pleasure. These centers of well-being corresponded to anatomical areas in the brain containing high concentrations of biogenic amines, such as norepinephrine and dopamine, which apparently were released by the electrical stimulation.[42]

Surgical research in animals has also helped to demonstrate that negative feelings, as found in depression, seem centered in the right hemisphere of the brain. When the neocortex of the right brain is removed, immune function is enhanced, apparently as a result of eliminating the source of depressive images.[52] When the cortex of the left hemisphere is removed, T-cells are lost and immunity diminishes. Activation of the left brain is associated with optimism.[53]

Probing the Mystery of Schizophrenia

Amphetamines in high doses lead to a rise in dopamine and are accompanied by symptoms resembling schizophrenia. Some researchers suspect excessive dopamine is a factor in producing schizophrenia.[54]

Dopamine was found to be the neurotransmitter the brain uses for communication between the corpus striatum part of the brain (near the base) and higher centers, mainly the limbic system and the frontal lobe of the cortex.[55] In people with schizophrenia, amphetamines have been shown both to increase the amount of dopamine and aggravate the disease.

On the other hand, it was found that antipsychotic

drugs, such as Thorazine, have effects because they block the amount of dopamine that reaches the upper brain from the corpus striatum. Such drugs, however, can produce serious side-effects, since they may also block dopamine in the motor centers of the brain, where muscle movement is controlled. Tardive dyskinesia, which causes a restless, jerky moving of the limbs and mouth, is the most striking example. Now scientists are searching for a drug that will block excessive dopamine to the limbic system and cortex without interfering with the needed neurotransmitter in the motor centers.

The aim of much brain research today is not only to identify all the neurotransmitters present in the central nervous system and understand their functions but also to synthesize drugs that will relieve mental illness. Since deficient or excessive transmitters are associated with major disorders such as depression and schizophrenia, one prospect is that drugs can be fashioned that will restore chemical balance.

But affecting the brain is not just a matter of finding drugs that work. Our very diets may have a potent influence also.

5. Mood, Food and Pain

Foods are chemicals, and some people may be medicating themselves with food because it makes them feel better.[1]

What you eat for lunch can affect more than physical fitness . . . certain nutrients can have a noticeable impact, within hours, on attention span, memory and mood. The effect is like that of a drug.[2]

Because we can get temporary relief from psychic pain by the food we eat, our moods affect what we eat just as our diets can affect our moods. Findings now confirm that what kind of mental or emotional state we are in, how confident or uncertain we are about coping with the problems we face, can determine what foods we seek.[3] People who are anxious, depressed or chronically under stress, for example, often crave sweets or junk food as a daily diet while those who have more of a sense of control prefer regular, more-balanced meals.[4]

Candy and pastries, as well as high carbohydrates found in snacks and take-out food, often lead to increases of serotonin in the brain and a temporary calming effect or satisfied feeling. If we chronically feel down, we may turn to carbohydrate snacks as a way to modify our moods by elevating serotonin. Most antidepressant drugs have similar action—that is, they raise the amount of serotonin available in the brain (see also Chapters 4 and 12).[5]

Turning to food to comfort us when we feel distressed is often learned early in life when cookies or other goodies are offered to children to distract them from a hurt or problem behavior.[6] When people feel distressed as adults, they often seek sweets to give them a lift. The effect is both psychological and physical, since the natural opiates we have in our brains seem to be triggered by perceptions of stress. For a while, at least, our hurts are blunted by what food does for us.

The two-way link between mood and food, then, involves our sensitivity to pain, both physical and psychological. Just as snack food can result in more serotonin, binge eating or excessive sweets seem to release endorphins, the natural opiates that relieve pain. Raised serotonin levels, as well as the endorphins, are known to diminish pain sensitivity.[7] In addition, gorging on food has been reported to relieve tension by reducing norepinephrine in the brain.[8]

Changing Brain Function with Food

Regardless, then, of whether the brain is being acted on by the natural drugs in our food or whether our choices of food are being determined by our moods and coping appraisals, clinical researchers are giving more attention to nutrients and their influence on cognitive function. The primary focus has been on the essential amino acids tryptophan and phenylalanine, neither of which can be synthesized by the body and must come from what we eat, and the nonessential amino acids tyrosine and glutamine, which the body manufactures but certain foods also contain.

Measurable changes in brain chemistry have been linked to what a person has eaten at the last meal. The evidence suggests that amino acids in the food we eat can have profound effect on depression and anxiety as well as our concentration, motivation and memory. The discovery that neurotransmitters in the brain could be enhanced by diet came as a surprise.[9] It had been assumed that the production of substances needed by all important systems in the body was kept at equilibrium and was not subject to increase by what was eaten. But ingesting more of the precursors that the brain uses to make its transmitters does seem to increase the neurochemical supply. Richard Wurtman, a physician who is professor of neuroendocrine regulation at MIT in Cambridge, has commented:

> It remains peculiar to me that the brain should have evolved in such a way that it is subject to having its function and chemistry depend on whether you had lunch and what you ate.[9]

Pasta or Shish Kebab?

We can increase our alertness and concentration by eating a high-protein meal a few hours before an important meeting, or if we want to be calmer at the risk of feeling lethargic, we can produce that effect if we have pasta or any other high-carbohydrate food.[10] Although such effects will vary depending on age (older people are more sensitive), sex (women get sleepy, men calmer from carbohydrates) and time of day, experiments have confirmed that "what one eats can affect the way one feels and behaves."[11]

Laymen may consider this an obvious point, but research has recently demonstrated which constituents in food may produce what specific effects. Also, the mechanism by which nutrients affect the brain and thus our moods and behavior is becoming clearer. In general, the food elements work by supplying brain cells with what they need for synthesizing certain key neurotransmitters—catecholamines, serotonin and acetylcholine.[12] Not all the nutrients that act as precursors for our neurotransmitters are amino acids. For instance choline, which is reported to aid memory, has been classed as a vitamin although it can be synthesized in the body.[13]

Foods Acting Like Drugs

Since some of the nutrients—such as tyrosine, tryptophan and choline—seem to have an effect on brain or mood disorders, including depression, they may serve as drugs and are being investigated as possible treatments. Just as drugs have neurochemical effects in the brain by producing changes in important transmitters, a food may bring about the same changes and have similar influences on our moods and behavior.[14]

Tyrosine, which is present in many protein-containing foods, has been tested in depression because it helps elevate norepinephrine and dopamine, which have been found deficient in depressed people. Harvard and MIT researchers, in one pilot study, reported improvements in 67 percent of the depressed patients who received tyrosine versus 38 percent who were given a placebo.[15] Tyrosine may also be useful in Parkinson's disease, which results from a deficiency of dopamine. This neurotransmitter depends on the amino acid tyrosine as its precursor.

Many of the pioneering studies on tyrosine and other nutrients affecting brain and behavior have been conducted by Wurtman's laboratory at MIT. Among other things, he has found that, based on experiments with rats, tyrosine is also useful for lowering blood pressure.[4] Since tyrosine is a precursor of norepinephrine and, in hypertensive animals, norepinephrine acts to lower blood pressure, increased doses of the nutrient boosts the brain's ability to control the body's hypertension.

Tryptophan, which is found in one percent of all dietary proteins, is another nutrient that may be useful in what is being called "precursor treatment." Tryptophan is necessary for the manufacture of serotonin, a neurotransmitter that lowers our sensitivity to pain, decreases our appetite and calms our moods. Tryptophan may also be useful in treating obesity and insomnia.

As for choline, it is present in lecithin, which is found in egg yolks, liver, soybeans and, in lesser amounts, in fish and cereals. It is converted at the terminals of certain brain cells into the neurotransmitter acetylcholine, which is deficient in Alzheimer's.[14] In a six-month study in London, half of the Alzheimer's patients given large doses of lecithin showed an improvement in certain cognitive functions and self-care.[4] Since acetylcholine is critical to the proper functioning of muscles and action of the body, food rich in lecithin has also been used to treat movement disorders, such as tardive dyskinesia.

Calm or Sleepy

Both tryptophan and tyrosine have been implicated in the changes that healthy people experience in mood, concentration and task performance after eating certain foods. Psychologist Bonnie Spring of Texas Tech University in Lubbock, who previously worked with Wurtman in Cambridge, headed a research team that tested the effects of both high protein and high carbohydrate meals on 184 normal adults.[16]

Women reported greater sleepiness after eating carbohydrates. Men felt calmer. When the meals were eaten for breakfast, but not for lunch, people 40 or older reported feeling more tense and less calm after a protein meal. Those in this age range experienced a decline in attention and concentration after a high-carbohydrate lunch.

A meal rich in proteins (and tyrosine) may act on the brain by increasing the synthesis and release of catecholamines. A high-carbohydrate lunch, on the other hand, increases the amount of tryptophan that reaches the brain. The more tryptophan that is available to serotonin-producing neurons in the midbrain—particularly the raphe—the more serotonin is synthesized and released, resulting in sleepiness for women and calmness for men.[16]

High carbohydrate meals may also lead to people making more errors at work and being at higher risk of accidents.[17] In fact, any big meal—1,000 calories or more—eaten at lunch seems to act on the brain in such a way that a person's performance that afternoon is impaired.

Perking Up

Finally, phenylalanine is also being investigated. It is an amino acid found, for instance, in aspartame, a sweetener used in many food and drink products—diet colas, puddings, fillings, chewing gum, cold breakfast cereals. Phenylalanine, as is true of tryptophan, tyrosine and other amino acids that can influence mood or brain function, is also sold in tablet or capsule form across the counter in many health food stores and pharmacies.

In the brain, phenylalanine manufactures a neuroregulator called 2-phenylethylamine (PEA), which has effects like amphetamine.[18] One food containing phenylethylamine is chocolate, which, somewhat facetiously, has been recommended for the blues of a broken romance. Some scientists speculate that the basic mechanism in depression may not be too little norephinephrine or dopamine but deficient PEA. However, PEA may not act alone but in combination with the other two neurotransmitters to affect our moods.

In any event, phenylalanine is chemically related to both phenylethylamine and amphetamine. Some athletes use phenylalanine, which is safer than amphetamines, to lose weight, promote alertness and avoid depression. L-phenylalanine has been found to improve memory, learning and motivation. Glutamine, another amino acid, also seems to enhance memory and concentration and has been used to help people addicted to alcohol and tobacco since it eases anxiety during the withdrawal period.[13]

The amino acid L-phenylalanine has shown limited promise as a treatment for depression. In one study it was given to 40 depressed patients every day for two to six months.[19] Of 31 patients who reported improvement in mood, 10 were completely relieved of symptoms.

Possible Headaches

On the down side, phenylalanine may contribute to migraine headaches in some people. Approximately 100 food products and beverages have in them aspartame, which contains the protein building blocks aspartic acid and phenylalanine. People who use food and drink products containing "Nutrasweet" (aspartame) reported a significant decrease in migraines when they eliminated the sweetener from their diets.[20]

Phenylalanine's tie to migraine headaches is believed to be through tryptophan and its neurotransmitter serotonin. At the onset of a migraine headache, serotonin levels drop in the brain, resulting in a dilation of blood vessels. The dilation, which follows vasoconstriction, is thought to produce the migraine pain. Serotonin depends for its production on tryptophan, which must compete with five other amino acids for entry into the brain, as we will see. When phenylalanine is in a person's diet, it crowds tryptophan out, leading to the drop in serotonin.[20]

In tests that Wurtman did of aspartame's effect on the amount of phenylalanine in the brain, he found that levels almost doubled in rats.[21] He used a dose of aspartame that was consistent with the amount that an 8-year-old child might consume during a hot afternoon—three cans of diet soft drink (500 milligrams) and 100 milligrams from other foods. Although aspartame has been approved as safe by the Food and Drug Administration, people should know that it can have effects on neurochemicals in the brain.

Competition for Brain Access

Increasing the production of a neurotransmitter in the brain is not simply a matter of consuming more food containing the compound's precursor amino acid. The effect of nutrients is influenced by the ratio of carbohydrates to proteins in the diet, by the frequency of cell firings and other factors.[14]

If we want to feel calmer and more relaxed by increasing tryptophan and serotonin in the brain, a high-protein meal will have the opposite effect. Even though tryptophan is found in dietary proteins, it drops after high-protein meals, and a person often feels tenser or more alert, not calmer or relaxed. A primary reason for this is that tryptophan must compete with five other more numerous amino acids in protein meals to cross the blood-brain barrier and affect brain function.

When a high-protein meal (steak, for example) sends amino acids into the bloodstream, tryptophan is at a disadvantage in attaching to the carrier molecule that "opens the gate" for crossing the blood-brain barrier. However, after a meal high in carbohydrates (pasta, for instance), insulin levels rise, sending the more numerous amino acids into muscle cells. Tryptophan has the unique ability to escape the insulin action by attaching itself to the blood protein albumin. It then is left free to enter the brain and make serotonin.[22]

In general, findings indicate that a high-carbohydrate, low-protein lunch will promote a more relaxed feeling and less sharpness in performing tasks or paying attention. A high-protein, low-carbohydrate lunch is more likely to do the opposite. One other effect of tryptophan, as we noted, is that it reduces sensitivity to pain and acts as an analgesic, like aspirin.[22]

"Precursor Treatment"

The use of food to treat the brain—using nutrients that act like drugs—is gaining popularity. As neurologist John Growdon of Massachusetts General Hospital in Boston has observed, precursor treatment "has great appeal because it is using the body's own mechanisms, but you're making it work in your favor . . . and it's unlikely to have toxic side effects or longterm deleterious effects that some synthetic drugs have."[23]

One theory on why some people start using cocaine is that they have deficiences of dopamine, norepinephrine or serotonin in key areas of the limbic system. At Columbia-Presbyterian Medical Center in New York and at UCLA, clinical researchers are using L-tyrosine and L-tryptophan to treat cocaine addiction.[24] As we have noted, tyrosine is a precursor amino acid for dopamine and norepinephrine and elevates levels of these two neurotransmitters. The amino acid tryptophan, necessary for the production of serotonin, increases the activity of that important psychochemical. At Temple University's Maxillofacial Pain Control Center in Philadelphia, tryptophan and a high carbohydrate diet are being used to relieve migraine headaches and temporomandibular joint pain.[25]

Some depressed people report a sense of euphoria when they get increases of tryptophan and serotonin in their brains.[17] Some people who are trying to stop smoking may also benefit from high-carbohydrate meals and doses of tryptophan.[26] The aversive effects experienced when smokers are deprived of nicotine appear to be relieved by tryptophan and serotonin.

Whether a given chemical messenger in the brain is excessive, deficient or otherwise disregulated may be the result not only of our diets and stressful interactions with the environment but also of our genetic predispositions. Some people, for instance, who are manic depressive or have other mood disorders seem to be born with an overabundance of receptors for the neurotransmitter acetylcholine.[27] "Perhaps two-thirds" of people who suffer both manic and depressive episodes and one-tenth of those with other mood disorders have "a genetic supersensitivity to acetylcholine that can be identified by skin testing."[28]

Food and Coping

When people feel anxious or depressed, one way they try to cope with those feelings is by eating. An example is the "carbohydrate craving" or uncontrollable quest for sweets that some persons have when they feel depressed.[4] They may be needing more serotonin in their brains and are turning to foods that will increase the levels of tryptophan, which is the transmitter's precursor. As we have seen, serotonin seems to relieve pain and has a calming effect.

The carbohydrate craving that preoccupies some people seems to have more to do with their brains' need for serotonin than it does with taste—having a sweet tooth—or an inability to control food intake. Judith Wurtman, a Ph.D. researcher at MIT's laboratory of neuroendocrine regulation, has shown that when obese people who crave snacks—potato chips, cookies, munchies of various kinds—are given a choice of sweets or nonsweet foods, they demonstrate no special appetite for cookies or candy.[5] They also do not have uncontrollable urges to overeat at regular meal time or increase their caloric intake. What her experiments suggest is that they have a specific need to increase serotonin in their brains. When, for instance, the carbohydrate cravers are given a drug—d-1 fenfluramine, which releases serotonin in the synapses of brain cells—the craving for carbohydrates is significantly reduced. Total calories consumed at regular meals also goes down.

Treatment of obesity or a craving for snacks, then, may not only be more effective if serotonin is increased (by drug or diet) but also by probing for the reasons behind the neurotransmitter deficiency or disregulation. Serotonin, as are other key psychochemicals, is apparently affected by our appraisals and the amount of control we believe we have. Increasing coping skills, particularly cognitive coping, may offer considerable promise for improving our moods, which then may improve our eating habits. From learning cognitive coping, we can enhance our sense of control and self-efficacy, which leads to less depression and greater pain tolerance (see also Chapters 12 and 16).[29]

What we eat, as well as how much, when we are

stressed has the potential of adding to our problems over the long haul. Junk food, high in fat, may lead to impairment of the immune system.[30] Eating carbohydrates to the exclusion of proteins may produce a protein deficiency, which interferes with the ability of T-cells and phagocytes to kill incipient cancer cells.[31] In the shortrun, a diet of snacks and junk food may give us a lift. We may not only get some sense of tranquility from an increase in serotonin but, if we eat enough, we may also enjoy a release of beta-endorphins, which deaden pain and elevate moods. Binge eating particularly has been linked to triggering endorphins. What is important to remember, however, is that this neurotransmitter, like others, can have both good and bad effects.

Endorphins: Positive Effects

That release of neurotransmitters is affected by our perceptions of stress and our reactions has been well documented in research. One of the peptides released in stress is the endorphins, which have attracted wide interest because they act like morphine in the brain and reduce pain. Three families of natural opiates or opioids in the body have been discovered. They include a variety of endorphins (a word meaning "endogenous morphine") and the enkephalins (Greek for occurring in the head), which are less potent, and the dynorphins ("dynamic endorphins"), the most powerful of the innate analgesics.[32]

The discovery in 1973 of receptors for opiates (see Chapter 2) triggered the explosion in brain research that continues today on an ever-growing list of neurotransmitters.[33] Scientists reasoned that if the brain has receptors for pain-reducing substances, then such chemicals must occur naturally in the head or body. Nature was not likely to put opiate receptors in our brains just to accommodate the use of pain-killing drugs.

The search for the innate analgesics uncovered the first enkephalins in 1975 and three of the endorphins shortly afterwards. The enkephalins and endorphins, although closely related and coming from the same mother molecule (lipotropin), have different pathways and tracts in the brain. Beta-endorphin was found to have the greatest opiate-like activity until dynorphin was identified in 1979.[32] These intrinsic opioids turned out to be pharmacologically identical to narcotic analgesics, which means that morphine is addictive because it mimics the molecular shape of natural transmitters that inspire a sense of well-being and freedom from pain. Various therapeutic devices are now being used with people who have chronic pain in an attempt to stimulate release of endorphins. One of these is a "neuroprobe," a small electrical instrument that is applied to painful areas of the body.

Some dentists are using transcutaneous electrical nerve stimulation (TENS) instead of novocaine to prevent pain for patients. A low-voltage electrical shock is administered and seems to provide anesthesia without side-effects and no need for hypodermic needles. One theory is that TENS may stimulate the release of the neurotransmitter serotonin, a psychochemical that blocks pain.[34]

1,000 Glands from Iran

In an early effort to purify what he later named beta-endorphin and to determine its sequence of amino acids, Choh Hao Li of the University of California at San Francisco made arrangements to obtain 1,000 pituitary glands from Iranian camels.[35] He had been told that camels are virtually pain-resistant, suggesting that their pituitaries are rich in natural opiates. Li got the camel glands, but it developed that camels do feel pain and the pituitary is only one source of endorphins.[36] Nevertheless, Li described the compound (a fragment of beta-lipotropin) as 48 times more potent than morphine and named it accordingly—endogenous morphine or endorphin.

A number of other neurotransmitters and peptides are now known to participate in the body's analgesic systems and the amount of pain we experience. These include norepinephrine, serotonin, substance P and dopamine.[37] Researchers are discovering that for pain-killing drugs to work, the body's chemical messengers must be in place. Analgesic drugs interact with the neurotransmitters and their receptors and if the chemical messengers or their receiving sites are disturbed, the drugs do less good. As with the endorphins, scientists are now trying to determine all the sites where these neurotransmitters and peptides are present in the body and what determines when they relieve pain or enhance health and when they may contribute to disease.

Endorphins, for instance, are present not only in the brain and pituitary but also in the intestinal tract, adrenal glands and other parts of the body. When we perceive something stressful, CRF brings about the release of beta-endorphin from the pituitary gland. Other opioid peptides (opiate-like substances made in the body) are also released from both the brain and peripheral nervous system, and there is some evidence that immune system cells have receptor sites for endorphins and enkephalins.[38]

As we saw in the last chapter, our bodies use endorphins to relieve psychological as well as physical pain. Some researchers postulate that the good feelings we experience when we get a pat on the head or succeed at something important come from a burst of endorphins. This psychobiological process is programmed into us from early age, and we become dependent on endorphin stimulation to maintain a normal emotional and physiological state.[39] But no matter how positive our childhood experiences are or our adult successes, if we have a genetically weak endorphin system, we may get inadequate release of the neuropeptide and be particularly sensitive to psychological pain. Similarly, if we have a strong endorphin system but constantly perceive situations as stressful and threatening, we may also experience frequent distress and possibly depression from depleting our endorphin supply.

Less Beneficial Endorphins

The action of endorphins may not be all beneficial. Some may promote tumors and impair learning or memory, according to animal experiments. A few reports have suggested that beta-endorphin, which increases under stress, might enhance our immune system or our ability to fight cancer and other disease.[40] However, other experiments have found that alpha-endorphin and other opioid peptides, secreted under inescapable stress, suppress the function of T-cells in the immune system and reduce the effectiveness of NK (natural killer) cells.[41] NK cells, as we have noted, seem to play a central role in protecting the body from development of cancer and viral infection.

Japanese researchers have reported that beta-endorphin promotes cancer growth.[42] They injected mice with the substance after the animals had received grafts of cancer cells. Tumors were accelerated in the injected mice. When the animals were given naloxone, a drug that blocks endorphin activity, the mice's survival rate increased. On the other hand, researchers in this country recently reported that beta-endorphins and met-enkephalins stimulate macrophage activity and may enhance immune function.[43]

Although the controversy continues, the majority of the evidence indicates that a perception of helplessness causes opioids in the body to increase, which in turn leads to diminished immune defenses and faster growth of tumors.[44] Natural killer cells, as well as other leukocytes, seem to be suppressed by the endorphins and enkephalins. The consensus seems to be that while the endorphin system may be vital for handling pain and emergencies, it is not useful in healing and may, in fact, dampen our immune defenses.[45] One other negative effect of endorphins is suggested by the finding that opioid peptides may encourage obesity because they seem to stimulate appetite and reduce energy expenditure.[46]

As for affecting learning and memory, psychologist Joe Martinez of the University of California, Berkeley, has found that leu-enkephalin injections induce cognitive deficits in rats.[47] No matter whether it is given before or after a learning task, leu-enkephalin results in impaired learning, according to his experiments. Since three major stress systems in the body—the posterior pituitary, anterior pituitary and adrenal glands—all produce enkephalins, there may be a connection between stress, increase in the peptides and effect on learning or memory. Endorphins may also play a role in schizophrenia, but the evidence is mixed as to whether an excess or deficiency is the problem. When naloxone, the endorphin antagonist, was given to a group of schizophrenics who had auditory hallucinations, a significant number stopped hearing things.[35] However, in other experiments, when a smaller group of schizophrenics was given injections of beta-endorphin, mild improvement occurred.

Swiss researchers have speculated that beta-endorphins may be involved in sudden infant death syndrome (SIDS), since high concentrations have been found in the brainstems of infants on whom autopsies were performed at the University of Zurich.[48] The theory is that the endorphins were triggered by stress—the stress, for instance, of some innocuous illness—and then may have suppressed normal breathing function in the sleeping babies. The opioids are known to suppress the breathing reflex as well as the immune system.

Inner Thrills and Chills

Although the negative effect of endorphins is still not well defined, repeated findings do suggest their usefulness in promoting a sense of well-being as well as relieving pain. Endorphins can apparently be triggered by vigorous physical exercise, such as running, which is frequently followed by increased feelings of well-being.[49] The role of endorphins in producing "runner's high" must be interpreted with caution, however, since stress may release endorphins in the body without increasing them in the brain. But in terms of pain relief, endorphins do seem to "turn on" in the placebo response when people strongly believe that a certain pill, procedure or coping skill will reduce their discomfort or disorder.[50]

In addition, endorphins seem to be released when we are moved by music, the beauty of a sunset, a work of art or some similar experience, and we get goose bumps at the back of our necks or a tingling feeling of chills running up and down the spine. This hypothesis was tested at Stanford by pharmacologist Avram Goldstein with students who listened to their favorite music and were given the drug naloxone. They were compared with a matched group who received a placebo.[51] Since naloxone blocks the effects of endorphins, Goldstein predicted that the students given the drug would not experience the sense of euphoria that normally comes when endorphins are turned on. He was right; many students did not get the same sensation from the music as they usually did or that the control group did. The reason seemed to be that the euphoria-producing endorphins were not allowed to do their job because of naloxone.

As part of the same study, Goldstein surveyed 249 students, faculty members and staff on what kind of experiences most commonly produced "thrills"—goose bumps, tingling, chills, hair standing on end or other signs of intense feeling.[51] Musical passages ranked first, followed by scenes from a movie, play, ballet or book, great beauty in nature or art, touching, nostalgic moments and sexual activity. (For more on endorphins and Goldstein's work, see Chapter 16).

The Brain's Valium

Just as the brain will release substances that block pain and promote a sense of euphoria or well-being, it also seems to have neurons that secrete Valium-like chemicals that produce calming effects.[52] Related to the endorphins, these transmitters—the benzodiazepines—quiet anxiety, relax muscles and help to induce sleep.[39] Compounds have been isolated that act on the molecules that serve as benzodiazepine receptors on cells. Through these, researchers are identifying possible ways to help people with sleep disorders. Both the opioid and benzodiazepine systems seem to be intrinsic to the brains of animals from insects to humans. This suggests that we have the built-in potential to deal with both pain and anxiety by tapping these internal systems.

But the brain also has a naturally occurring peptide (DBI) that increases anxiety.[53] This recently identified compound blocks the effects of drugs such as Valium and Librium and a chemical messenger in the brain (GABA) that inhibits and slows down activity of neurons. It does this by occupying cell receptors that are target sites of GABA or tranquilizing drugs. Tranquilizers like Valium and other benzodiazepines apparently work by stimulating the production of GABA—gamma-aminobutyric acid—and quelling heightened activity in brain synapses. DBI works in the opposite direction.

Although the brain seems to have its own anxiety compound, it also is well endowed with keys to self-healing processes and calming mechanisms. Faith, love and positive expectations, as we will see, are now being researched as a means by which the mind may activate the body's intrinsic healing processes, which serve to protect our health and promote recovery from disease. These processes seem to be largely regulated by neurotransmitters and peptides. When we increase our resistance to disease through a sense of control and support in life, we may be inducing our neuro-regulators to trigger the body's self-healing mechanisms.

PART 3
Coping

6. How Ties That Bind Benefit Our Health

Friends can be good medicine.[1]

"A problem shared is a problem halved" is certainly true, at least in terms of its toll on physical and mental health.[2]

. . . the quality of our relationships may have more to do with how often we get sick and how soon we get well than our genes, chemistry, diet, or environment.[3]

We now know that people's reactions to the same stressful experience vary widely and those who have a greater sense of control, support and satisfaction in their lives are at less risk of illness. Those who get sick most seem to view the world and their lives as unmanageable while those who stay healthy have a greater sense of coherence and control though faced with the same problems.

A wide range of illnesses reflects the role that ineffective coping and inadequate support play. The highest rates of tuberculosis have been found among isolated and marginal people who have little social support, although they may live in affluent neighborhoods.[4] Similar findings have been reported for other respiratory diseases. People who lack a sense of control or support have also been found to have higher rates of accidents and mental illness.[5] In England during World War II, children who were separated from their parents and evacuated to safer areas experienced more deleterious effects than did those who remained with their families during the blitz.[6] More recently in England, civil servants with the highest rate of death from coronary heart disease have been found to be workers who have less contact with neighbors, relatives or friends—who have, in other words, little social support.[7]

Social support can be helpful in a number of ways: If something bad happens to us and we have people who stand by us, our view of the problem is likely to be less pessimistic or hopeless. Someone may give us useful information on how to deal with the problem. Or the support may be even more tangible in the form of money or material aid. We may be given emotional support and understanding that is important to us. Or, if nothing else, we may be invited to go somewhere or do something that will get our minds off our trouble for awhile.

Permanence and Continuity

Although social support may help us view problems less stressfully and thus protect our health, it may do so by enhancing not only our sense of control but also our sense of permanence and continuity. As we saw in Chapter 3, people who believe in the value of certain central principles, places or relationships seem to be at lower risk of some disorders. Their sense of permanence and continuity, of attachment to home, place or religion apparently attenuates the effects of negative experiences and promotes well-being. These are people who believe in the importance of stable relationships, of routines in daily life, of spiritual principles that suggest a universal order. They seem to draw strength from places they love.

When Boyce and his coworkers at the University of Arizona School of Medicine tested 89 unmarried pregnant adolescents for their sense of permanence and continuity, they found that mothers scoring low were much more likely to give birth to infants who experienced neonatal complications.[8] Mothers who scored high on a perception of permanence and continuity had significantly greater psychological well-being. Socioeconomic status was not significantly related to sense of permanence. There was a strong association, however, between social support and sense of continuity and permanence.

The researchers suggest that the reason social support is positively related to less illness and better health is that it increases our sense of permanence and continuity, which in turn influences how we view the world and react to it. They also argue that if we have a sense of permanence, we are more likely to have a sense of meaning in life, which is another factor that may protect us against illness.

Social support, sense of permanence, continuity and meaning, our appraisal of life experiences—all, then, seem interconnected in terms of how they can have beneficial effects on our health.

Friends, Church Ties and Health

A widely quoted study, which tracked the health of people in Alameda County, California over nine years, showed that those with many social ties—such as from being married, having friends and contacts with relatives, participating in church affairs and belonging to other groups—experienced significantly lower mortality rates.[9] Even middle-aged men who had insufficient income but much social support lived longer than did affluent men with poor social ties. And even people who smoked, drank and engaged in other unhealthy behavior found a surprising degree of protection from the ties that bind.

A separate study on the relationship between cancer and social ties followed 6,848 men and women in the Alameda County survey for 17 years. Women who were socially isolated were found to be at a significantly higher risk of dying of cancer.[10] In addition, isolated women who *felt* they were without support were much more likely to get cancer. Social ties did not seem to affect whether men got cancer. However, among men who developed cancer, those who were socially isolated died much sooner than did those who had social ties.

As suggested by the Alameda County study, social support can be found in a variety of settings—at home, work, church. Support on the job from supervisors and coworkers has been identified as increasing resistance to a number of illnesses, including heart disease, ulcers, chronic respiratory ailments, rashes.[11]

People who attend church regularly have less reported cardiovascular disease, pulmonary emphysema, cirrhosis of the liver, abnormal cervical cytology and lower blood pressure.[12] This has been found true even when allowances are made for age, race, sex, social class, weight and smoking history. In addition to the social support people may experience from regular church attendance, their health may also benefit from the calming effect of prayer or increased faith.

Researchers at Howard University reported in a 1985 study that among 800 black persons surveyed in Norfolk, Virginia, involvement in religion offered an important protection against depression.[13] Along with having close friends and confidants, participating in church activities and listening to religious programs on the radio and watching them on television were found associated with fewer symptoms of depression.

Less Heart Disease

Another community that demonstrated the positive influence on health of the ties that bind was Roseto, Pennsylvania (see Chapter 10).[14] In this closely knit community of Italian-Americans, heart disease rates were significantly lower than those in neighboring towns and the rest of the United States. This was true despite the fact that the Rosetans had a high-fat diet. However, when the close ties and strong support system began to weaken as younger generations broke away and adopted other lifestyles, the heart disease rate climbed substantially and began to equal national norms.

In Israel, men who were diagnosed as having a high risk of heart disease were almost two times less likely to develop angina pectoris—chest pain from restriction of blood to the heart—if they felt they had loving and supportive wives.[15] Almost 10,000 men were studied over five years. Researchers from Tel Aviv University and the Israel Ischemic Heart Disease Study were surprised to find that some of the effects of heart disease risk factors—such as hypertension and high cholesterol—could be "counteracted" if a husband believed he had his wife's love and support.

The amount of obstruction in arteries may also depend for some people on how much social support they get. Persons with Type A behavior, which is characterized by a sense of time urgency and a struggle to dominate, have been found to have less arterial blockage—from cholesterol build up and fatty deposit—as a function of social support.[16] It may be that Type As with a sense of support alter their chronically stressful perceptions and lower their stress hormones, which reduces their level of cholesterol.

Group Ties and Longevity

Perhaps the most persuasive evidence for social support comes from the impressive longevity and significant resistance to major disease of the Japanese, whose culture emphasizes close group ties. As noted by Leonard Syme, professor of epidemiology at the University of California, Berkeley, the causes of our health problems are often attributed to "industrialization, urbanization, technology, pollution, smoking cigarettes and a fast pace of life."[17] But the Japanese have all these problems yet do not have as high incidence of disease. Japan is a highly industrialized, urbanized technological society that has a pollution problem worse than ours, its people smoke more than Americans do, and the pace of life in its cities is at least equal to that found in our metropolitan areas. Despite these "health hazards," Japanese now have the highest life expectancy in the world, the lowest heart disease rate among nations that keep health statistics and a low rate of death from all causes.[17] How is this possible?

The easiest explanation would be that the Japanese have an exceptionally favorable genetic inheritance. But the evidence fails to support this hypothesis. Japanese who migrate to the United States and adopt western ways become just as vulnerable to heart disease and other illness as Americans are. Those, however, who keep close ties to Japanese values and community enjoy protection from higher death and disease rates. This is true even for the Japanese migrants who eat American diets—food high in fat and cholesterol.

What may explain the protection found among the Japanese is "Amae," a characteristic they value. "Amae" emphasizes a belief that the well-being of the individual depends on cooperation with others and goodwill from the person's group.[18] In other words, social support is central to the values Japanese practice and continues to provide a source of resistance to disease even when migrants adopt unhealthy habits like eating food rich in cholesterol and not exercising enough.

Various kinds of health problems have been alleviated or avoided by what seem to be the beneficial effects of support. Among women under high stress who perceived they had support in their lives, complications of pregnancy were nearly one-third lower than among those who believed they had little support.[19] Because a pregnant woman's belief that she is supported can have powerful physiological effects, it is the tradition in many cultures for a mother in labor and childbirth to be accompanied by a friend or relative. A study in Guatemala found that women attended by a friend had far fewer complications and experienced an easier delivery.[20] They also stroked, smiled at and talked to their newborn babies more. Among 100 married men whose manufacturing plants shut down, those who saw themselves as receiving support from wives, relatives or friends experienced lower levels of cholesterol, fewer illness symptoms and less depression than did the men who considered themselves as having little support.[21]

Persons with chronic conditions, such as asthma, also seem to react less negatively to high stress if they perceive a support network around them. Asthmatics who had recently undergone a number of stressful experiences but had high support required less than a third amount of the steroid drugs than did those who had an equal amount of stress but low support.[22]

Immune System Affected

When social contact is increased or loneliness reduced, the immune system seems to strengthen. A group of 30 elderly people in retirement homes showed increased immune competence in terms of both NK (natural killer) cells and antibodies from being visited three times a week for a month.[23] Support can also affect T-cells when a person is under stress.[24] Lack of support has been found to reduce suppressor T-cells and is associated with recurrence of some illnesses, such as herpes simplex, Type II.

Princeton psychologists have found that undergraduates with low social support perceive their environment as significantly more stressful.[25] They also have lower levels of IgA (upper respiratory defense) antibodies than do students with high support. In women, the immune system seems to be sensitive to the social support that comes from a good marriage. In a study of 38 married women, researchers at Ohio State University College of Medicine found that marital quality was significantly associated with immune functioning, including percent of helper T-cells and ratio of helper to suppressor lymphocytes.[26] The women who perceived their marriages as satisfying and supportive had less depression and loneliness as well as better immune defenses.

Close Relationships the Key?

Having frank and confiding relationships may be a critical element in whether social support protects our health. In other words, it may be more important to have at least one person with whom we can share open and honest thoughts and feelings than it is to have a whole network of more superficial relationships. Researchers at the University of New Mexico School of Medicine found that, among 256 healthy elderly people, individuals with confiding relationships had significantly higher indices of immune function, lower serum cholesterol and uric acid levels.[27] As noted in Chapter 2, both elevated cholesterol and high uric acid have been associated with heart disease.

We have suggested that one way social support seems to protect our health is by reducing the intensity with which we look at stressful events and react to them. If we know we have someone "in the wings" who will support us and help guide us, we tend to view a threatening situation less pessimistically. We thus lower the levels of our stress hormones and diminish their potential effect on our immune defenses. Some authorities have taken the position that the way social support promotes our health is by encouraging us to eat regular meals, get plenty of sleep, exercise and practice other healthy behaviors.[28] In other words, if we have people who are close to us, they are likely to care about our health and urge us to adopt lifestyles that are good for us.

Pets as a Companion or Support

Although the effects of social support may in some instances come from the benefits of having loved ones monitor our health, this is not true in all cases. For example, it has been found that pets as well as people can serve as sources of support, love or companionship. With persons who have experienced heart attacks, their survival rates increase if they have pets waiting for them at home.[29] Patients in hospitals, including mental hospitals, are reported to recover faster and are discharged sooner when pets are around. People

with high blood pressure have been found to have "significant reduction in blood pressure in the presence of a pet."[29]
The fact that animals we deeply care about may contribute
to our health suggests that a key ingredient in how distressed we become both physically and psychologically is
whether we have relationships in our lives that we view as
loving or supportive.

Aaron Antonovsky, an American-educated sociologist who migrated to Israel and joined the faculty of Ben
Gurion University, developed an extensive theory of what
keeps people healthy by observing those who have undergone extreme stress—such as the experience of a concentration camp, poverty, racial discrimination—yet remain "at a
fairly high level of health."[30] The key, he concluded, was
that they had a number of "generalized resistance resources," including social support, which contribute to a
"sense of coherence" (see Chapter 3).

The University of Chicago study of stress also found
that the business executives who stayed healthy were those
high in "resistance resources."[31] Although psychological
hardiness—a sense of control, challenge and commitment—
offered the most powerful benefit, social support also was
found to have a protective influence. Exercise was another
buffer for the effects of stress. Psychologists Kobasa and
Maddi found that for executives under high stress who had
all three of these resistance resources, the chances of suffering a severe illness in the near future were less than 1 in 10.
In contrast, for the high-stress manager who had neither
psychological hardiness nor support and did not exercise,
the severe illness probability was more than 9 chances in 10.

Not All Support Is Helpful

Despite many reports on the positive effects of support, recent research has confirmed that its mere existence cannot

be automatically equated with being beneficial to our health. Whether support is helpful or not depends on its type, the kind of stress a person is facing and the personality of the individual.

A man who has high stress at the office probably needs problem-solving support from his boss or coworkers more than emotional support from his wife. In fact, high support at home may be detrimental. In the study of executives under stress, those who had low psychological hardiness but high support at home reported more illness than those who had less support.[31] It was as if the executive who could count on much sympathy from his spouse was "more likely to give up the fight . . . and simply stay home and let his family take care of him."[32] Managers who perceived they had support from their bosses had lower illness scores under stress.[33]

In other studies, it has been found that people who are high on internal control—they see themselves capable of influencing situations and are not just at the mercy of events—make best use of social support and experience less distress when they have it.[34] Support that is helpful at one time may not be later. A bereaved person may benefit from family support immediately after the death of a spouse but be kept from reestablishing other relationships and renewing outside activities if that kind of support continues indefinitely. In the case of some illnesses, "expressions of support received during times of severe and chronic disability may only serve to highlight the person's inability to reciprocate that support" and diminish the individual's self-esteem.[35] A cancer patient may need support and information from health professionals or other patients more than expressions of concern from friends and relatives.[36]

Whether support is stress-relieving, then, depends on the context and circumstances in which it is given, as well as on how the person perceives it or uses it. Another factor that must be considered is the nature of the group giving "support." Friends or groups that reinforce smoking and drinking habits or encourage the use of other drugs cannot be considered helpful. Some kinds of support are clearly unhealthy.

How It Looks to the Person Involved

The importance of how we perceive support cannot be over-estimated. We must not assume that because a person is married, he or she will feel supported and enjoy greater resistance to disease than someone who is divorced, widowed or single. For example, among 4,581 men of Japanese ancestry living in Hawaii who were studied over nine years, those who were married or remarried experienced a higher incidence of cancer.[37]

In the San Antonio Heart Study of more than 3,000 Mexican-Americans and non-Hispanics, men living alone had lower triglyceride, total cholesterol and LDL (low-density lipoprotein, "bad" cholesterol) levels than did males living with others.[38] The men living alone also visited with friends more and may have perceived themselves as having good support in life. The marital quality study at Ohio State also emphasized the point that it is not just the presence of support that is important to health, it is the quality.[26]

The Way Physicians are Perceived

Physicians, by definition, are in supportive roles, but the way they are perceived by patients can produce marked physiological effects that may be quite negative. For instance, our blood pressure often shoots up in the presence of a doctor. A group of 48 persons, consisting of both "hypertensives" and "normotensives" were monitored for 24 hours to establish their average blood pressure.[39] They then made a 15-

minute visit to a physician. After a two-minute contact with the doctor, their systolic pressure (upper reading) was an average of 27 millimeters of mercury higher and their diastolic (lower) was 15 points greater. Even after 10 minutes, average blood pressure remained mildly elevated. And during a second visit with the same physician, blood pressure went up, almost as much as the first time.

This study highlights the powerful effects our thoughts and anticipations can have on important bodily functions and the time it takes for us to adapt to an authority figure—even someone in a supportive role. At hospitals, similar effects occur as a result of perceptions by patients. The effects are particularly pronounced when the staff is new or unknown to the person under treatment. One study showed that people in the hospital with heart attacks were five times more likely to experience sudden death when unfamiliar staff were making rounds.[40]

Even heart attack patients who are improved enough to be transferred out of the coronary care unit to a general medical section of the hospital may react negatively to the change in surroundings, equipment and personnel.[41] Five of seven patients making such a move had increases in levels of catecholamines (the "fight-or-flight" stress hormones). With a second group, the patients were given information in advance about the move and the same physician-nurse team from the coronary unit accompanied them during the transfer. Patients in the second group showed significantly lower levels of catecholamines.

The Familiar and Predictable

What is familiar to us is often less threatening because it seems more predictable and manageable. Animal studies have confirmed the important influence unfamiliarity has on stress reactions. Experiments showed that if pigs with induced coronary occlusions (blockage of heart arteries) were kept in a laboratory and tended by staff with whom they were familiar, no lethal, irregular contractions of the heart muscle would occur.[42] But if the pigs were in a laboratory new to them and tended by a unfamiliar crew, fatal arrhythmias of the heart resulted. When J.P. Henry and his research group at UCLA School of Medicine used crowding to induce hypertension in their laboratory mice, they noticed that high blood pressure occurred only when the animals were strangers to each other.[43] If litter mates were used in the experiment, little conflict over territoriality resulted from the crowded conditions and high blood pressure failed to develop.

When people move to strange or unfamiliar locations that they perceive as stressful, their risk of ill health often increases. For example, cigarette smokers who were born in rural areas and migrated to cities had a considerably higher death rate from lung cancer than did lifetime urban dwellers with the same smoking histories.[44] The rural smokers' stress reactions, with chronic elevation of catecholamines and cortisol, may have markedly impaired that part of the immune system that helps protect against development of malignant tumors.

Although having family, friends and familiar faces around us can markedly modify how stressfully we view something, we can also gain a sense of control from other sources. We can learn better coping skills, take more responsibility for ourselves, acknowledge our successes and recognize that our failures do not mean the world has come to an end. The evidence shows that our very beliefs are in themselves important in our resistance to illness.

7. Taking Charge and Living Longer

You can't control the world, but you can control your response to it.[1]

. . . the belief in personal control . . . is basic to human functioning—regardless of who the person is or where he or she may be.[2]

I f viewing life and its difficulties with pessimism or helplessness increases our risk of illness, then whatever enhances our sense of confidence and control is likely to reduce our vulnerability. Research findings indicate that not only can we learn to look at problems less stressfully but we can also add to our feelings of self-efficacy and control by taking more responsibility for ourselves and not handing over to others the job of "fixing" our health or taking care of us.

Psychologists Ellen Langer, now of Harvard, and Judith Rodin of Yale demonstrated the beneficial effects on health of self-responsibility and positive outlook in the elderly.[3] They gave one group of nursing home residents potted plants to care for and offered suggestions on doing more for oneself instead of letting the staff take all the responsibility. A second group—matched with the first in terms of degree of ill health or disability—received the usual nursing home treatment with the staff announcing that they would be responsible for the care of the residents and make all the decisions.

Within three weeks, the first group showed significant improvement in health and amount of activity engaged in. Even more dramatic were the results after 18 months. The death rate of the "self-responsibility" group was one-half that of the other group.

Positive Self-Statements

Patients in the first group were also taught coping skills, which helped them make changes in their environment and gave them techniques for dealing with stress. They were told how the negative statements they made to themselves when they confronted a problem were a major determinant in increasing the stress they experienced. Group members were taught positive self-statements to use when they faced a stressor. Compared with the residents who were not given training in coping skills, the intervention group showed significant improvement in stress hormone levels and perceived control as well as in physical symptoms and longevity.[4]

The care of both their plants and themselves seemed to be a big factor in an added sense of control for the residents. Making more of their own decisions contributed to this sense. They became convinced that by changing their "internal environment"—their attitudes and self-statements—they could take more effective action on external problems and conditions they identified as sources of stress.

If we believe that control in life is "internal" more than "external," that we have influence over what occurs to us and are not simply pawns of fate, chance, luck or powerful forces, then high stress does not seem to have much impact on our health. For example, psychologists James Johnson and Irwin Sarason of the University of Washington found that depression and anxiety were high among students with multiple life changes only for those who believed they had no control over what happened to them.[5] Those who perceived themselves as in charge of their lives showed no depression or anxiety despite high stress.

The risky effect of an external locus of control on depression has also been demonstrated in a study of institutionalized elderly people.[6] Two nurse researchers from Pennsylvania State University tested 60 men and women, age 65 to 95, who were residents in two longterm care facilities in rural Pennsylvania. Those who believed that what happened to them was more controlled by external sources than by their own actions were more depressed and had lower self-esteem. The more depressed elderly also perceived themselves as having less social support.

When Events are Beyond Control

Even when control over external events is impossible, how we react *is* under our control. In fact, as we saw in Chapter 3, control is defined by some psychologists as a *belief* that we have the ability to reduce the aversiveness of something stressful.[7] Since we can reduce the intensity of our stress by looking at problems without "catastrophizing" about them, we have within us the ability to control the effects that adversity has on us. By reducing the internal effects of how stressful something is, we are better able to deal with the external problem.

Closely related, then, to this sense of inner control is a belief in our own self-efficacy, in our ability to cope effectively. The evidence shows that perceived self-efficacy—that is, the *belief* that we can manage adverse events or their effects—is strongly correlated with both psychological and physical well-being.

People with an efficacy belief are less likely to be depressed and, when exposed to stress, their sense of control keeps stress hormones and endorphins from reaching such levels that their immune systems are impaired.[8] Because a sense of control or self-efficacy means toned-down physiological and biochemical reactions for our bodies, it is a crucial element, therefore, in staying healthy. In some instances, it can even play a role in whether we survive.

For example, one of the most stressful events in the lives of elderly people is being moved from one location to another, from one institution to another. A marked increase in death rate often occurs, particularly in the first three months after relocation. When a home for the elderly in Chicago was closed, the mortality rate was substantially lower for those who accepted the news of relocation philosophically but not with a sense of defeat or helplessness.[9] Those who got angry had the next lowest death rate. Residents who became depressed had a high mortality rate. The very highest was found among those who tried to deny the reality of the impending move. Physiologically, an angry reaction may have been helpful in this instance because it mobilized the residents to take care of themselves by eating, keeping as active as possible and not giving up.

Information Increases Control

A sense of increased control can come from a number of sources—from building a support system, learning new coping skills, placing faith in someone or something we deeply trust, or from adopting a less negative outlook (which gives more control over the intensity of physiological reactions). Another important source is information. Giving people useful or relevant information can help them prepare for what is coming and make the situation more predictable and manageable. Even more importantly, such information can lead to our interpreting the situation as less threatening and reducing our anxiety and physiological response.

The effects of information, emotional support, training in relaxation exercises and other coping skills—all provided to groups of hospital patients—have been analyzed in 34 controlled studies.[10] Sociologist Emily Mumford and her collaborators at the University of Colorado found that the benefits included shorter stay in the hospital, speedier recovery, lower blood pressure and fewer posthospital complications.

Recently in England, 63 patients undergoing a gynecological operation (laparoscopy) were studied to determine the effects of giving 20 of them an informative booklet on the surgery, telling them how to deal with preoperative fear and postoperative symptoms and how best to promote their recovery.[11] These women were compared with 26 others who received routine care only and 17 who got a booklet that gave global, reassuring statements but little information on the surgery. Results demonstrated that women in the first group had less fear and anxiety, lower heart rate and blood pressure and reduced pain after surgery. They also recovered faster in the hospital and after going home, returning to normal activities sooner than did patients in the other two groups.

At Massachusetts General Hospital in Boston, a team of physicians tested the effects of giving patients information before their operations on why pain occurs after abdominal surgery and what the patients could do to gain relief.[12] The doctors taught a group of 46 patients how to relax their abdominal muscles, which are subject to spasm after incision. For comparison, a group of 51 patients who underwent the same type of surgery was not given any special instructions. After surgery, the first group needed less pain-relieving medication and was ready for discharge from the hospital an average of almost three days sooner than was true of the second group.

A group of heart attack patients was given explanations about the causes, effects and treatment of myocardial infarctions and an opportunity to participate in their treatment.[13] They had access to cardiac monitors so they could obtain an EKG tracing whenever they experienced symptoms, and they were taught mild isometric and foot-pedaling exercises to do under supervision. These patients had short hospital stays compared with a comparable group that was given minimum routine information and no chance to participate in their own recovery.

Getting more physicians and hospitals to offer patient education and support programs on a regular, systematic basis is seen as a promising way not only to promote recovery of patients but also to reduce the costs of medical care.[14] Such education and support clearly affect what patients think and feel while they are sick and in the hospital, and what they think and feel clearly affects their recovery.

> It is often argued that the medical care system cannot afford to take on the emotional status of the patient as its responsibility. . . . However, it may be that medicine cannot afford to ignore the patient's emotional status assuming that it will take care of itself. . . . The psychological and physiological expressions of emotional upheaval may be themselves disastrous. . . .[15]

Letting Patients Decide

Whatever information helps make our situation more comprehensible and manageable is likely to contribute to our sense of control and a reduced risk of pain and illness. But letting patients decide what they want to know—and how much—is an important point.[16] By letting them decide what information they want, they can augment their sense of control.

How much explanation people are given about their impending surgery or cardiac damage and what they are told about how they can contribute to their own recovery need to fit their own coping styles.[10] Some people prefer to place all their faith in someone else—a doctor, God, some powerful figure—to control the illness they have or the situation they are in. They may want little or no information about their problem. With most people, however, getting information that tells them what to expect, when, and what they can do about it helps them deal with the situation better. For instance, studies in both humans and animals have demonstrated that pain can be more easily tolerated when the recipient is able to predict when it is coming.

Chronic pain also has been relieved by teaching people to change the negative statements they make to themselves in stressful situations. A group of people who had chronic pain was trained by psychologists Donald Meichenbaum and his associates at the University of Waterloo in Ontario and Dennis Turk at Yale in how to use positive internal dialogue for keeping fear reactions under control during high stress.[17] Compared with a group that did not receive such instruction, those who did had a significant reduction in their pain.

Less Effect from Noise and Crowding

Regardless of the situation or setting, whatever leads us to believe we have some control seems to help us cope better and experience fewer bodily effects. In urban environments, for instance, high levels of noise produce few symptoms or aftereffects when people believe they have some control over it.

Interestingly, believing we have control is more important than whether we actually do. A group of students in a University of Texas study were subjected to loud outbursts of noise (102 decibels) at random intervals and given arithmetic problems to do.[18] Half were told they could stop the noise by pressing a button on the side of their table. The others were not given such control. No one pressed the button (which actually had no effect), but those in the first group reported significantly fewer symptoms from exposure to the noise. Sweaty hands, racing hearts, ringing ears and headache were the most common symptoms in the group with no control. A sense of control seems to lead people to view the noise as less stressful.

Psychologists David Glass, now of State University of New York, and Jerome Singer of the Uniformed Services School of Medicine did pioneering studies on noise and urban stress and were impressed by how city dwellers manage to adapt. They found that to combat the intrusion of unwanted sounds, many people mask the noise by covering it with an overlay of music from their own radios or tape players.[19] Such strategies put the noise under the person's control.

Another common source of stress in cities is crowding. The effects of crowding are also a function of our perception of control. Early studies blamed crowding for disease, discomfort, delinquency, psychological problems and other types of distress.[20] Since then, researchers have made a useful distinction between population density and crowding.[21] Density is the number of people per unit area. Crowding is a person's negative experience or evaluation of the area.[22] The fact, then, that many people are in an area does not automatically mean they feel crowded. A sense of being crowded depends on whether the density of a space interferes with our goals or behavior. If we perceive a high density situation as unpleasant or unmanageable—such as being in a subway car at rush hour—we are likely to see it as crowded. If the same "crush" of people were at a cocktail party or in some situation we viewed as pleasant, we would be less likely to react negatively and experience it as crowded.

Big-city dwellers reduce their sense of crowding by "shielding," by giving little attention to peripheral sights, sounds and stimuli, and even to people passing them. The higher the population density, the more filtering occurs. Patrons in a Manhattan department store were less able to recall details of the store when it was full of people than when it was not.[23] As we have noted, a feeling of being crowded occurs when population density keeps us from sensing some control over the environment. Actually, a person may feel less crowded when more people are present. For instance, one research team showed that individuals regarded a setting as more crowded when there were not enough people present for the group to perform assigned tasks.[24] Perceived crowding was significantly less when the density was increased and there was enough manpower to do the tasks.

149

Again, giving a person information about a situation can constitute a form of control and contribute to a more favorable outcome. Even information about what people are likely to feel or experience in a crowded store seems to help them perform better. Psychologists Ellen Langer and Susan Saegert, then at City University of New York, tested the effects of such information on women entering two super-markets.[25] Each woman was given a long shopping list on which they were to select the most economical purchase in the store for each item. One group was told, "While you are carrying out the task, the store may become crowded. We know from previous research that crowding sometimes causes people to feel aroused and sometimes anxious. We just wanted you to know this so that if you feel aroused or anxious, you will know why." The other group did not get this information. Under crowded conditions, the informed group got more shopping items correct, were more satisfied with the store and felt more comfortable than was true of the "no-information" group.

Having information about possible reactions in a situation can free people from "searching for explanations" about their feelings and bodies and increase the amount of attention and energy they give to a task. When any chance of control in a crowded situation seems gone and people must carry on unwanted contact with others, behavioral and physiological disorders may result. In one study, stress associated with lack of control and population density was linked with an increase in death rates.[26]

Commuting with Less Stress

Commuting is another part of urban life that many people find highly stressful. Surprisingly, less intense reactions may be found among commuters traveling longer distances to work than among those spending less time on the road.

In Sweden, a comparison was made between men who boarded a commuter train 79 minutes out of Stockholm and those who got on at a stop 43 minutes from the city.[27] The first group had a significantly smaller increase in adrenaline or epinephrine than did the second group. Passengers from both train stops had seats, but those who got on first—at the start of the line—had greater options. They could select where they wanted to sit, with whom, and they had greater freedom to arrange coats and parcels.

8. Our Influence Over Infections

Only a fraction of those infected with a pathogen become ill, and psychological factors may play a major role in determining who does and does not get sick.[1]

I have come to the tentative conclusion that there is . . . an "immunosuppression-prone" personality.[2]

Many people with . . . the AIDS virus never manifest the symptoms, and it may well be that . . . emotions, attitudes, beliefs, life style are a contributing cause of the disease.[3]

Our vulnerability to illness seems to increase not only when we appraise difficult situations as if our very lives are at stake but also when we behave in a way that fails to resolve the external problem or makes it worse. Our coping efforts can take a variety of forms. If the external problem we are trying to handle involves another person, we can attempt to bargain or negotiate, we can be assertive, placating or attacking. Some people's style is to capitulate or be passive. Others will rebel and be defiant.

To understand better how susceptibility to illness is linked to how we not only perceive situations but also act toward them, three researchers at Boston University School of Medicine compared a group of college students who suffered upper respiratory infections with a matched group who remained free of sore throats and other URI symptoms for a year.[4] Those who went to the student health service with infections reported having recently experienced substantially more stressful events than did students in the well group. The ill students particularly perceived themselves as having more failures, disappointments and problems related to their identity and roles in life.

As to how the students tried to handle their external problems, those who got sick would characteristically rebel, attack and become defiant. Because such responses fail to solve problems, and often make them worse, the ill students also experienced a greater intensity of unpleasant feelings—more depression, helplessness, anxiety and hostility—than did those in the symptom-free group.

The researchers hypothesized that people become ill and require medical treatment when they perceive (1) a distressing life situation, which (2) cannot be resolved effectively, resulting in (3) a sense of helplessness and intense unpleasant feelings, thereby (4) weakening their resistance to disease, and thus (5) making them more vulnerable to ever-present pathogenic agents.[4]

Since the Boston study, evidence has repeatedly suggested that certain ways of coping—such as being hostile or giving up—weaken the immune system and increase risk of illness. Such a coping pattern constitutes what George Solomon calls an "immunosuppression-prone" personality.[2] Solomon, a professor of psychiatry at the University of California, Los Angeles, is a longtime researcher in the field of psychoimmunology.

How Beliefs Affect Health

How we look at our life situations depends in large part on our assumptions about what we "need" to feel okay about ourselves or maintain a sense of well-being. The assumptions that underlie our perceptions are shaped by early experience, cultural messages and possibly genetic makeup. They become our beliefs about the world—beliefs that have a powerful effect not only on how easily we feel threatened but also on how chronically we stay aroused or depressed.

The profound influence of our beliefs on our bodies' vulnerability or resistance to disease was long conjectured but has been subjected to rigorous scientific testing only in recent years. One study that produced empirical evidence of the influence the mind has on the body was done at West Point by researchers from Yale University School of Medicine.

Stanislav Kasl and his colleagues in Yale's department of epidemiology and public health were interested in why some people who have infectious mononucleosis virus come down with the disease while others who also are infected do not.[5] The agent in infectious mononucleosis (IM) or "kissing disease" is the Epstein-Barr virus. Out of an entering class of some 1,400 cadets at West Point, 194 became infected with the virus during the next four years but only 48 developed the disease. (The majority of the new cadets already had an immunity to IM from having previously been infected). In comparing the infected cadets who developed mononucleosis with those who did not, the Yale researchers found that the most significant difference could be traced to the values and beliefs the students had about succeeding.

The cadets who became ill had fathers who imparted extremely strong values about the need to achieve to be worthwhile. The fathers themselves had occupational attainments that exceeded their education and were described by the researchers as "overachievers." Although their sons apparently adopted the belief that they too must excel, they were caught in a bind because their grades at the military academy were consistently below average. In contrast, infected cadets who did not develop mononucleosis had both less intense needs and better grades.

The researchers concluded that the cadets who became ill were under constant pressure from their beliefs that they must excel even though their academic ability did not allow for such success. The pressure was accompanied by a high level of chronic physiological arousal, which in turn apparently increased the cadets' vulnerability to illness.

As we have seen, frequent arousal involves high levels of stress hormones, which may depress the immune system. For instance, Army recruits who got respiratory illnesses during basic combat training had elevations in both catecholamines ("fight" and "flight" hormones) and cortisol ("conservation and withdrawal") hormones.[6] Students at the University of Waterloo, Ontario, who had acute infectious disease episodes also experienced increased catecholamine activity before the onset of symptoms.[7]

Low Moods and Herpes

When we have unduly pessimistic attitudes toward tough situations and we stay physiologically aroused, the peaceful coexistence we have with many microorganisms seems to get upset. Most of the microbial inhabitants to whom we play host reside in our digestive and respiratory tracts and some serve very useful functions, such as helping us synthesize vitamins.[8] More than 150 different viruses have been recovered from human hosts, although fewer than half have been identified with disease or illness.

For about a third of us, one of the viruses we carry is a type of herpes simplex agent that is found in cold sores, fever blisters and small ulcers inside the mouth. Physical or psychological stress can turn these normally latent Type I herpes against us. Sources of the stress vary: sunburn, overexertion, fever, menstruation, a scratch on the lip or some combination of these. In addition, our moods, outlooks and reactions to frustrations and disappointments may predispose us to herpes illness or precipitate outbreaks.

For instance, 10 persons who had repeated attacks of herpes simplex shared a similar reaction pattern to frustrations and conflicts, marked by high anxiety or guilt.[9] They got relief from the attacks by psychotherapy. In two other studies, demonstrating the effect of cognitions on herpes, recurrent activation of the virus was produced by suggestion during hypnosis.[10] Also, students facing examinations have been reported to have an increased incidence of cold sores.[11]

Researchers from the department of psychiatry at the University of Pennsylvania and Veterans Administration Hospital in Philadelphia found that people with typically unhappy moods had a greater number of cold sore episodes in the year that followed.[11] The group tested two classes of young women entering nurses' training and reported that those who were characteristically unhappy also had more illness in general during their first year. More recently, health diaries kept by 589 adults in Detroit showed that bad moods consistently triggered physical problems.[12]

Loneliness and Decreased Immunity

At Ohio State College of Medicine, studies were done on how stress and loneliness might affect the ability of the immune system to defend against herpes viruses.[13] Greatest effects were found among students with high loneliness scores. Immune system depression was also found during examination periods. Effects tested were on the IgG antibody as a defense against herpes simplex Type I, Epstein-Barr virus and cytomegalovirus.

Type II herpes, which is venereal herpes, has also been found to recur when people with the latent virus anticipate stressful events ahead, experience negative moods or lack social support.[14] A study at the University of California School of Medicine in San Francisco showed that both helper and suppressor T-cells are affected by perceptions of stress and by negative moods.

Psychologist Margaret Kemeny and her coworkers found among 36 people with genital herpes that those who were depressed experienced more recurrences of symptoms.[15] The depressed individuals also had significantly lower levels of suppressor cytotoxic T-cells, which apparently keep outbreaks from occurring. Depression, stress, anxiety, hostility, fatigue—all were found to be significant predictors of poorer functioning of suppressor T-cells.

Latent bacteria as well as viruses may be activated by negative moods and distress.[8] For instance, bacteria normally residing in the mouth may produce trenchmouth sores, technically called acute necrotizing ulcerative gingivitis (ANUG). People who become stressed before examinations and have depression of their IgA antibodies, which are a firstline defense against infection, have been found to get trenchmouth sores.[16] In a study comparing 35 patients who had ANUG with a matched group of people free of any symptoms, the patients were found to have recently experienced significantly more negative life events, anxiety and emotional distress.[17] They showed higher levels overnight of cortisol in their urine and had depressed lymphocyte function and other impairment of immune system activity. Even the bacteria in our mouths that contribute to dental caries have been found to increase when we perceive situations as stressful. When we relax, such salivary bacteria decline.[18]

Relaxation Skills Increase Immunity

The importance of relaxation in keeping the immune system strong has been demonstrated by psychologist Janice Kiecolt-Glaser and her research group at Ohio State. They found that medical students had decreases in helper T-cells on the day of examinations. But when half the group were taught relaxation exercises, their T-cells increased. The percent of their helper T-cells could be predicted by how frequently the students practiced relaxation.[19] The researchers suggest:

> These data provide further evidence that relaxation may be able to enhance at least some component of cellular immunity, and thus perhaps ultimately might be useful in influencing the incidence and course of disease.[20]

Other studies have shown that stress hormones, such as cortisol and the catecholamines, decrease after relaxation.[21] Because our immune defenses tend to weaken when we generate stress hormones, relaxation exercises may be one way to keep our resistance up.

Psychoimmunologist Joan Borysenko of Harvard and her colleagues have found that certain diabetics benefit from learning and practicing relaxation techniques.[22] These were diabetics with an "inhibited power need syndrome"—a high need for dominance that is kept restrained. Relaxation resulted in lower blood glucose levels, which means that more "sugar" was fueling their cells instead of building up in the bloodstream.

Tipping the Balance

The balance between the microbes we harbor and the antibodies protecting us against them can be tipped, then, by the way we react to stress and what we do to cope with it. What we do will help decide how much effect our stress hormones have on our immune defenses. Since our lymphocytes have receptors for such hormones, both branches of our immune system—the B-cells that produce antibodies and the T-cells that monitor the body for invaders—can be depressed by stressful reactions and faulty coping.

As we have seen, people who have trouble coping may also end up with lower activity of natural killer or NK cells—a special, "null" lymphocyte—that destroys certain viruses and cancer cells.[23] Impaired immunity may explain why people who are recently widowed have a significantly higher rate of death and sickness. Many of the bereaved experience diminished activity of lymphocytes.[24]

People with strong needs to dominate and make an impact, as we noted in Chapter 3, have depressed immune defenses when they face certain stressful situations. Students who have such "power" needs but inhibit them have been found to have diminished antibody activity as exam times approach.[25] Apparently they become so stressed from believing they absolutely must excel and make an impression that their overreactive sympathetic nervous systems depress their immunity.

Although prolonged elevation of stress hormones may lower immune defenses, not everyone who has such arousal gets ill. Not every cadet who was driven by beliefs about the need to excel or every nursing student with unhappy moods became sick. The beliefs and moods were risk factors and increased the likelihood of illness, but a given cadet or nursing student might have had other resources that offered protection from such a consequence.

Between a stressor at point X, reactions at Y and illness at Z, many mediators interact.[26] The majority of smokers do not develop lung cancer. They either escape other risk factors associated with the disease or have "protection" for reasons not yet understood. This point, however, does not negate the fact that smoking increases the chances of illness.

Our Influence over Serious Infections

If how we cope with our life stresses is so important in whether we come down with colds, sore throats, fever blisters, mouth sores and the like, what influence might we have on more serious infections? Is there no single "physical cause" of tuberculosis or polio, for example, which places such diseases completely beyond our control? The answer to such a question seemed simple in 1882 when Robert Koch, the German bacteriologist, discovered the tubercle bacillus. The medical world promptly embraced the bacteria Koch discovered as "the cause" of the great white plague. Scientists set out to find a single, specific agent for every other disease to prove that germ theory could explain all illness.

Koch himself knew differently. He later proved that healthy humans can carry even cholera bacteria without suffering from disease.[8] Meanwhile Louis Pasteur, the French chemist and bacteriologist who developed germ theory, had been challenged on induction into the prestigious French Academy on the grounds that he believed external agents were the cause of all disease.[27] His opponent, H. Pidoux, said: "Disease is the common result of a variety of diverse external and internal causes. . . ."[28] By the time Pasteur died, he agreed that the "internal causes" were important, that how people react to life and their environment can be even more decisive in disease than the influence of a germ. On his deathbed, he said: "Le germe n'est rien, c'est le terrain qui est tout." ("The microbe is nothing, the soil is everything.")[29]

But the appeal of a simple cause-and-effect explanation for disease was so powerful that it reigned supreme for decades. Before Koch's discovery of the tubercle bacillus, the causes of TB were regarded as a combination of heredity, climate and "depressing emotions."[30] Emphasis quickly shifted to controlling the spread of bacilli in communities. Although the presence of tubercle bacillus is a necessary condition for tuberculosis, other factors must also be present for the disease to occur. Control of the bacteria has proved difficult as demonstrated by the fact that the majority of adults today are tuberculin positive—are infected—although most never show clinical signs of the disease.[30] In fact, "for every 100 Caucasian Americans now becoming infected with the tubercle bacillus, 98 or 99 do not develop the classic pulmonary disease."[31]

In the midst of his pioneering studies on stress, Selye observed that reactions to psychological as well as physical threats and challenges could trigger a person's latent bacilli.[32] He noted the importance that rest—freedom from stress—continued to play in the treatment of the disease.

Holmes and his colleagues at the University of Washington studied people who became ill with tuberculosis in Seattle and found most were of "marginal status"—they lived isolated lives in transient neighborhoods.[33] The highest rates among nonwhites were for those living in white neighborhoods and vice versa. The researchers also compared a group of sanitorium employees who became ill after tubercle bacilli infection with a matched group who had equal exposure to the bacteria but remained free of symptoms. In the year preceding the onset of their illness, the first group had experienced many more perceived difficulties and distressing events having to do with work, marriage and finances. They also felt they were less able to handle such problems. Holmes concluded they became ill because of a combination of their reactions to stress and the presence of infection.

As a demonstration of how a stress-related hormone can destroy resistance to tuberculosis, a scientist at the Institute of Experimental Medicine and Surgery at the University of Montreal injected a group of 20 rats with ACTH (adrenocorticotrophic hormone) and human-type tubercle bacilli.[32] Despite the fact that such rats are resistant to human-type tuberculosis, all died. When a second group of 20 rats received the same injections plus a shot of STH, a hormone that countered the effects of ACTH, none of the rats even became ill.

ACTH and hormones it releases from our adrenal cortexes act to depress antibodies and prevent inflammation from occurring.[32] If we have an infection from tubercle bacilli in our lungs and no barricade is placed around the microbes by inflammatory tissue, the germs can easily spread and produce tuberculosis.

Tubercle bacilli are not the only virulent agents that humans may harbor that produce serious disease when other risk factors are present. At the height of the outbreak of poliomyelitis, many people carried polio virus but had mild, if any, symptoms. Microbiologist Dubos noted that a number of people also may have latent viruses for meningitis and harbor bacteria associated with amoebic dysentery.[8] In such instances, genetic resistance, high immune levels or the absence of other risk factors protects people from developing disease.

Influenza and "Psychological Vulnerability"

The fact that only a proportion of infected persons becomes sick during a viral epidemic was also demonstrated in a study of psychological factors and the Asian flu.[34] When an Asian influenza outbreak was predicted for the Baltimore area, researchers gave 600 federal employees a battery of psychological tests to see if the scores would later correlate with which workers came down with the flu. Three months later, when the flu epidemic arrived, the rate of illness was three times higher among the "psychologically vulnerable"—those who had lower morale, coped less well and reacted more strongly to physical symptoms.

The same study also showed that psychological factors affected the length of time it took the federal employess to recover from the flu.[35] Among those who got sick, a little more than half reported they were completely recovered from their illness when they returned to be checked at a dispensary three to six weeks later. Slightly fewer than half stated that they still had symptoms. When the pre-illness psychological tests of the two groups were compared, it was found that those who still had symptoms had scored significantly higher on depression.

Psychosocial Factors in AIDS

Increasing evidence suggests that psychosocial factors and coping ability may also play a part in acquired immune deficiency syndrome (AIDS). When the AIDS outbreak struck this country, the unmistakable impression given the public, and found among health professionals as well, was that the disease kills everyone who gets it, and since no known cure existed, nothing could be done to keep the inevitable from occurring. But from the start, there have been "longterm survivors" of AIDS.[36] The public, however, seldom heard of them because of the universal assumption that it was just a matter of time before they too died. Also from the beginning, there were many more people who became infected with the dreaded AIDS virus than developed the disease.

So overwhelming was the preoccupation with the newly discovered retrovirus (HTLV-III), which was assumed to be all it took for anyone to fall victim to the disease, that hardly anyone dared to ask the question: "If the virus is 'the cause' of AIDS, how can so many people who get infected with it fail to develop the disease?" and, "If HTLV-III is such a killer virus, how does anyone survive?"

Slowly a few psychologists, psychiatrists and psychoneuroimmunologists began to study such questions. They were aware that in many infectious diseases, viral and otherwise, psychosocial factors can play an important role in who becomes sick and who does not—and who survives and who does not. There was little reason to believe that AIDS was completely exempt from such influences. The researchers wanted to determine what effect a person's attitudes, moods and ways of dealing with problems may have on whether he develops symptoms of AIDS—or its milder form ARC (AIDS-Related Complex)—and if he does, what influence psychosocial factors then have on whether he lives or dies.

Many More Infected Than Ill

By 1985, an estimated 2,000,000 people had been infected with the virus identified as the primary AIDS agent.[37] By 1987, some 30,000 had been diagnosed as having the disease—which means that many people are infected but have no symptoms.

From 5 to 20 percent of those with the virus go on to develop symptoms of ARC (also known as AIDS-Related Conditions). An estimated 10 to 30 percent of those with ARC go on to develop the full-blown symptoms of AIDS.[38] More than half of those diagnosed with AIDS have died. Among homosexual men, who are most at risk of getting AIDS, only an estimated 1 percent have the disease.[39] Many are believed to be healthy carriers. The blood test to screen for antibodies against the AIDS virus shows that many people have been exposed to the agent but do not have the disease. Estimates are that for every living adult with AIDS there are from 100 to 300 infected, antibody-positive people with no disease.[40] In a three-year study of homosexuals, drug users and hemophiliacs, 10.1 percent of those who had been infected developed the disease.[41]

Intensive investigations have been launched to determine what distinguishes people who get the AIDS virus but not the disease from those who are infected and get sick or die. Ability to cope with stress is one possible influence, both in terms of whether someone develops symptoms and how serious the symptoms may be.[42] As we have seen, coping deficiences can contribute to impairment of the immune system and vulnerability to viruses and other disease agents. Once infected with the AIDS retrovirus—its RNA makes an enzyme that permits it to incorporate into a host's DNA—a person is believed to carry the agent for life.[43] The latency period between the time when a person becomes infected and when he develops the disease, if he does, may range from 28 to 62 months.[41]

The serious threat that AIDS represents comes from the "opportunistic infections" and unusual tumors that may take over the body when the immune system is severely depressed. The most common of these are *Pneumocystis carinii* pneumonia (PCP) and Kaposi's sarcoma (KS). Some of the agents or organisms responsible for the infections already reside in the body or are commonly found in the environment.[44] They are held in check by lymphocytes, particularly helper T-cells, which signal B-cells to make antibodies. People who get AIDS have lost a large portion of their helper T-cells.[45] Poor coping, as well as other cofactors, may be involved in impairment of the helper lymphocytes.

Healthy persons generally have two helper T-cells (also known as T-4 cells) for every suppressor cell (T-8 cells). One theory is that from birth homosexuals are inclined to have helper/suppressor cell ratios different from those of the general population and that this "special immune configuration" makes them particularly susceptible to the AIDS virus, which has an affinity for T-4 cells.[46] The AIDS retrovirus uses the DNA of helper cells to replicate itself and, in the process, destroys the T-4 lymphocytes. A gene in the virus seems to produce a protein that takes over the infected T-lymphocytes and causes them to make new viruses so rapidly that the cells appear to age prematurely and die. Depleting the number of T-4 cells has serious consequences: B-cells are unable to produce adequate antibodies, and T-cells that ordinarily kill foreign invaders are impaired.[47] In addition to attacking a critical component of the immune system, the AIDS virus also seems capable of invading fluids and tissue of the spinal cord and brain, leaving some patients with dementia and meningitis.[48]

Coping Factor in AIDS

Ability to cope with stress, however, seems to be a factor in who remains asymptomatic or undergoes mild illness and who gets the fully developed disease.[49] Psychologist Hal Knooden of New York City, whose patients are mostly homosexual men, has observed that all of those who developed AIDS reported experiencing unresolved stressful situations prior to the onset of the disease.[39]

In a study at the University of California School of

Medicine in San Francisco, poor coping ability has been found to be associated with some of the opportunistic infections and tumors of AIDS.[50] Psychotherapy appeared useful in heading off full expression of Kaposi's sarcoma, which is one of the serious complications that may result. Stress management and development of coping skills offer some promise in helping to prevent "lesser AIDS" (ARC) from becoming the full-blown disease.[51]

Tentative findings from longevity studies at UCSF have indicated that cognitive factors make a difference in survival. For instance, among AIDS patients with *Pneumocystis carinii* pneumonia (PCP), a significant correlation was found between survival and sense of control.[36] The survivors had substantially greater ability to view problems in more optimistic ways and to believe they had some control over them. Similarly, those still alive sought out significantly more help from others to solve problems. When stressful events occurred, those who later died showed more passivity and helplessness.

In doing follow-up studies on men with ARC, project psychologists found significant associations between attitude or mood and immune defenses. For example, those with greater anxiety, a sense of hopelessness and no control had significantly lower white blood cell counts.[36] Substantially lower helper/suppressor T-cell ratios or other immune activity levels were found among ARC patients who scored high on loneliness and depression or who had poor coping skills.[52] Those with ARC who believed they could do something to help themselves seemed better able to ward off progression of their disease.[36]

Virus Not Sufficient

HTLV-III (human T-cell leukemia virus), which has been reported as the AIDS agent, was isolated in 1984 by a research group headed by Robert Gallo of the National Cancer Institute.[53] The media hailed the development as meaning "the cause" of AIDS had been found. French scientists, led by Luc Montagnier of the Pasteur Institute in Paris, had identified a similar virus, lymphadenopathy-associated virus or LAV, as the AIDS agent.[54] The HTLV-III agent is now being referred to as human T-cell lymphotropic virus, and LAV as the lymphadenopathyAIDS virus. A third virus, ARV (AIDS-associated retrovirus) also has been reported as the agent in AIDS. Studies now confirm that all three viruses are variants of the same virus.[55] The name that may be agreed upon for all three is "human immunodeficiency virus (HIV)."

But, regardless of what it is called, the agent is not "the cause" of the disease. The agent may be necessary for symptoms to develop, but it alone is not sufficient to produce the disease.[56] Other conditions affecting susceptibility must be present.

Just as everyone exposed to hepatitis B virus does not get sick, many people who actually carry the AIDS virus do not develop symptoms. As with AIDS, hepatitis B seems to be transmitted mostly through close sexual contact. An estimated 40 percent of people infected with hepatitis B virus develop no symptoms at all.[57] In San Francisco, according to another estimate, 80 percent of the adult male population have antibodies to chronic hepatitis but only 10 percent get symptoms.[58] With AIDS, some researchers have proposed that symptoms occur in those who already have some degree of immune depression.[59]

Something Already Wrong

Within a few months of the report of a human T-cell leukemia virus being "the cause" of AIDS, scientists in San Francisco and Paris and at the Centers for Disease Control in Atlanta were noting that "other cofactors in addition to viruses may be involved in the causation of AIDS."[60] And one of the cofactors that determines whether an exposed person gets AIDS or not may be deficient coping ability and its effect on the immune system. Another may be use of amyl nitrite—in vogue as a sexual stimulant—and other drugs that depress immunity. Whether the person is infected with other viruses, such as hepatitis B or cytomegalovirus, also is a consideration, as is poor nutrition.

John Zaia, director of virology at City of Hope in Los Angeles, believes people "get set up for HTLV-III" by cofactors.[61] He is convinced that "something's got to be wrong with you in the first place to make you susceptible to AIDS," and whatever that "something" is, it has weakened the immune system. His own research has centered on cytomegalovirus, a herpes virus that is carried by some healthy people but is capable of depressing immune defenses.

In any event, the finding that cofactors seem to be involved means that prevention of AIDS does not depend solely on developing a vaccine.[62] Drug education programs as well as stress management may be useful. Learning to cope without suppressing immunity seems critical. An important lesson that AIDS teaches us, according to one clinician-scientist, is that such diseases are "truly multifactorial."[63] They not only have several factors contributing to their cause but they also lend themselves to being treated or prevented by more than one approach.

Legionnaire's disease also illustrates the point that a potentially pathogenic agent is is not the sufficient cause of a disease. Ten years after the disease struck Legionnaires at a convention in Philadelphia and was given a name, researchers were noting that *Legionella pneumophilia*, the agent involved, is a common bacterium that "really doesn't hurt you unless you have a tremendous dose of the organism or you have something wrong with you."[64]

As we have seen, an already depressed immune system may be what is wrong. Older people, particularly those who have smoked for a number of years, often have compromised immune function and are at higher risk, as are hospital patients. One source of *L. pneumophilia* is in the cooling towers of some air conditioning systems, such as used by the hotel where the initial outbreak of Legionnaire's disease occurred in Philadelphia.[65]

Why One Person and Not Another?

The fact that no illness, infectious or otherwise, can be explained strictly on the basis of a germ or some other single agent has left medicine without an adequate theory for disease.[66] Without such a theory, few truly comprehensive treatment and prevention programs can be developed. Drug therapy must necessarily be relied upon as the response by most physicians to health problems. Herbert Weiner, a widely published clinical researcher now at UCLA School of Medicine, has observed that medicine's one existing theory or model "derives from infectious disease and is generally acknowledged to be unsatisfactory because it is linear, restrictive and oversimplified."[67]

In addition to limiting severely the approaches to prevention and treatment, this deficient model also leaves medicine without answers to such questions as: Why do some people get sick and others do not when they are exposed to the same infectious agent or noxious conditions? What decides whether a person is at risk of acquiring a particular disease? Under what circumstances will a predisposed person develop a disease?

The prevailing medical model cannot explain why the same virus or microbe may "cause" different diseases or none at all. For example, the microorganism *Treponema pallidum* may result in inflammation of the aorta in one person, syphilis of the brain in a second and no disease at all in a third.[66] An adequate theory must be able to account for such differences and explain the conditions and circumstances that predispose people to disease, as well as the factors that precipitate illness and maintain it. Even injecting virus directly into an organism often will not produce disease. It takes a combination of factors. Animal studies have demonstrated that when a combination of stress (electric shock) and an injected virus (Coxsackie B) was applied to mice, disease developed, but neither alone was sufficient to cause illness.[68]

One of the reasons that medicine has been described as being in a crisis is that its prevailing theory of disease, which largely ignores psychosocial influences, cannot answer so many important questions or account for individual outcomes.[69] Although modern medicine has outgrown the idea that every disorder is caused by its own specific agent, the theory of infectious disease—which once seemed to explain so much and lead to so many advances—remains the guiding light to many practitioners and lay people.

The Major Killers and Our Behavior

Our susceptibility to infectious disease, as we have indicated, has now been convincingly linked to the way we cope with our life and environment. And the way we cope starts with how we view events and situations. But important as infectious diseases are, the fact remains that they no longer account for the major illnesses most Americans develop.

The emergence of noninfectious diseases as the leading causes of death and disability has weakened even further the cherished theory that external agents, such as germs, are responsible for our health problems. Heart disease, cancer, strokes, accidents—in fact, all the leading causes of premature death and disability—are increasingly being linked to behavioral risk factors, to smoking, drinking, bad diets, lack of exercise and faulty stress management.[70]

Since many of our ill-advised habits, lifestyles and

171

other behaviors represent attempts to cope and make ourselves feel better, the way we react to life's stresses is a central determinant of the major chronic diseases as well as the acute, infectious illnesses. Yet the training of physicians and the practice of medicine still largely neglect mind and behavior in explanations of why we get sick or what can be done about our health problems.

PART 4
Vulnerability

9.
Dissatisfaction and Illness

What does it mean
if you . . . wake up anxious,
dreading the day? . . .
What about continuing in roles,
jobs or relationships you hate.
. . . if you are like most people,
you are likely to continue
as you always have—
even if you give yourself
high blood pressure.[1]

The unhappy person is the
target for any and every
kind of illness.[2]

Research findings on health indicate that the degree of satisfaction that we derive from our work and home life is more important than the number of jobs we are doing or how many roles we perform. For instance, a study of employees and homemakers in Detroit found the best health among active people, men and women, who were satisfied with both their jobs and family lives.[3]

Dissatisfied homemakers had numerous illness symptoms, which they frequently tried to relieve with various drugs. People dissatisfied generally, whether at work or home, tended to smoke, drink more and experience greater stress.

Air traffic controllers, widely acknowledged as being in a stressful occupation, also have been found to vary in health according to how negatively they perceived their work and "the system" that employs them. When psychiatrist Robert Rose, now of the University of Texas Medical Branch at Galveston, and his colleagues (see Chapter 1) did examinations and on-the-job testing of the 416 air traffic controllers over three years, they observed that those with the highest dissatisfaction developed the most psychological disorders or the most mild-to-moderate medical illnesses.[4]

In the longterm studies at Cornell Medical College of employees and other groups (see Chapters 1 and 3), Hinkle and his colleagues described those with the highest rate of illness as unhappy and discontented and as having a large number of interpersonal problems.[5]

For both men and women under high stress, those who have adopted the values, beliefs and expectations of "the masculine role" report more distress and dissatisfaction.[6] Three aspects of the masculine role identified with physical as well as emotional distress are (1) restrictive emotionality—difficulty in expressing feelings and being self-disclosing; (2) inhibited affection—limited expression of affection and tenderness toward others; and (3) success preoccupation—persistent preoccupation with career to the exclusion of interpersonal pursuits and commitments.[7] Findings from a study of 567 men and women undergraduates showed that those with the masculine role values and beliefs were significantly predisposed to experience distress and dissatisfaction in the face of high stress.[6]

Healthy Women under Stress

As was true of the Chicago business executives and lawyers (Chapter 3), people who have a sense of control or ability to cope seem to escape certain ill-effects when under high stress. Women with a great deal of occupational pressure were believed to be at risk of menstrual dysfunction and reproductive problems. But this did not prove to be the case in a study of 72 women in high-paying, high-stress positions who seemed to cope well and have a sense of control.[8] Although they had a number of tension symptoms, such as neckache and backache, they did not report menstrual symptoms in any significant number or have other problems associated with chronic elevation of adrenocortical stress hormones (such as heart trouble, high blood pressure and ulcers).

Another assumption about women and work has been that if they try to carry on careers as well as roles of homemaker, wife and mother, they will run a high risk of hurting their health. The evidence suggests that the opposite is true, that women may promote their health by working. In San Antonio, 422 Anglo working women and housewives plus 623 Mexican-American women were studied for risk factors of coronary heart disease.[9] The working women had three indicators of better health: higher levels of high-density lipoprotein, the "good" cholesterol that helps protect against coronary heart disease; lower levels of low-density or "bad" cholesterol, and decreased levels of triglycerides, fats in the blood that may increase the risk of CHD.

Helen Hazuda of the University of Texas at San Antonio, the psychologist-epidemiologist who did the study, suggests that health may be promoted for women who look upon their jobs as a challenge. She believes that multiple roles, rather than producing overload, may buffer the effects of stress if they are rewarding.[10] Another study, based on a national survey, found that employed women tended to have a higher sense of well-being than did their nonemployed counterparts.[11]

Also, in a representative sample of married, middle-aged women in the United States, those with favorable and positive attitudes toward their employment had better health, as confirmed by a follow-up five years later, than did housewives.[12] A University of Michigan survey found that women who held three, four or five roles did not report experiencing greater stress or conflict than did women with only one or two roles.[13]

David Duncan, professor of health education at Southern Illinois University at Carbondale, and his colleague, Rita Whitney, have reported that for both men and women over age 54, those who work full-time—or are active in volunteering—find their lives "more interesting and satisfying" than do those who are retired, work parttime or do little volunteer work.[14] The two researchers surveyed all persons who visited the Senior Center at the Illinois State Fair in 1984.

Conflict on the Job

Dozens of outbreaks of illness on the job have been traced to feelings of great dissatisfaction with the job, boredom, conflict with the boss, lack of support or other perceived stress. Often a physical stressor—a strange odor, noise, poor lighting—is blamed by workers for their symptoms. But investigations by outside authorities, such as from the National Institute for Occupational Safety and Health, often find that either there is no physical stressor present or, if there is, it is not at a level to be injurious or toxic. Nevertheless, affected workers experience nausea, dizziness, headaches, weakness and other symptoms.

Two NIOSH staff members reviewed 16 "epidemics" of illness at five plants, one data processing center, nine schools and one hospital.[15] At the plants and data center, affected workers perceived their jobs as boring and repetitious or stressful. Poor relations with management also were often reported. At the schools, many of the affected students had records of numerous absences and disciplinary problems. At the hospital, where a number of nurses got sick, those affected had been ill more in the past and were more inclined to overreact when stressed.

What all this suggests is that if a substantial number of people on a job start seeing their employer as uncaring or nonsupportive and the work as stressful, boring or meaningless, then the chances for "mass illness" increase greatly. For instance, when employees are moved to renovated quarters, which may have a stuffy odor, those who are most dissatisfied with their jobs or who feel little control may come down with a variety of symptoms.

The "stuffy building syndrome" occurred at both the National Broadcasting Company and New York University in Manhattan when some employees were moved into hermetically sealed renovated space.[16] At NYU, where 23 women and 13 men complained of burning eyes, dizziness, sore throat, chest tightness, fatigue and headache, inspections were made by the school's medicine department, the city health department, various consultants and NIOSH. No problems of toxicity could be found. Yet the employees abandoned the building. At NBC, similar symptoms and investigations occurred. In both cases, giving workers a chance to air grievances and to have more of a voice in the conduct of their jobs helped to overcome the trouble.

This is not to say, however, that "the cause" of illness outbreaks among employees is "all psychological." Inadequate ventilation or improper temperature and humidity control, particularly in tightly insulated buildings, may escape detection by conventional testing and contribute to widespread symptoms of headaches, fatigue and mucous membrane irritation. As is the case with most illnesses, no single factor is "the cause" and both the psychological and physical are involved.

Lack of Control at Work

How much latitude we have in changing the pace of our job or making other decisions about our work has a stronger influence on our health than high stress does. Rena Pasick, research associate at the University of California School of Public Health, Berkeley, views the question of job control as including how closely a person is supervised, how routine the work may be and whether one's education or skills fit the complexity of the job. In a recent probability sample of 787 working adults in Alameda County, California, she found an association between job control and health status.[17] Although managers and other white-collar employees may have considerable pressure on the job, many have better health because, compared with blue-collar workers, they have more job control.

Heart disease in particular has been of concern among people on jobs where control is minimal. The incidence of coronary heart disease is greater among waiters and assemblers than among managers who are faced with equally high job demands but have more "decision latitude" and control.[18]

Women clerical workers have also been found to have

twice as much heart disease as do housewives or women in other occupation groups.[19] These findings, from the Framingham heart study, suggest that clerical workers may "experience severe occupational stress, including a lack of autonomy and control over the work environment, underutilization of skills, and lack of recognition of accomplishments."[20] A sense of little control at work triggers a rise in blood pressure and an increase in stress hormones. Women in high demand/low control jobs have more than three times the risk of heart disease than do women in jobs with lower demand and more control. Librarians, natural scientists and billing clerks are examples of those with lower demands and more control.

No Joy in Life

Work satisfaction has been found to be a powerful predictor of how long we live as well as how likely we are to remain healthy (see Chapter 3).[21] Conversely, dissatisfaction with not only work but life in general is associated with significantly higher risk of illness. As we saw in Chapter 1, long-term studies have shown that employees who get sick most often are usually those who have high job dissatisfaction, difficulty in coping or are unhappy in their lives. Dissatisfaction off the job, as well as on, seems an important determinant.

In Sweden, researchers studied identical male twins— all adults—and found that, in each pair, the one having greater dissatisfaction with his childhood experiences, educational level and achievements in life had signficantly more severe coronary disease.[22] Life dissatisfaction, in fact, was a more powerful predictor of severity than were blood pressure, serum cholesterol or obesity. In a Swedish study of people who had experienced heart attacks—as compared with matched healthy persons—the postinfarction patients reported substantially greater work dissatisfactions.[23]

Similar findings have come from studies of some 10,000 American workers—including professors, lawyers, farmers, accountants, printers, librarians, sales and clerical personnel.[24] Stewart Wolf, then a professor of medicine and psychiatry at the Oklahoma University Medical Center, concluded that people at higher risk of myocardial infarctions go through life striving without joy, in the manner of Sisyphus, the character from Greek mythology who was condemned to push a heavy stone to the top of a hill only to have it always roll back down. In a nine-year prospective study of 65 people who had experienced heart attacks, Wolf and his research team were able to predict which in the group would suffer new myocardial infarctions, based on how much they tended to view life as a striving without satisfaction.[25]

Low Stress, High Distress

We have seen that people's attitudes and appraisals, their sense of satisfaction and control, have a pervasive influence on their health. The influence of these factors contradicts the theory that high stress automatically produces physical or psychological distress. If that theory were true, then low stress should yield the absence of illness and other worries. In other words, if we could just escape from stress, then we would be free of problems. Again, the evidence is otherwise.

For example, people who live in low-stress communities fail to show low rates of mental disorders or illness. In North America, the Hutterites are a prime example.[26] They are a religious sect that first came to the United States in 1874 and established self-sufficient farming communities. Work is shared on a cooperative basis, and there is no threat of unemployment, financial insecurity or a need to strive for status through competition. The community provides "social security from the womb to the tomb." The group offers a support network to all members.

Yet, despite the absence of external pressures, illness seems to be as common as anywhere else. People still get depressed and anxious. They perceive themselves as not living up to the expectations of the group and thus experience strain and other reactions that we associate with stress.

"Country people," free from the pressures of urban living, also have been pictured as less distressed psychologically and more healthy physically. Yet recent studies have shown no significant differences in health and general well-being between rural and urban dwellers.[27] In fact, greater depression was found in rural areas.

Even vacations, where stress is minimum, can be distressing to certain people. Type A people, who constantly need to be in control of situations, seem to have great difficulty dealing with periods of leisure, where demands and challenges are largely absent. While most people unwind fairly quickly in such settings, Type As often continue to show elevated adrenal hormones.[28] They are in constant "need" of challenge and continually struggle to dominate whatever faces them. When there is nothing to control, they can be in even greater distress.

The lack of external stress in people's lives can be a grossly misleading indicator of how distressed they actually are. A person may appear to "have everything," yet be extremely unhappy or sick. The last two stanzas of Edwin Arlington Robinson's poem on Richard Cory illustrate the point:

> And he was rich—yes, richer than a king,
>   And admirably schooled in every grace:
> In fine, we thought that he was everything
>   To make us wish that we were in his place.
>
> So on we worked, and waited for the light,
>   And went without the meat, and cursed the bread;
> And Richard Cory, one calm summer night,
>   Went home and put a bullet through his head.[29]

Well-Being and Happiness

Finally, the failure of stress-strain theory has raised serious questions about the connection between "objective" physical or social conditions and personal well-being. Recent evidence suggests that such measures as income, housing, transportation, public health, level of education and crime cannot be used as indices of people's life satisfaction.

When attempts were made to correlate objective conditions in 15 American cities with the level of satisfaction of residents, no connection between the two was found.[30] Large differences in physical and social conditions were present among the cities but not in the general level of people's sense of well-being. Objectively, Milwaukee was found to be 20 times safer than Washington, D.C. in terms of crime. In public health, Philadelphia was much worse off (as measured by infant mortality) than Cincinnati or Los Angeles. But there were no corresponding marked differences in satisfaction of residents. As one researcher reported:

> In short, there appears to be no evidence at all that . . . the objective social conditions of cities have any relationship with the levels of subjective life quality of their citizens.[31]

In another recent study, six of the 11 states that were part of the Confederacy during the Civil War ranked low on objective indices of "quality of life." But when people in these states were asked to rate their personal well-being, they were more positive than were persons living elsewhere under better physical conditions.[32] Because personal support and satisfying relationships play such a major part in how we evaluate the quality of our lives, external conditions can no more be equated with internal reactions than stress can with distress.

Despite Viet Nam, Watergate, double-digit inflation and high unemployment, Americans have reported little difference in their level of well-being and happiness over the last three decades.[33] In the 1980s, 30 percent of the population said they were very happy, compared with 35 percent in the 1950s. National crises do not seem to cause significant deterioration in people's well-being any more than do other forms of major stresses.

Media Doom and Gloom

The media would have us believe the world is going to end every night, and the public dutifully shows grave concern about news developments while "it continues, on the whole, to be satisfied with life."[34] Personal well-being is shaped more by how we perceive the quality of our intimate relationships and our ability to cope in our everyday lives. A national increase in divorce rates is not as important as how well our own marriage is doing. Inflation and unemployment may go up, but if our standard of living rises over the years, that will count more in the satisfaction we report.

Objective stress, then, does not tell us much about people's distress, since their well-being or lack of it is determined more by their own attitudes and appraisals and their sense of control and support in their individual lives. We adapt to life on a personal level, and our efforts at doing so are deeply influenced by whether we feel loved or lonely, confident or unsure, in control or helpless.

The "cause" of our distress or what "makes" us ill or unhappy is not to be found in simply the external conditions or stressful events of our lives. In fact, newer concepts of disease question whether there is any such thing as "the cause" of illness. As we have seen, whether we get sick is more often a matter of how we look at life and cope with its problems—which largely determines how much resistance we have.

10. What Wishing to Die Does

Those who know how close the connection is between the state of mind of a man . . . and the state of immunity of his body will understand that the sudden loss of hope and courage can have a deadly effect.[1]

Perhaps the most dramatic evidence suggesting the connection between what we do in our heads and what happens in our bodies comes from the documented cases of people who die after giving up or insisting that they no longer want to live. Equally intriguing are the cases of people who postpone their deaths until after their birthdays or some other occasion that they are determined to live for.

As remarkable as these cases are, the scientific and medical literature has paid them little attention because they have been mostly anecdotal and—more importantly—no biological mechanisms explained *how* they happened. Privately, clinicians have long acknowledged that our frame of mind can profoundly affect whether we live or die. But scientific proof has been lacking.

Attempts began in the last half century to make more systematic observations of the powerful effects that giving up or seeing no solution seems to have on the human body. These studies come from diverse sources: sudden deaths of people who have experienced losses they perceive as unbearable; experiments with animals put in uncontrollable situations; unaccountable deaths of people who believe they have violated a sacred taboo; concentration camp experiences in which the difference between living and dying seemed to depend on giving up or not.

The influence of thoughts and expectations on *when* we die has been suggested by research studying the "postponement" of deaths by people who decide to live for a special day or occasion. The folk wisdom of many cultures has accepted as fact that it is possible for the mind to control the body even to the point of determining when death will occur. But no one has explained this phenomenon, and science has remained skeptical.

For a wish (such as wanting to die) or a belief ("I will live until Christmas") to have biological significance, it must register itself not only in the head but also in the body, in our physiological processes. Biofeedback instruments, the polygraph and other psychophysiological devices, have presented graphic evidence of the mind-body connection. Even more dramatically, the linkage has been illustrated by the recently developed ability to "image" the brain as we think and anticipate and to measure chemical changes in the body as we lose a sense of control or believe we are helpless. A psychobiology of thoughts—of the effects on the body, for example, of giving up—is emerging as a new frontier in health science.

Bereavement and Impaired Immunity

In grief, when a widowed spouse believes life is no longer worth living, the ability of the immune system to fight infection can be markedly impaired. Activity of our lymphocytes, the white blood cells that counteract bacteria and other intruders, is suppressed. The immune function is lowered for both T-cells, the monitors in our bodies that detect and attack foreign invaders, and B-cells, which generate antibodies.

The first evidence that people may experience depressed immune function after the death of their spouses was reported in 1977.[2] Four researchers in Sydney, Australia, studied immune activity in 26 persons two weeks after the subjects had lost their spouses and again six weeks later. On both occasions, compared with a control group, there were significant effects on T and B-cell activity. At Mount Sinai School of Medicine in 1983, researchers measured the immune function of 15 men whose wives had terminal breast cancer.[3] After the women died, there was significant suppression of lymphocyte activity in the men, and this effect continued up to 14 months.

In Florida, another research group found that men who became depressed after deaths or serious illness in their families had significantly reduced responsiveness of lymphocytes.[4] The doctors, from the Veterans Administration Medical Center and the University of Miami School of Medicine, studied 60 men—average age of 54—who had experienced family deaths or serious illness among family members in the previous six months.

Inability to cope with loneliness as well as separation and loss has been found to depress the immune system. Among 76 first-year medical students, those who had the highest loneliness scores and highest stress—in terms of life changes—had the lowest levels of natural killer (NK) cells on the day that examinations began.[5] Students with the highest levels of NK cells, suggesting no impairment of immunity, had the lowest loneliness and stress scores. This study was done at the College of Medicine of Ohio State University (see also Chapter 8).

More Deaths Among the Bereaved

The diminished immunity now found among the bereaved, lonely and depressed may help explain the increased mortality and illness such people have long been known to experience. For example, a substantially higher death rate was found among 4,032 persons in Maryland who had become widowed.[6] For both men and women, moving into a nursing home was associated with greater mortality, as was living alone. In Australia, the death rate among recently bereaved widows was 3 to 12 times that of their married counterparts. In England, among 4,486 widowers over 54 years old, death rates increased more than 40 percent during the first six months of bereavement.[7] In Wales, 903 close relatives of 371 residents who died during a five-year period were studied. Almost 5 percent died within one year of being bereaved, compared with 0.7 percent for nonbereaved individuals of the same age in the same community.[8]

In the United States it has been estimated that 700,000 persons 50 years old or more lose their spouses through death in any given year. About 35,000 deaths occur annually among persons newly widowed, and of these some 7,000 are directly linked to the death of the spouse.[3] We cannot assume that giving up, which leads to a suppressed immune system, is "the cause" of the significantly higher mortality among the bereaved. Some of the widowed simply may not take care of themselves. Failure to eat properly, to take prescribed medication or seek medical help when needed may be factors contributing to the problem apart from suppression of the immune system.

How "No Control" May Affect Immunity

The "psycho-immuno-suppression" often present in those who perceive their loss as unbearable has also been seen in cancer. Women with early breast cancer who reacted with extreme distress or helplessness had significantly reduced activity of natural killer cells in their immune systems, compared with patients who did not respond with such hopelessness.[9] Other evidence of the link between appraisal and immunity has been found among workers who believe they have no control over their jobs (the pace and other conditions).[10] Their stress hormones—cortisol and catecholamines—rise and, in turn, depress the immune system.[11]

Laboratory animals that are put in no-control situations also often lose their ability to fight infection or cancer. In one of the first demonstrations suggesting a connection between lack of control and illness or disease, a team of Colorado researchers in 1983 subjected rats to electric shocks from which the animals could not escape.[12] A second group of rats was given the same shocks but under conditions that allowed them to escape. The first group had a reduction in lymphocyte activity whereas the second group's immune system was not affected. The researchers concluded that "the controllability of stressors is critical in modulating immune functioning."[13]

Later experiments have shown that both lack of support and deficient control seem detrimental to our immune defenses. When animals perceive that they are in uncontrollable situations, they suffer a decrease in activity of natural killer (NK) cells, which protect against development of cancer.[14]

Believing that a situation is uncontrollable also affects key neurotransmitters in the brain, such as dopamine. Animal experiments at Carleton University in Ottawa, Canada, have shown that chronic stress that is inescapable results in a drop in dopamine in certain areas of the brain.[15] Dopamine has been found to be important to a sense of reward and pleasure.

A Stanford University School of Medicine group found suppression of a specific antibody, IgG, in infant squirrel monkeys that were separated from their mothers and placed in new quarters.[16] In contrast, monkeys of the same age—all had been weaned—that were separated and put in familiar surroundings with peers and unrelated adult monkeys showed significantly less effect in their immune function. They also had markedly lower stress hormone (cortisol) levels than did the monkeys that lacked both social support and a familiar environment.

People Who "Will" Their Own Deaths

Mounting evidence, then, of some of the ways that our cognitions (thoughts, appraisals, expectations, associations) can make our bodies vulnerable is helping to explain how people who give up or see no point in living can "will" their own deaths. A giving-up appraisal can apparently contribute to death and disease not only through effects on the endocrine and immune systems but also by direct action on the nervous system. In the face of a shocking, unexpected loss or a setback perceived as traumatic, a belief that "I can't go on" or "all is lost" may precipitate death through overstimulation of the autonomic nervous system, particularly if the person is old or already ill.[17]

Throughout most of the history of medicine, physicians have spoken of cases in which people die suddenly from extreme emotional distress. "Grief" used to be listed as a cause of death.[18] But as medicine became more scientific, with requirements to identify mechanisms or processes by which disease occurs, most physicians have confined their observations on grief, loss and extreme distress "causing" death to private conversations. However, a few investigators have systematically tried to identify the common denominator of the circumstances and conditions under which death and disease occur. Most notable among these workers was George Engel of the University of Rochester Medical Center. In one series of studies, Engel collected 275 examples of sudden or unexpected death reported in the daily press over a six-year period.[19] Where possible, he verified the facts and cause of death with physicians on the cases. Here are some of the cases:

A 71-year-old woman rode in the ambulance with her 61-year-old sister, who was pronounced dead on arrival at a hospital. The older woman "collapsed at the instant of receiving the news." An EKG (electrocardiogram) was done and showed she had suffered myocardial damage. She then developed ventricular fibrillation—an electrical derangement of heart rhythm—and died.

A 52-year-old man had a wife who died of lung cancer. Although six months earlier he had had an EKG showing no evidence of coronary disease, the day after her funeral he died suddenly of a massive myocardial infarction.

An 88-year-old man, with no known heart disease, was told of the sudden death of his daughter and began wringing his hands and asking: "Why has this happened to me?" As he talked on the phone with his son, he developed acute pulmonary edema and died just as a physician reached his house.

Unfulfilled expectations, resulting in extreme disappointment, also illustrate the influence of cognitions on physiological processes. For example, a 53-year-old physician who had recovered from a heart attack two years earlier was certain he would be appointed to succeed his chief. When he learned he would not get the promotion, he reacted with outrage but soon composed himself. Four days later, however, after a chance meeting with his chief, "he again became angry in the presence of witnesses." He then collapsed, went into ventricular fibrillation (as confirmed by EKG) and died.

Not all sudden deaths are heart related. A young woman, 22, with a malignant paraganglioma—a cancer in the sympathetic nervous system—was still able to take drives with her mother. On one outing, an accident occurred, and the mother was killed when thrown from the car. Her daughter was not injured. However, in a few hours she lapsed into a coma and died. An autopsy showed widespread metastases but no evidence of trauma.

A 31-year-old woman had been having headaches, nausea and eye problems when her close friend and neighbor, also 31, suddenly died of an abdominal hemorrhage. She herself died two days later of a brain tumor.

Sudden Death in the Healthy

Sudden death may also occur in younger people who are apparently healthy but seem to decide life is unbearable when they unexpectedly lose a twin or other relative to whom they are extremely attached. For instance, a 14-year-old girl dropped dead when told of her 17-year-old brother's unexpected death, and a 18-year-old girl died when informed of the death of her grandfather, who helped raise her.

A recent example, although of inseparable older persons, comes from Engel's hometown, Rochester, New York, where two cousins died 12 hours apart.[20] Pete and "Re-Pete" were the same age, lived within two blocks of one another their whole lives and married sisters. At 69, Pete died of liver cancer. Re-Pete had a heart attack and died at the same hospital early the next morning.

Two other researchers, psychiatrist Ian Wilson and pathologist John Reece, reported on twin sisters in North Carolina who were inseparable.[21] Neither ever married or stayed away from the other for any prolonged period. At about 21, both young women began to show signs of schizophrenia—emotional flattening, suspiciousness and delusions. Ten years later they had to be hospitalized. During the next year they were in and out of the hospital several times, becoming worse on each readmission. Finally, they refused to eat. Hospital authorities separated them on the theory that they reinforced each other's behavior and refusal to take food. Early one morning, twin A was found dead. Twin B on a floor below was immediately checked and was found dead at a window. Another patient reported she had been looking up at the window of the room where her sister was and slumped to the floor.

Animals, as well as humans, seem to give up when they experience the loss of a lifelong companion. Because the effects of giving up have been found across species, Engel regarded it as a basic biological phenomenon. The most poignant of his cases concerned "Charlie" and "Josephine," who had been inseparable for 13 years.

> In a senseless act of violence, Charlie, in full view of Josephine, was shot and killed in a melee with the police. Josephine first stood motionless, then slowly approached his prostrate form, sank to her knees, and silently rested

her head on the dead and bloody body. Concerned persons attempted to help her away, but she refused to move. Hoping she would soon surmount her overwhelming grief, they let her be. But she never rose again; in 15 minutes she was dead.

The remarkable part of the study is that Charlie and Josephine were llamas in the zoo! They had escaped from their pen during a snowstorm and Charlie, a mean animal to begin with, was shot when he proved unmanageable. I was able to establish from the zoo keeper that to all intents and purposes Josephine had been normally frisky and healthy right up to the moment of the tragic event.[22]

Testing the Theory

As a test of Engel's hypothesis that sudden death is often preceded by a giving-up reaction, psychiatrist William Greene and his colleagues at the University of Rochester studied 26 cases at Eastman Kodak Company in which employees died suddenly.[23] In the vast majority, the workers had been depressed for a week up to several months. Combined with the depression was an increase in pressure at work, longer hours on the job and often a conflict at home.

One 55-year-old employee, for instance, became depressed over the failure of his oldest son to finish high school and go to college. The son also got into trouble for stealing. On the day after the son was again caught stealing and was held by police, the father had a massive myocardial infarction at work and died despite attempts at the plant to resuscitate him.

Effects of Anniversaries

A sense of giving up or helplessness from loss can be revived and exacerbated by an anniversary or memorial.[19] For example, a 17-year-old boy collapsed and died at 6 AM on the June 4 exactly one year after his older brother had succumbed to multiple injuries sustained in an automobile accident. The brother had died at 5:13 AM the year before. Cause of death of the younger boy was listed as a massive brain hemorrhage from a ruptured arterial aneurysm.

The widow of Louis "Satchmo" Armstrong was stricken with a fatal heart attack as she played the final chord of "St. Louis Blues" at a memorial concert for her husband. A 70-year-old man who had established a music conservatory in memory of his late wife, a piano teacher, dropped dead during the opening bars of a concert marking the fifth anniversary of her death.

Engel reported on the effects of a traumatic event in his own life—the unexpected death of his identical-twin brother of a heart attack. Eleven months later, on the last day of mourning, according to the Jewish faith, Engel himself suffered a myocardial infarction. "This occurred," he said, "during the emotional strain of anticipating the first anniversary of my twin's death."[24]

Some people believe they are destined to die at the same age as their mother, father or some other close relative and feel helpless to keep the "inevitable" from occurring. In this sense, they give up. For instance, a woman was convinced she would die in her 42nd year as had her mother and aunt.[25] As the time approached, she became increasingly agitated and was admitted to a mental hospital, where she collapsed on the anniversary of her mother's death and died the next day, in the seventh month of her 42nd year.

Overt Wishes to Die

Most giving-up appraisals and perceptions of helplessness are not expressed overtly as a deliberate wish to die, but in some instances people will openly insist that they do not want to live or that they welcome death. A 27-year-old woman with asthma got into conflict with her family, who cut off her funds, forcing her to quit college and take menial jobs.[26] She kept losing the jobs because of asthmatic attacks. As she described her plight she became increasingly upset and cried, "That's why I wanted to die and want to die all the time, because I am no good, no good!" She then collapsed and died, apparently of cardiac arrest.

Some people have a "predilection to death" and see dying as both desirable and appropriate. Avery Weisman and Thomas Hackett, two Harvard psychiatrists, were struck by the unshakable conviction such people have that they are going to die—even when medical findings suggest otherwise.[27] One patient, in the hospital for a duodenal ulcer, had stewed for 20 years over a fight he had with a friend and an unsuccessful court battle he launched as a result. His only revenge was to outlive all those who had opposed him. Finally, when his last "enemy" had died, the man announced that now it was time for his death. After surgery on his ulcer, he seemed to be recovering without complications. Then suddenly on the third day, he began having difficulty breathing, his heart started beating irregularly, and he died. An autopsy revealed a clot that blocked his pulmonary valve.

Another patient who was convinced it was time to die was in the hospital for a broken leg. He stated that he was an illegitimate member of an illustrious New England family that had left him on the doorstep of an orphanage as an infant. After a career as a merchant seaman and later a robber, he grew old in isolation. Finally, he decided there was no point in continuing to live. After surgery on his leg, he asked his doctor what sense there was in remaining in the world when he no longer had an interest in it. On the eighth day after his leg operation, he suddenly died of a pulmonary clot.

Death from Hexes

The manifest loss of will to live and the welcoming of death have also been observed in voodoo deaths. Walter Cannon, the Harvard physiologist who discovered the fight-flight response, became interested in voodoo deaths because of what could be learned about the mechanisms involved when someone dies who believes he has been hexed or "boned" or put under a spell.

Cannon found numerous instances of tribe members in South America, Africa, Australia and New Zealand who were convinced they had been singled out by a sorcerer to die, and they did.[28] Others believed they had violated a sacred taboo and were expected to die, which they did. For instance, in the Congo, a young man had been told that the food he was being served for breakfast was not a wild hen, which was strictly tabooed for the immature. The young man then ate heartily. A few years later, he again met the person who had served him the food and was told that he had eaten a wild hen. The young man had been solemnly charged not to eat that food. On discovering his transgression, he trembled and was overcome by fear. He died in less than 24 hours. In New Zealand, a Maori woman died after learning she had eaten fruit from a tabooed place and had therefore profaned her chief.

Not all cases of being put under a curse come from less developed parts of the world. The mother of a 53-year-old asthma patient forecast dire consequences for him for disobeying her.[29] His first asthmatic attack had occurred some months earlier when, with his wife's support, he made a major decision counter to his mother's wishes. On learning of his decision, his mother predicted, "something will strike you." After that, the son had frequent attacks and hospitalizations. He was stricken with a fatal convulsive attack after he made another decision without consulting his mother, and she reminded him of her dire warning. He died an hour later.

Cannon recognized that in voodoo or "curse" deaths, people have deep beliefs about being hexed, put under a spell or being in violation of a taboo, and these beliefs can induce feelings of fear and terror or a sense of helplessness. Under such conditions, he reported, the sympathetic-adrenal medullary system mobilizes the body to flee or fight—high epinephrine levels, fast heart beat, increased glucose in the blood—but when no physical action is taken, "dire results may ensue."[30] The epinephrine and sympathetic nerve impulses cause constriction of small arterioles in various parts of the body, and if this state is prolonged it can lead to loss of blood plasma into interstitial space and to a "disastrous fall of blood pressure, ending in death."[31]

Believing a Situation Is Hopeless

The phenomenon of being literally "frightened to death" has also been observed in people who have terrifying experiences that cause no physical harm but lead to emotional shock or extreme anxiety. Cannon concluded that the same physiological mechanism is at work in persons who enter surgery believing that they are going to die and thereby place themselves at high risk.

A 43-year-old woman underwent a complete hysterectomy and appeared to withstand the operation well.[28] However, that night her blood pressure fell alarmingly, her heart rate increased to 150 beats per minute and her skin was cold and clammy. There was no bleeding to account for her condition, which was diagnosed as "shock brought on by fear." Cannon said that "a calm and reassuring attitude by her surgeon resulted in a change of attitude in the patient, with recovery of a normal state."[32]

J.M.T. Finney, for many years professor of surgery at Johns Hopkins, stated publicly that he would not operate on people who entered surgery believing they would not come out alive.[33] More recently Theodore Miller, senior attending surgeon at Memorial Sloan-Kettering Cancer Center in New York, told the Society of Surgical Oncology:

> After operating on several patients who expressed great apprehension and fear of death, only to have them die in spite of what appeared to be a normal operative course, I no longer operate on a patient who expresses the fear that he would not survive the operation.[34]

A person, then, who believes he is doomed, whether it is from being hexed, violating a taboo or facing serious surgery, may apparently "die from fright" by hyperstimulation of the sympathetic nervous system and adrenal medulla, leading to shock and blood pressure failure. Other people may believe their situation is hopeless and simply give up, activating a persistent parasympathetic response and causing the heart to slow to a dangerous degree as opposed to speeding up. Their feeling is not so much extreme fear as perception of no solution and defeat.

Rats That Gave Up

Psychologist Curt Richter of the psychobiological laboratory at Johns Hopkins was one of the first to describe the giving-up phenomenon.[35] He found that rats put into situations where they could not flee or fight would quickly die. Both domesticated and wild rats succumbed from being held under a bag or immersed in a jar full of water. Wild rats put in the water died within one to 15 minutes, not from drowning but from a slowing of the heart and respiration until the heart stopped. Electrocardiographic tracings showed that the first response to restraint under the bag or confinement in the water jar was an accelerated heart rate. This shifted to progressive slowing of the heart as the stress was prolonged, and the animal saw no escape.

The rats died even more quickly if their whiskers, a principal source of sensing the environment and orienting themselves, had been clipped. Richter postulated the mechanism in the deaths to be overstimulation of the parasympathetic system, which—in opposition to the sympathetic—causes the heart to beat slower. He observed:

> The situation of these rats scarcely seems one of demanding fight or flight—it is rather one of hopelessness; whether they are restrained in the hand or confined in the swimming jar, the rats are in a situation against which they have no defense. . . . they seem literally to "give up."[36]

That the sudden deaths of the rats were induced by their giving up was confirmed by the fact that when hopelessness was eliminated, the animals did not die. If the rats were briefly held under the bag or in the water jar on several occasions and let go each time, they would later swim in the jar for long periods without signs of giving up or dying.

Richter hypothesized that humans who appraise any situation as hopeless may give up and succumb to "parasympathetic death," as the rats did. He suggested the same mechanism may be involved in unaccountable deaths among healthy members of the armed forces who, in time of war, die in this country even though autopsies demonstrate no pathology. In addition, coroners in large cities report that a number of people die each year after taking small, nonlethal doses of poisonous substances or inflicting superficial wounds on themselves. Richter said the victims "apparently die as a result of the belief in their doom."[37]

A Forum on Coronary-Prone Behavior, which brought together authorities on heart disease from around the country, has agreed that no evidence of structural pathology may be found when death follows bradycardia (slowing of the heart).[38] The panel of experts noted that when an animal is placed in a situation where it has no hope of control, this kind of death may occur. It may also occur when "a submissive animal has no escape from a victor." Giving up and dying, apparently from parasympathetic overload, seems the only way out.

The traumatic effects on the body of having no sense of control in a stressful situation were also illustrated in a series of experiments with squirrel monkeys.[39] Six pairs of the animals were confined to chairs for eight hours a day. One of the monkeys in each pair had to turn off a light once a minute to prevent a shock from being delivered to the tails of both monkeys. The monkeys in control of the light developed high blood pressure, suggesting excessive arousal of their sympathetic nervous systems. But their yoked partners fared worse. Of the six monkeys that had no control over the light and the shocks, five collapsed from excessively slow heart action (bradycardia) and four died from irregular cardiac rhythm (asystole).

Living for a Special Occasion

Our beliefs, then, have powerful influences over our bodies and our health, even to the point of contributing to death. But do thoughts and other cognitions have equally profound effects for prolonging life? The mounting, though indirect, evidence indicates that they do. Again, much folk wisdom suggests that some people, even the terminally ill and very old, do not die until after observing a certain day or ceremony that has particular significance and meaning to them or their families. They either believe they must live until a certain time (such as for a wedding or Christmas) or they have something they very much look forward to (a reunion). In any event, they simply refuse to give up until after the special occasion is over.

The difficulty in investigating such phenomena scientifically has kept research on the questions to a minimum. However, sociologists have made some progress by investigating whether a dip in deaths occurs before such occasions as birthdays, an important religious event (such as Yom Kippur) and a noteworthy national happening (a Presidential election). David Phillips and Kenneth Feldman of the State University of New York at Stony Brook theorized that the more people feel part of a society, culture or family, the more they want to participate in its ceremonies and special occasions.[40] They believe in such events and attach much importance to them. "Such people," the researchers suggested, "postpone death in order to participate in social ceremonies."[41] On the other hand, and in line with Durkheim's theory of suicide, those who become increasingly alienated no longer believe that these occasions have any meaning and become isolated from society, their culture or family. Such people tend to die prematurely.

Phillips and Feldman looked at the association between birthdays and dates of death for 400 "notable Americans," since good public records could be obtained on such people. Also, birthdays were likely to bring more recognition for someone notable, and a true test could be made of whether an event important to a person could have an effect on when that individual died. The sociologists found that the notables were not inclined to die in the month preceding their birthdays. They observed that "there is a statistically significant death-dip in the month before the birthmonth."[42] As to whether there is a giving up after a birthday, Phillips and Feldman reported a "death peak"—a rise in number of deaths—in the following four months.

Important religious occasions seem to have similar effects. The researchers examined mortality before the Day of Atonement (Yom Kippur), the holiest day of the Jewish year. Again, they found a death-dip during the month before the event. Since the day has more meaning for Jews than for others, the sociologists expected that non-Jews would show no decline in mortality. An analysis of the data confirmed this.

The third identified death-dip occurred in September and October of presidential election years. Other events and ceremonial occasions seem to have different effects on people, depending on the sex, age, residence and subculture of the individuals. For instance, preliminary findings indicate that a death-dip occurs before the Olympic Games in cities that hold the contests.

Meaning and Support in Life

Believing, then, that we have something to live for seems to deflect our perceptions away from giving up or seeing no solution or feeling overwhelmed. Feeling part of a support network or having a sense of cohesion may help keep us from adopting attitudes of no solution and increasing our risk of disease. In Roseto, Pennsylvania, for example, the incidence of myocardial infarction among Italian-Americans was remarkably low (see Chapter 6).[43] Even among those in older age groups who experienced a heart attack, the death rate was low after the myocardial infarction. All this was true despite the fact that most of the Italian-Americans were overweight and ate a diet rich in saturated fats. Death rate from heart attacks was one-half that of neighboring towns and the United States at large.

Stewart Wolf, a pioneer in clinical stress research, studied the community and observed that "unlike most American communities," Roseto was "cohesive and mutually supportive with strong family and community ties."[44] But with each new generation, the ties began to weaken and the offspring who moved away or adopted new lifestyles experienced heart attack rates equal to those in the rest of the country. When stress is encountered, people with support and cohesion in their lives seem better able to keep from making appraisals of no solution or feeling life has no purpose.

Feeling unsupported and seeing no purpose or solution was a common experience among prisoners in Nazi concentration camps. But many who became prisoners survived. Bruno Bettelheim was one of the first psychologists to report on this phenomenon.[45] He based his observations on his own experiences in Gestapo political camps. Bettelheim identified a "musselmann" reaction that was closely followed by death. Those demonstrating the reaction, which was characterized by a giving up, soon died. They were the prisoners who came to believe the repeated statements of the guards that there was no hope for them and that they would never leave the camp alive.

In contrast, those who were determined to control some aspect of their life, despite an oppressive environment that seemed overwhelming, were among the survivors. In the concentration camps, once it was fully realized that the purpose of such places was extermination, the mere act of staying alive became an expression of autonomy and control. Small achievements could be perceived as evidence of personal control. As one former prisoner told psychiatrist Joel Dimsdale (also see Chapter 3): "The thing that kept me alive was to focus on where I could find a blanket, something to chew, to eat, to repair, a torn shoe, an additional glove."[46]

Viktor Frankl, an existential psychiatrist, also wrote of his experience in concentration camps. He observed that the risk of death was greatly increased if the prisoner could perceive no sense of purpose or meaning in life, both of which undergird personal control and militate against giving up.[47]

Determination not to give up has been reported as a critical factor in survival among cancer patients. When two groups of people—all of whom had been diagnosed as having incurable malignancies—were compared as to which patients lived longer than expected and which did not, it was those who had refused to give up who were the "exceptional survivors."[48] Patients in both groups had metastatic, stage IV cancer, but those with greater coping skills (ego strength) and self-sufficiency lived in excess of two years past their diagnoses while those who gave up died within 13 months.

Also in Less Extreme Conditions?

Thus from terminal cancer, concentration camps, sudden deaths, drowning rats and violations of taboos and hexes have come clues about the powerful effects of giving up, which means perceiving no control or solution, feeling helpless and withdrawing from life.

Most of us do not face problems under such extreme or traumatic conditions. We do not die in the throes of acute emotional distress. But we do get sick, sometimes seriously, while trying to adjust to a stressful situation. If the giving-up appraisal is truly a common risk factor, then its effects should be present in a variety of circumstances and conditions, in different people reacting to a wide range of problems. Can it, in fact, be found as a prelude to illness in general?

11.
Getting Sick
When We Do

---

*... most lay people take it for
granted that a person's frame
of mind has something to do
with his propensity to fall ill and
even to die. ... But physicians
... rarely regard this as a
legitimate area for their
scientific interest.*[1]

*Physical illness ... can
become ... the only control
one has over life.*[2]

In an attempt to answer the question of why we get sick when we do and what makes us vulnerable, a group of psychologically trained specialists in internal medicine in Rochester, New York, spent 20 years formulating the "giving up-given up complex."

They wanted to account not only for unexplained sudden deaths but also for the reversals in health people experience and the times when these setbacks take place. Germs, genes, nutrition and other single "causes" of disease do not adequately explain why one person gets sick when someone of similar age and background, exposed to the same environment, does not.

The University of Rochester School of Medicine team set out to identify the conditions under which illness occurs and to determine if there is a common setting conducive to disease. They conducted dozens of studies, involving clinical observations and interviews of hundreds of patients, and concluded that people who get sick have recently experienced some stressful situation—or a reminder of one—that they perceive as being beyond their control, having no solution or leaving them helpless.[3]

The case the doctors made for the giving up-given up complex as a common precursor of illness and disease was built upon investigations of patients with many kinds of diseases, disorders and symptoms: leukemia, colitis, psychiatric disturbances, multiple sclerosis, and all the disorders found in a random sample of persons treated in the medical division of a large hospital. The group came up with the term "giving up-given up complex" after noting that people who are at high risk of illness not only seem to believe that they themselves can do nothing about their problem but no one else can either.[4] They give up on themselves and believe others have given up on them as well. The Rochester researchers also used "giving up" and "given up" to designate separate stages. In the process of experiencing a loss or setback, a person struggles with giving up some important gratification or source of need fulfillment. The second stage comes when the person perceives no solution to regaining what was lost.[4]

Giving Up Found in 80% of Cases

George Engel, Arthur Schmale, William Greene, Franz Reichsman and their associates, all in the departments of medicine and psychiatry at Rochester, never claimed that giving up or helplessness was "the cause" of our getting sick. It is *one* factor that contributes to our vulnerability. They compared their research to an "epidemiologic approach to malaria, in which information about geography, climate, breeding conditions of mosquitoes, the life cycle of the mosquito, the conditions necessary for survival of the malarial parasite, the conditions necessary for transmission of the parasite from vector to human host and back again, the factors of host resistance and many others all combine to define the conditions necessary and sufficient for the development of the disease malaria."[5]

In other words, as we have noted, no one condition or agent is sufficient for disease to occur and each must be identified to understand how pathology starts and develops. What the Rochester group set out to do was to identify the psychological setting or conditions that precede illness and contribute to the onset of disease. They were aware that simply counting how many stressful life events a person had recently had did not tell them much. They were convinced that how the individual appraises such events and what personal meaning is attached to them spell the difference between being vulnerable to illness and being resistant.[4]

Identifying the personal interpretations and meanings that people give to their dilemmas and difficulties is just the beginning, however. Appraisals give rise to emotions and emotions to behavior, and all three generate physiological and somatic responses. When we encounter problems in life and we look at them as if there were no solution or "everything is out of control," we start feeling helpless, perhaps even hopeless, and we begin to withdraw and retreat into a shell. The physiological effects of our appraisal, our emotions and our behavior pave the way for illness by the neural, endocrine and immune responses that result.

"Needing" to Be Ill

To answer the question of why we get sick when we do, we must also look at the meaning that illness itself has for people. If we feel overburdened or unable to meet the demands of our jobs, families or other people, sickness may give us "permission" to stop trying and give up.[6] We may perceive illness as something we "need."

For some people, illness can provide an excuse for failure, for others it can make asking for love easier. Even a cold, transitory as it usually is, may provide us a reason to give up or give in for awhile—to go to bed, to take it easy, to nurture ourselves.[6]

Giving up, then, seems to be linked to illness not only as a precursor but as a consequence. As a factor that precedes sickness, giving up may be an unspoken, even denied, cognition. As something that comes after illness, it may be more conscious and acknowledged. The illness itself becomes the reason for giving up. In either case, the body responds to the message that our minds give it.

Although illness seems to result when we believe we

have little control over our lives, it may paradoxically become the one way some people establish control. Sick people may use their illness to manipulate others and to take over the very lives of family members and friends who become victims of their control.[6] For some victims, the only solution they can perceive is to give up and become sicker than the one in control of them.

"Cause" or "Effect?"

After more than 20 years of observations, the Rochester researchers concluded that in 70 to 80 percent of all illness the giving up-given up complex precedes the onset of symptoms.[3] This estimate of incidence was based largely on recorded interviews with people already sick who were asked to recall any stressful or emotional episodes preceding the development of symptoms. Relatives also were interviewed. Since sick people, particularly those seriously ill, may clearly be depressed because their normal activities have been disrupted, their recall of events may well be colored by their low morale. In other words, a giving-up outlook might not have preceded the onset of symptoms as much as it was a result of being ill. It might be more "effect" than "cause."

The Rochester group was aware of this criticism but noted that independent interviews with relatives confirmed that giving up or helplessness on the part of the person who became ill preceded symptoms rather than followed them. More importantly, among the hundreds of patients studied were some whose cases were followed for 12 to 15 years by the doctors. They were able to correlate the presence and absence of giving up with relapses and remissions.

Not a Fixed State

Both Engel and Schmale emphasized that giving up is not a fixed "psychological state"—it waxes and wanes as people make new efforts at coping, try new approaches, receive support or garner hope from other sources.[7] In the face of stress, people may alternate between seeing no solution to their problems and coping actively as circumstances change or new resources are mobilized. Engel found that bleeding episodes in ulcerative colitis came and went as patients experienced feelings of helplessness during some stressful situation or perceived new strength when a crisis was overcome.[5]

Sometimes years separate illness episodes. For instance, a 19-year-old girl was in bed for two weeks with Bell's palsy and leg weakness after graduating from business school and being confronted with going to work at a secretarial job.[8] Thirteen years later, she found herself trapped in a marriage to a man who beat her and their children. When she began to consider separation, she developed multiple sclerosis. In MS, myelin—the white material that sheathes and insulates nerves—incurs multiple scars, perhaps from immune cells mistakenly attacking normal cells that manufacture the myelin. Difficulty in coping and psychosocial factors seem to contribute to the onset of symptoms.

In a study of multiple sclerosis in Israel, Varda Mei-Tal, who worked with the Rochester physicians, described a 26-year-old married woman who had a sudden onset of symptoms after making a decision to have a second child.[8] She was working as a teacher and she and her husband had postponed the decision because their first born was an unusually difficult child. After the woman became ill, the pregnancy was postponed and she experienced a complete remission. Later, however, she became pregnant and suffered a relapse.

An 18-year-old high school student who had been

bothered by chronic eczema since childhood received notice at midsemester that he was failing a course.[9] He was terrified to tell his father, whom he believed had excessive expectations of him. When the father responded to the news by simply saying, "do better next time," the boy still felt "lousy." He worried about what the teacher must think of him to give him a failing grade and could not bring himself to discuss it with her. Within a week, he had a flareup of his dermatitis, which spread to his arms, neck, face and chest, and suffered a secondary infection.

In a woman with leukemia that two of the Rochester doctors checked weekly for more than 12 years, they noted that the severity of her case, as reflected in peripheral blood counts, varied with the amount of control she believed she had over problems and events that occurred.[10] A major aggravation of the disease developed when she accepted the fact that her third marriage was failing. A further relapse occurred when her son left home for military service.

Sense of Helplessness

In these and other cases studied by the medical-psychiatric liaison group at Rochester, the predominant theme was a sense of helplessness brought on by perceiving a situation as having no solution. This was true of situations involving loss or separation, conflicts in marriage, at work or school, broken romances, impending surgery and a wide range of other problems. In fact, the nature of the situation or problem was not important. It was the meaning that the person ascribed to the event that mattered.

A dilemma or disappointment that might not seem serious to an objective observer can have profound effects on the individual involved, who interprets it in an entirely different way. For example, a young college graduate left home to seek employment in another city.[9] In the five months he was gone, he and his mother exchanged four visits, traveling 400 miles each time. The young man was lonely and "uneasy" in his new surroundings, but he arranged with a friend to go bowling. The friend was an hour late. As the young man was waiting, he kept thinking, "isn't this the way things always work out?" He was reminded of the time when he was 8 years old and his father died and his mother had to go to work. He felt alone and on his own. Still waiting for his friend, he began bowling alone and was suddenly stricken with pains in the lower back. He had to return to his mother's home and was hospitalized.

"Can't Stand it Any More"

To understand the kind of meaning and appraisal a person may attach to a troubling situation, the researchers made a systematic study of the words used to describe the event and the reaction to it. People typically expressed a giving-up appraisal in language like this:

"I had the feeling life wasn't worth living" (woman in hospital with a depressive reaction after her youngest child started to school).[11]

"How much can I take? There's never any end" (woman hospitalized with headaches after daughter became sick with pneumonia).[11]

"There are dozens of things that come up in a business that can discourage you, especially if you haven't got the fight left in you to fight back" (62-year-old man whose toy business went bad and he was hospitalized with a bone marrow tumor).[12]

"Well, you just simply give up fighting any more. What's left to fight for?" (40-year-old factory worker whose wife divorced him after 22 years of marriage. He was diagnosed as having congestive heart failure and was later admitted to surgery with a clot in the femoral artery).[13]

"I have thought of that [dying] many times" (44-year-old widowed man who despaired of getting his teen-age sons to go to school and was admitted to the hospital with pneumonia).[14]

"People expect far more than you can produce" (37-year-old man who described himself as being "like a rat in a corner." He struggled with feelings of frustration and failure over not being able to support his family and his wife's going to work. He developed multiple sclerosis).[15]

"I just can't stand it any more" (man hospitalized with a diagnosis of antisocial personality disorder after renewed conflict with his parents over his wedding plans).[16]

"My whole world came apart when she died" (19-year-old young man who suffered paralysis of one leg after his mother's death).[17]

"Things are too much for me . . . I want to run but there's no place to run" (45-year-old mother who was hospitalized with headaches after criticism and rejection from her husband).[18]

"I really should have done more for her, but I just don't know what to do" (43-year-old woman in the hospital with digestive complaints that began increasing on the anniversary of her mother's death at age 43).[19]

"I felt lost as to what to do" (young schoolteacher who was admitted to the hospital for migraine headaches, which started after several of her pupils misbehaved and played pranks on her).

Words that carry thoughts of giving up and helplessness lead to excessive levels of stress hormones, which, as we have seen, may impair a person's immune defenses, constrict or damage arteries, and disregulate other bodily functions.

Too Much Conservation-Withdrawal

In addition to seeing situations as having no solution and feeling helpless, people at high risk of illness also often change their behavior, increasing their vulnerability even more. They may withdraw into a state of inactivity or immobility, a state Engel and Schmale called the "conservation-withdrawal response."[20]

Drawing on earlier animal studies, the Rochester researchers viewed all living creatures as having two basic emergency systems—fight-flight and conservation-withdrawal. Each of these encompasses a wide range of behaviors, with the first system focusing on activity and the second on inactivity. Both are means to deal with our environment and problems that come up, but when either one is used excessively or inappropriately the system then becomes maladaptive and turns against us. The purpose of the conservation-withdrawal response is to permit us to disengage from a source of pain or trouble (physical or psychological) so that we can save our energy, rest and wait for better times. But when we overdo the reaction and become virtually unresponsive to everything around us, physiological changes may occur that place us at risk of illness or even death. It is as if we have carried "playing possum" too far, held our breath too long or "hibernated" to such an extreme that there is no return.

All living organisms use inactivity as a means of coping.[20] Even the lowly amoeba will contract and cease to move when a stimulus is intense. If the stimulus is prolonged and powerful enough, the organism will remain contracted until it dies. Otherwise, it resumes locomotion. The doodle bug will roll up into a ball and become immobile in a threatening environment, and similar creatures also use "encystment" to adjust to adverse conditions. Larger animals go into varying states of dormancy through hibernation, sham death and "tonic immobility" to cope with excessive heat, cold, moisture or other unfavorable changes in the environment. Whether the stressor is physical or nonphysical, the conservation-withdrawal response is triggered when no control of the environment seems likely. The conservation-withdrawal response can be seen in infant pigtail monkeys whose mothers have been removed from the colony. In a sitting position, they put their heads between their legs and bring their arms in to support and protect their faces.

Engel and Schmale identified similar behaviors in humans under extreme stress.[20] A child dying of starvation hunkers into a tightly closed, knees-to-chest position. At scenes of devastating earthquakes, people can be seen with their hands to their faces, their shoulders drooped and rounded, their knees flexed, as if they are ready to slump to the ground and curl up into a ball.

Physiological Changes

The Rochester group did detailed observations of a 15-month-old baby girl admitted to the hospital whose esophagus had been closed since birth from a congenital defect.[21] An artificial passage—a gastric fistula—had been established from her body surface to her stomach so that she could be fed until she was old enough to have an operation correcting the defect. Corrective surgery was performed when she was 5½ months old. Because her mother was only 19 and had problems of her own, "Monica" suffered early neglect and had to be hospitalized from time to time. Engel and his coworkers did their study when she was admitted at 15 months until she was discharged six months later.[20]

The doctors noticed that when a stranger came to Monica's bedside, or some other threat appeared, she would assume a position much like the infant monkeys separated from their mothers. She would become motionless, her head and eyes averted, her arms and legs limp. Engel and Schmale measured differences in the baby's physiological states during the withdrawal response compared with periods when she showed contentment, joy, irritation and anger. Her gastric secretion of hydrochloric acid was significantly lower during withdrawal than at any other time. If she was given histamine during periods when she was outgoing and relating actively with those around her, her stomach secreted considerable amounts of hydrochloric acid. But when she was in the withdrawn state, the histamine had little or no effect. Similar differences were found in heart rate and respiration. Whereas there was marked acceleration of heart rate and respiration during anger and irritation, the opposite was true during withdrawal. The conservation-withdrawal response, then, is marked not only by behavioral changes but also by physiological alterations.

"At the End of Their Rope"

When we repeatedly perceive no solution to whatever trouble we are in, or when we persistently have no sense of control in our lives, the conservation-withdrawal response seems to stop being protective and puts us at risk of illness and, in some instances, even death.[3] Other researchers have noted the physiological effects in people who believed they were "at the end of their rope" or felt helpless and hopeless.[22] Cardiac slowing, drop in blood pressure, arrhythmia, decrease in urinary water and sodium, diminished gastric secretion—all are consistent with what Engel called conservation-withdrawal.

But the most powerful feature of the response is what happens to the nervous system. It is the action of the autonomic nervous system, which controls our internal organs, that is directly or indirectly responsible for many of the significant physiological changes that occur in the body during conservation-withdrawal. The autonomic's two major divisions, the sympathetic and parasympathetic nervous systems, are normally in a reciprocal balance when the body is functioning smoothly. One system acts as a check on the other. The sympathetic, for example, accelerates heart action while the parasympathetic decelerates it.

If someone perceives that a problem can be controlled by fighting, running or some other direct activity less motoric (such as assertion or persuasion), then the sympathetic may take over and mobilization for action is appropriate. If disengagement, detachment or insulation seems to be the only option, then the parasympathetic dominates. Fight-flight and sympathetic activity are part of the body's "ergotrophic" system—the system that alerts, arouses or excites.[23] Conservation-withdrawal and the parasympathetic engage the "trophotrophic" system, which inhibits action, decreases muscle tone and restricts responsiveness to the environment. The ergotrophic system involves "catabolic" hormones, which means the body is expending energy and interacting with the environment. The trophotropic response involves "anabolic" hormones, meaning the body is seeking supplies or rest from the environment for repair, renewal and growth.

Our first line of defense is activity—attempts to change the environment so that our needs, as we perceive them, can be met. Our last line of defense is disengagement and resignation, a refusal to deal with the environment. If our final conclusion is that no solution is possible, then giving up becomes permanent, with all its attendant trophotropic, parasympathetic consequences.

In between active efforts to cope and a final giving up is often a "freeze" response—a stopping of action to watch and wait, to see if things will change or an opportunity will present itself. Lizzy Jarvik and Dan Russell of the department of psychiatry and biobehavioral sciences at UCLA consider "freeze" as a third basic emergency response, different from both fight-flight and conservation-withdrawal, which they identify with giving up.[24] Freeze, they believe, is an optimal response under threat for people with declining resources, such as the elderly. In vigilant watching and waiting, the response may trigger sympathetic hyperarousal. In fainting or swooning, it may engage parasympathetic hypoarousal.

Uncertainty and Rapid Shifts

Rapid shifts between sympathetic and parasympathetic responses seem to predispose people to illness and death as much as giving up does. Such alternations occur when we are caught in relentless uncertainty about what to do.[25] The disorganizing effects on behavior and the body have been graphically illustrated in experiments in which dogs, for instance, have been put under overwhelming stress. Before a final giving up, they rapidly swing back and forth between fight-flight and conservation-withdrawal. They bite, crouch, tremble, move about aimlessly, bark, whine, salivate, urinate, defecate, pant and sometimes even momentarily doze, all in rapid succession.

Psychoanalyst L.J. Saul had a 45-year-old patient who found himself in a situation that the man perceived as unbearable and required him to move to another town.[26] But just as he was ready to make the move, trouble developed for him in the other town that he believed made it impossible for him to go there. Now he did not know what to do. He went ahead and boarded a train for the new town but half way there, he got out to pace the platform at a station stop. When the conductor called "all aboard," he felt he could neither go on nor return home. He dropped dead on the spot.

In the 26 cases of sudden death at Eastman Kodak (see Chapter 10), the majority of the men had been depressed for some time and then experienced an increased work load or some conflict that resulted in arousal.[27] The researchers proposed that the shift from depression to arousal produced an incompatible variety of reactions resulting in arrhythmia, infarction or both. The shift was like that between conservation-withdrawal and fight-flight or alternations between parasympathetic and sympathetic responses.

How Giving Up Does Us In

Details of the neural, physiological and biochemical changes that seem to accompany helplessness, uncertainty and giving up are still being unraveled in research. But in addition to profound effects in the autonomic nervous system, an appraisal of no control also registers in the pituitary-adrenal cortical system.[28] Cortisol and other adrenocortical hormones are emitted, which, as we have seen, tend to suppress our immunity to disease. J.P. Henry and P.M. Stephens of UCLA School of Medicine showed that when animals sense some opportunity to control a challenge they face, their brains activate the adrenal medullary system—the fight-flight response first identified by Cannon.[29] But when the animals perceive no control, conservation-withdrawal sets in and Selye's adrenocortical hormones are activated.

In humans, those who have a driving need to control and dominate often show chronic elevation of fight-flight hormones and a higher risk of coronary heart disease and respiratory illness.[30] Those who are inclined toward depression and giving up have higher levels of cortisol and a greater risk of cancer from suppression of natural killer cells in the immune system. A sense of helplessness leaves us more susceptible to illness in general and cancer in particular. Experiments have demonstrated that when animals see themselves as helpless, they experience both suppression of natural killer cells and faster growth of tumors.[31] Giving-up reactions also bring a higher risk of sudden death or cardiac arrest from overstimulation of the parasympathetic nervous system.

Diabetes and Hopelessness

Even before the Rochester group began to identify how health is affected by giving up, clinical researchers at Cornell University Medical College in New York were making similar observations. Harold Wolff of Cornell had been one of the pioneers in stress research who showed that illness and disease are a function of how we react to noxious events and the way we interpret them.[32] One of the techniques the Cornell researchers used to demonstrate the link between appraisal and physiological changes was the "stress interview."[33] Using material from a patient's medical and social history, the doctors could observe how blood pressure, heart rate, electrocardiogram, blood flow and other measures fluctuated as a function of the conflicts, dilemmas and difficulties discussed in the interview. With diabetic patients, there was a marked drop in blood glucose and a rise in ketones (products of fat metabolism), which can lead to an acidosis chemical imbalance and possible coma.

In longterm studies of diabetes mellitus conducted by Lawrence Hinkle and Stewart Wolf, then at Cornell, a sense of helplessness and hopelessness was linked with the onset and exacerbation of the disorder. Hinkle and Wolf traced the ups and downs of a 17-year-old school girl who was diagnosed as having diabetes when she was 10.[34] Early stresses in the child's life—rejected by mother, spoiled by older sister, starting school, moving three times—all could be correlated with bouts of illness and bodily changes finally culminating in the diabetes diagnosis at 10. After the diagnosis, episodes of ketosis and coma could be linked with the girl's hopeless attitude toward stressful situations that came up. She had to be admitted to the hospital 12 times over five years for diabetic acidosis and coma. These admissions came after fights between her parents, arguments with her mother, changing to a new school and the departure of her sister ("the only one who loved me"). The doctors asked her to keep a diary of daily events and her accompanying feelings about situations. Every two weeks they reviewed these and checked her condition. Her insulin dose was maintained constant throughout. Hinkle and Wolf had already noted that diabetic flare-ups could often occur despite careful regulation of the patient's diet, insulin and physical activity.

This point was dramatically illustrated during one of the hospital stays of the girl. Although her diet, insulin and activity were being closely monitored, she had a marked change in her condition after a visit from her mother. She perceived her mother as being extremely angry with her and also believed that her physician (her "only" friend) was also angry. Although she became increasingly anxious and depressed, she was unable to express her feelings. Tests showed that she was losing large amounts of glucose in her urine and that ketones, the compounds that indicate the body is having to turn to fat as a source of fuel, were rising sharply. She also had a rapid heart rate, dry mouth and skin. However, once she was assured that her mother was not angry with her and that her physician was still her friend, her ketosis and other symptoms all disappeared without additional treatment.

"As If" Reactions

The Cornell investigators were committed to the idea that disease represents the misuse of adaptive mechanisms in the body.[35] In other words, most disorders are the result of some normal, natural process of the body going awry by too much or too little stimulation—or being engaged inappropriately. For instance, waves of contractions in the stomach and bowel, accompanied by explosive diarrhea, are adaptive and appropriate when someone has food poisoning and the body is trying to eliminate salmonella. Such action by the same mechanism is maladaptive and inappropriate when it is triggered by the person's believing that he or she must get rid of a boss, mate or anyone else perceived as unbearable.[34] Similarly, the conservation-withdrawal, parasympathetic mechanism is adaptive when it is used to help us recoup so that we can reenter the fray. When it is employed as a permanent escape, by our giving up once and for all, then the consequences can be highly damaging or fatal.

If most disease is the end result of normally beneficial bodily mechanisms turned against us, how could the process responsible for diabetes be considered adaptive? This was the question raised by Hinkle and Wolf. They concluded that the diabetic mechanism was present and necessary in the body to help defend humans against starvation.[34] When there is no food, glucose—the body's chief source of fuel—must be conserved in the bloodstream as long as possible to supply energy for the nervous system and brain, which cannot use any other fuel source. It is adaptive, then, for fat stores and muscles to be raided for fuel and leave what precious little glucose there is for the brain.

In diabetes, the body reacts as if it must preserve glucose and burn fat. The glucose spills over into the urine, and the products of fat metabolism can build up to the point of causing a serious acid imbalance and coma. Hinkle and Wolf theorized that since food in many societies is closely identified with love and nurturing, some people who believe they are emotionally deprived will lead their bodies into reacting as if there were no food. The adaptive diabetic mechanism to defend against starvation then gets triggered and becomes destructive.

Wolf went on to identify further "as if" responses, suggesting that our misperceptions and faulty expectations can play havoc in our bodies.[36] The person who ends up with a peptic ulcer often acts as if he must be fed or devour something. The hypertensive individual may believe he must be constantly on guard for battle, and his body behaves as if it were going to be hurt and blood pressure must be kept high. Russian researchers did studies with baboons that supported the theory that hypertension is more likely to occur in persons who act as though they must be poised for combat, although their aggression is always held in check.[37] The Russians took pairs of baboons that had sought each other out as mates and separated them. The female was placed in a large cage with a strange male. Her mate was put in an adjoining smaller cage. The cuckolded male regularly developed sustained hypertension.

Predicting Effects of Helplessness

A number of clinical studies, outside of those at Rochester and Cornell, tended to confirm the influence of giving up and helplessness on vulnerability to illness. One that became a model for the concept that disease occurs from a combination of converging factors and is not caused by some single agent was done in the 1950s by Herbert Weiner and his colleagues at Walter Reed Army Institute of Research and the University of Pittsburgh School of Medicine.[38] They were the first to be able to predict, using a large group of Army recruits, who would develop an ulcer during basic training. As noted earlier, they demonstrated that recruits with high dependency needs, high secretion of pepsinogen in the stomach and an appraisal of high stress were most vulnerable. In being separated from their homes and those who took care of them, these recruits apparently were forced to give up gratifications they perceived they had to have and could not bear to relinquish. They thus tended to see themselves as helpless.

The same combination of genetic predisposition, environmental factors and a giving-up appraisal was used to predict the onset of symptoms in another digestive disorder, celiac disease, which is characterized by periodic diar-rhea, irritable bowel and fatty stools.[39] Of 30 symptom epi-sodes in eight families under study, 28 of them were preceded by a sense of giving up and food that included gliadin, a wheat protein that some people cannot absorb. But no symptoms occurred as the result of the diet factor alone. When giving up alone was present, irritable bowel problems occurred but not the other symptoms.

Ben Bursten of the department of psychiatry at Cin-cinnati General Hospital reported that he could predict changes in the condition of a hospitalized asthmatic woman based on periods when she exhibited a giving-up, helpless attitude.[40] When she reacted to events with a self-sufficient manner, her sputum contained few or no eosinophils, white blood cells often found in allergic reactions. When she re-acted with helplessness, the physician could successfully predict that her sputum would be laden with eosinophils.

Weakness of Early Studies

The predictive studies attempted to overcome a weakness of the original giving-up research, which made inferences about causes of disease after the disorder had already de-veloped. The next step was predicting physiological changes or symptoms in people based on whether they reacted to situations by giving up. But in most of the early predictive research, the number of persons studied was small and could have easily constituted a biased sample. Also, there was no systematic, objective way to measure giving up or helpless-ness. Appraisals and attitudes were inferred by the clinical researchers based largely on what the patients said and did.

Henri Parens, Brian McConville and Stanley Kaplan, in the department of psychiatry at the University of Cincin-nati College of Medicine, tried to avoid such drawbacks by using a larger sample and administering questionnaires.[41]

They studied two groups of freshman nursing students (total of 136) to see if frequency of illness could be predicted by adjustment to school. The researchers measured the extent that students became depressed or had feelings of helplessness/hopelessness during their first six weeks.

A standardized scale was available for measuring depression, but the researchers had to develop their own giving-up questionnaire. Even so, the results suggested that there was an association between giving up and frequency of illness—mostly respiratory, gastrointestinal disorders, headaches and backaches. More conclusive findings showed that the student nurses scoring highest on depression had the most illness.

Still, more carefully controlled studies were needed to establish just how powerful a sense of giving up or helplessness can be in making us vulnerable to illness and to clarify how the effect occurs.

12. From Feeling Helpless to Going with the Flow

Brain chemicals can be transformed . . . when a person feels he isn't in control . . . and this can produce depression.[1]

Rule No. 1 is, don't sweat the small stuff. Rule No. 2 is, it's all small stuff. And if you can't fight and you can't flee, flow.[2]

A pessimist is someone who, when confronted with two unpleasant alternatives, selects both.[3]

WHO GETS SICK

One of the most powerful effects our heads can have on our health comes from the explanatory style we use. When something bad happens to us, we invariably think about what caused it. Mounting research suggests that when we characteristically make "internal, stable and global" assumptions about the cause, we have an explanatory style that increases our risk of illness.[4]

It works like this: When bad things happen, people with this thinking style make the assumption that "it's me" that is the cause—an internal attribution. Then they go a step further and tell themselves, "it'll always be this way"— a stable attribution. And, third, they assume that "it's going to spoil everything I do"—a global attribution.

The opposite of this style is to make attributions that take into account the role of external factors in causing a problem—other people, outside circumstances or conditions—and to recognize that one negative event does not mean that all future happenings will also turn out the same way. Under stress, healthy people are more inclined to blame outside influences or not take total responsibility on themselves for what went wrong. People who get depressed and sick tend always to blame themselves.

How a healthy causal style differs from a pessimistic one can be seen in these examples:[5] When a person discovers that his checking account is overdrawn, if his customary style is to make internal, stable and global attributions, he would think that "I'm incapable of doing anything right." A healthier way of thinking would be to consider that the bank might have made a mistake—"all institutions make errors"—or to make allowances for special circumstances, such as the fact that "I've had the flu for a few weeks, and I've let everything slide, including keeping my checkbook balanced."

By measuring the degree to which people tend to think pessimistically, psychologist Martin Seligman of the University of Pennsylvania and his colleagues have been able to predict who is most likely to become depressed or sick or to fail on a job.[4] For instance, with 172 undergraduates who were rated for explanatory style, the researchers accurately predicted which students would be sick the most, both one month and one year later. In 13 patients who had malignant melanomas, the tendency to make internal-stable-global (ISG) attributions proved to be a more powerful predictor of survival than even their level of natural killer cell activity.

Bad Style and Poor Performance

Interestingly, the ISG thinking style is also correlated with performance on a job or in sports.[4] Seligman's group tested 100 new life insurance agents at one of the country's largest firms and predicted which would quit and which would perform best. In sports, at the end of a season in the National Basketball Association, he and his colleagues did content analyses of verbatim quotes of players published on sports pages during the year. The psychologists then correctly predicted which teams would perform worse the next season and which would beat the point spread in future games.

A depressive, ISG style also catches up with even young, healthy superstars as they live out their lives. The researchers rated the verbatim statements of members of the Baseball Hall of Fame over the last 50 years, again by doing content analyses of direct quotations carried on sports pages over that period. Since the health and longevity of the former stars were a matter of public record, the psychologists could determine the relationship between causal attributions and illness and death. They found that those who characteristically blamed themselves in defeat or had pessimistic explanatory styles died earlier and had more illness.

Immune System Effects

People who go through life with an ISG explanatory style seem to increase their risk of illness by adverse effects on the immune system. In one longitudinal study of 280 men and women, those who construed setbacks with a pessimistic style of thinking had significantly lower immune function in both T-lymphocytes and NK cells.[4] Such an influence might contribute to premature death as well as illness.

Seligman was given verbatim transcripts of interviews with 20 men who were in a large study of Harvard College graduates that has been underway for the last 45 years.[5] These interviews were done in 1946, and records have been kept since on the mental and physical health of all the men in the study. On the basis of rating the explanatory styles in the sample interviews and comparing the scores with health status more than three decades later, researchers found an impressive correlation between "bad style and bad health."

The damaging influence of negative style seems to come by robbing people of a sense of control in their lives. As we have seen, lack of control has a detrimental impact on both the cardiovascular and immune systems, as well as neurotransmitter networks.

Learned Helplessness

The growing research on the effects of thinking pessimistically follows in the wake of the early investigations on giving up. Although the pioneering studies on giving up not only linked our perceptions of no control to risk of illness but also specified a biological mechanism for the connection, many questions remained. For example, does everyone who gives up get sick? Why does one person who sees no solution to his predicament end up with multiple sclerosis and another with depression or diabetes? What happens in the brain when we have no sense of control and get depressed?

In the process of investigating these questions, researchers have shed new light on the key role that a sense of control plays in our physical, mental and social well-being. Led mostly by experimental, social and learning-theory psychologists, the research has implicated a perceived lack of control in a wide range of health-related consequences—from death among the elderly to depression, tumor growth and alcoholism.

Starting in the 1960s, Seligman and his coworkers at the University of Pennsylvania began developing a "learned helplessness" model, which has been used mostly to explain depression but has been modified and extended to account for a number of other disorders. In working with dogs in the laboratory, the investigators discovered that when the animals were given unavoidable, inescapable electric shocks, they just seemed to give up.[6] The same dogs were later placed back into a shock situation, but with an opportunity to avoid it by jumping over a barrier. Instead of acting to escape the shock, they would act helpless and do nothing to terminate the stress.

The researchers demonstrated that it was the perceived uncontrollability of the situation, and not any trauma from the shocks, that was responsible for the giving up and helplessness that resulted. In other experiments, they showed that when animals are exposed to the shocks but given a chance to control the stimuli, there was no later helplessness.[7] Out of these experiments came the theory that when people as well as animals are in a situation they appraise as being beyond their control, they then start expecting that their actions will not make any difference in other situations as well, and they end up feeling helpless. Such appraisals lead to changes in brain chemistry, which contribute to helplessness and depression.

Hurting Ourselves with "Causes"

In 1978 Seligman and his colleagues revised the theory to include another important cognitive process that occurs between perceiving an event as uncontrollable and experiencing a distressful outcome.[8] As we have seen, when people fail at something, such as being unable to control a situation, they start attributing the failure to certain "causes." If they explain the bad event in terms that are internal ("it's my fault"), stable ("I always have trouble with this") and global ("I'll never be able to do anything right"), then they predispose themselves to depression and other disorders.

For instance, the researchers found that students who tend to make causal attributions that are internal, stable and global will get depressed when they receive a low grade.[9] Another psychologist showed that when pupils who had this kind of attributional style were taught to consider other causes for failure, they did not get depressed.[10]

The experiments on control and learned helplessness not only helped bring psychology into the mainstream of health research but also added important links in the connection between our giving-up appraisals and vulnerability to illness. Unlike most of the early research on giving up, many of these studies have used comparison groups to demonstrate clearly that people who perceive no solution for a situation are at significantly greater risk of ill health and other distress than are others who are in the same "fix" but who do not take such a dim view.

While much of the earlier work was on people already sick, the later research has been done largely on nonclinical populations. Rather than depending on patients' recalling what stressful events occurred before they got sick, the newer generation of studies has made observations of outcomes as they occur in healthy people or animals that are placed in stressful situations where a certain percent perceive control and others do not. In addition to laboratory experiments, everyday environments are also studied. In homes for the elderly, for instance, tests have been made on the effects of teaching residents how to gain a greater sense of control in their lives.

Out of all this has emerged a richer notion of what effects no control has and what determines whether we appraise something as having no solution. It is not simply a matter of our appraising a situation as having no solution and then getting sick. We also start expecting that our actions will not make any difference in other situations, and we begin to feel helpless. We begin thinking about what "caused" our problem and our failure to cope with it successfully, and these causal attributions can add to our distress. If we attribute the problem or situation to some lasting defect in ourselves (particularly in our character) and expect that the defect will always plague us regardless of the situation, then we lower our self-esteem and compound our risk of illness.[9] Expectations and attributions, then, as well as appraisals, are part of the heady processes that can make us vulnerable.

The distress that is generated by a person's pessimistic causal style can occur in a variety of situations and settings. For instance, if such a person is giving a talk in front of a group, and two people leave in the middle of it, the speaker's internal attribution will be something like, "they're walking out because I'm boring." The stable attribution follows with "this always happen to me," and the global clincher is, "I'll never be any good at anything. I'm too dumb." Such stressful self-statements are cognitive distortions because they overpersonalize and overgeneralize besides attributing "cause" without adequate proof. The two people may have left because they had another appointment they could not break, and their action had nothing to do with the speaker. In addition, "always" and "never" are absolutes that grossly overstate the facts and selectively ignore times and situations when even the speaker would acknowledge he or she succeeded at something.

"Good Causes"

We put ourselves in a no-control, no-solution position when we perceive something as bad and then attribute all its cause to a personal defect ("I'm too dumb"), which we project across all future occasions. This does not mean that internal attributions for our problems are always damaging and that we should look outside ourselves for "the cause." In fact, attributing a problem to the way we behave, as opposed to the way we are, may facilitate well-being or performance rather than impair it.[10]

For example, in a study of persons with spinal cord injuries, those who coped best and were rehabilitated fastest were the ones who attributed their accidents to their own behavior (running around the sides of a swimming pool, diving into water too shallow, taking chances).[11] Those who attributed their injuries to the actions of others and to external forces made significantly less progress.

The difference was that the good copers believed they had some control and order in their lives. In attributing their problems to their own behavior, they recognized that it was something under their own control. They also seemed to recognize that the success of their rehabilitation depended on their own efforts and behavior, and they were willing to do everything they could to recover. The poor copers, in blaming others and outside forces, did not perceive control and order in their lives or in their chances of rehabilitation.

Similarly, among women who underwent mastectomies, those who believed that their own behavior contributed to "the cause" of their breast cancer made significantly better adjustments.[12] Those who attributed the cause of their cancer to personality defects or to other people— who were blamed for passing on faulty genes—were more likely to be depressed and not cope as well. The women who used behavioral attributions believed that they could keep from experiencing a recurrence of cancer by engaging in healthy behaviors, such as eating better diets, not smoking or taking hormones and avoiding injuries to their breasts. In other words, they had a greater sense of control.

Improving Health and Control in Old People

Our attributions have powerful effects on our well-being for the same reason that our appraisals do. We react to both. We do not respond to environments and events per se. We (our bodies) respond to how we see and interpret the situations (our appraisals), to how we explain what happened (our attributions) and what we expect next.

When people are taught to change their self-defeating attributions, striking changes can occur. In the study that two psychologists did in a home for the aged (see Chapter 7), a group of residents was given environmental explanations for their problems to substitute for their customary attributions, which blamed "old age" and declining health for nearly everything.[13] For instance, the group was told that just about anyone might have trouble walking on the floors because they were made of tile and slippery from frequent moppings. The residents invariably attributed their slipping on the floors to old age, weak knees or poor movement. They were also reminded that just about anyone who is awakened at 5:30 every morning is likely to be tired by evening, and increasing fatigue during the day could not all be attributed to advanced age. A second group in the home for the elderly was also given information, mostly from doctors' reports and journal articles, that could be used for alternative explanations for typical problems the residents had. A third group received no intervention.

When the three groups were later checked by psychologists Ellen Langer and Judith Rodin, the one that had been given environmental attributions to explain problems showed marked improvement in general health, memory and participation in activities. Declines in each of these areas were experienced by the other two groups, particularly among residents who had not received any intervention to change their usual attributions for problems. Importantly, those in the first group were found to have increased the amount of control they perceived having in their lives. As they stopped attributing all their problems to old age, which they could not change, and more to their environment, which they could, the residents also showed decreases in levels of the stress hormone cortisol.

Escaping the Hopeless Label

People in institutions often accept the attributions that others provide about the "hopelessness" or inevitability of their condition and are thus left with no sense of control. A change in environment sometimes leads to different attributions and a marked change in behavior and health.

A woman in a mental hospital who had remained mute for nearly 10 years was shifted to a different floor while her unit was being redecorated.[14] The unit where she had been living was known as the chronic, hopeless floor. In contrast, the floor to which she was moved was occupied mostly by improved patients with privileges, including freedom to come and go on the hospital grounds. It was an exit ward from which patients could anticipate discharge.

Soon after being moved to this ward, the woman surprised everyone by ceasing to be mute and becoming socially responsive and gregarious. But a little later the redecoration of her former unit was completed, and she was moved back. Within a week of returning to the "hopeless" floor, she collapsed and died. The autopsy revealed no pathology of note.

Importance of Purpose and Meaning

People who perceive no control in their lives often have little sense of purpose, meaning or competence. The concentration camp studies taught us how important purpose and meaning were for those who survived. In old age, deterioration seems to be a direct function of a person's not feeling needed or having no responsibility or anything to live for (see also Chapters 13 and 7). In institutions for the aged, people often give up from a sense of uselessness.

As we saw in Chapter 7, in their study of the elderly in the nursing home, Langer and Rodin investigated the effects of giving responsibility to a group of the residents and found dramatic changes.[15] Compared with a group that was given the usual treatment of being totally cared for by the staff, which retained all responsibility, the "responsible" residents became happier and healthier. They were encouraged to make the home something to be proud of, to arrange their rooms whatever way they liked, to decide which of many activities to participate in, and to take responsibility for deciding what needed to be changed and to make their complaints known. The improvement in the group's mood, morale and well-being came within three weeks. More surprising were the findings 18 months later. The death rate among those who had been given "responsibility training" was almost one-half that of the comparison group.

How Support Helps

Just as a sense of being useful and responsible can mitigate the tendency to give up, other kinds of resources, such as having loved ones support us, also may influence whether we perceive any control in a situation and experience less distress (see Chapter 6). When the situation involves the death of someone close, everything may seem lost or out of control. This is particularly true for a child whose mother dies. Such an early loss often intensifies reactions to later losses when the person is an adult.

For example, in a random sample of 458 women in London, researchers found that those who had suffered the loss of their mothers before age 11 were at significantly higher risk of depression when they experienced a later loss.[16] However, the risk was considerably reduced if they had a confiding relationship with their husbands and full or part-time employment. When people without support and other resources experience a loss, they seem more likely to see their situation as hopeless—particularly if they suffered the loss of their mothers at an early age and felt helpless then.

Hopelessness and depression, in turn, are likely to leave the individual more vulnerable to disease. As we have noted, the higher mortality among people who have recently lost their spouses may be traced to depression and impaired immune defenses. Also, researchers at Boston University School of Medicine have reported lower levels of immune function, including natural killer cell activity, among depressed or anxious persons.[17] Both depression and reduced NK activity have been associated with cancer.[18]

Depression and Brain Chemical Changes

When people are depressed in reaction to a loss or a sense of no control, they often become unmotivated and passive.[19] They are not interested in doing anything and make a minimum of physical movements. As we have suggested, many depressed people often believe there is no point in trying, that they always fail or the outcome is invariably painful. They have learned helplessness from failing and being seriously disappointed or experiencing problems that they believe have no solutions.

The biological reactions in the brain to a repeated experience of perceiving no control or being helpless may help explain the motivational deficit and restricted behavior of many depressed people, as well as their negative mood. Healthy motor activity, movement of the body, initiation of behavior and responsiveness all require undisturbed communication among cells in the brain (see Chapter 4). To some extent, the same is even true of our facial expressions. In depression, the triangularis muscles, which control the movement of the sides of the mouth, are affected. There is a typical gloomy or despairing look.

In depression, dopamine and norepinephrine are two neurotransmitters that seem to play key roles.[20] Serotonin has also emerged as having a critical function.[21] Nerve networks in the brain that contain and conduct these neurochemicals have branches to key areas having to do with sleep, appetite, sex, moods and movement.

Animal studies and some human research have shown that when there is no perceived control or chronic or intense stress, norepinephrine appears to become depleted, particularly in an area of the brainstem known as the locus ceruleus. Dopamine—which is associated with a sense of reward or pleasure—also seems to decline from perceptions of uncontrollability.[22] Both of these substances are critical to neurons "talking" with each other, relaying nerve impulses and carrying out vital functions, such as sparking motivation and movement. As we saw in Chapter 4, a disregulation—rather than simply a depletion—may occur in key psychochemical systems in the brain and involve failure of cell receptors to respond properly to the neurotransmitters.[23]

When there is a disregulation in aminergic neurotransmission in the neural pathways of the forebrain, particularly the area known as the limbic system, there is disturbance in centers having to do with reinforcement, reward, pleasure, mood, as well as psychomotor activity, appetite, sleep and sex.[24] As these sites "shut down" or falter, the individual sees himself as hopeless with everything beyond his control, thus adding to his depression.

What may start, then, as a way of looking at a stressful situation—believing it has no solution and expecting other problems to be beyond control—can lead to altered catecholamine metabolism and disturbance of neurotransmitters in the brain. This, in turn, can compound the person's sense of helplessness, further limit his motivation and movement and impair his ability to experience any reward or pleasure in life.

Suicide and Alcoholism

As we have seen (Chapter 4), serotonin disregulation is implicated not only in depression but also in suicide and alcoholism. This neurochemical is associated with relief of both psychic and physical pain. Among people who are depressed, significantly lower levels of this particular neurotransmitter have been reported for those who attempt suicide and those who have been diagnosed as alcoholic.[25] Depressed persons from alcoholic families have been found to have lower levels of a serotonin metabolite, 5HIAA, than was the case with depressives having no family history of alcoholism.[26] Low serotonin, which may be genetically controlled, has been particularly linked with violent suicides.[21] Some researchers have associated a deficiency of the neurotransmitter with impulsive and violent acts in general, not just suicide.

Low serotonin levels, then, may underlie both depressive illness and alcoholism in some families and may play a role in whether suicide is attempted and violent means are used. Again, no assumption can be made that serotonin deficiency is "the cause" of depression, self-destructive behavior or alcoholism as if these problems occur independently of psychosocial factors. How we cope and appraise events influences our neurotransmitters, which affect the functioning of the brain and body. As with most other disorders, both a genetic tendency and our cognitive coping may contribute to our risk of depression, alcoholism or attempted suicide. As suggested earlier, a person with both a genetically weak serotonin system and a coping style of being negative about everything may be at highest risk. A person with low serotonin levels who has a different belief system and way of coping with problems would likely be less vulnerable.

New insights have recently been gained into how serotonin binds to receptors of cells in the brain and can be influenced by steroid hormones.[27] Whether a stress hormone like cortisol, which is a corticosteroid hormone, may significantly interfere with serotonin functioning is being investigated. Alteration of serotonin binding may change the sensitivity of cells to neurotransmitters and modify the responsiveness of the brain to incoming stimuli. Researchers have discovered that changes in binding differ according to sex and seem to be linked to changes in the number of binding sites. Women, who are believed to have a higher rate of depression than men do, may be at greater risk due, at least in part, to hormonal influences on serotonin binding sites and receptors.

Some people who have periods of depression between manic moods may have an abnormally high level of receptor sites for yet another important neurotransmitter, acetylcholine. A study at the National Institute of Mental Health has shown that the elevated density of acetylcholine-binding sites may be inherited.[28] Several antidepressant drugs seem to work by blocking acetylcholine receptors.

Drugs or Cognitive Therapy for Depression?

Treatment for depression involves giving patients drugs, psychotherapy or both. The most widely used drugs are the antidepressants that are intended to restore the biochemical equilibrium in the brain. The most frequently prescribed antidepressants are the tricyclic compounds. Tricyclics apparently raise serotonin levels and seem to block pain.[29] As we saw in Chapter 4, the tricyclic drugs also increase norepinephrine and raise the levels of dopamine. The way they affect neurotransmitters is by blocking the re-uptake of the chemicals from the synapse between neurons. In other words, tricyclics seem to keep more of the neurotransmitters available for binding to receptor sites on the membranes of receiving cells.

Another group of antidepressants, the monoamine-oxidase (MAO) inhibitors, are designed to block depletion of neurotransmitters through other means.[30] These drugs reduce the activity of monoamine oxidase, which is an enzyme that breaks down neurotransmitters into their metabolites. This action occurs inside brain cells at the terminals where neurotransmitters are released. MAO inhibitors are often prescribed in cases when the depressed person is also very anxious and tends to oversleep and overeat. Both groups of drugs produce side-effects, with the more severe reactions coming from the MAO inhibitors.

Cognitive therapy, whose main aim is to correct the

person's distorted way of thinking about himself and his perception that problems are beyond control, has been reported to be more effective for some cases of depression than drugs are. For instance, psychiatrist Aaron Beck of the University of Pennsylvania School of Medicine and his colleagues took two groups of equally depressed, nonpsychotic outpatients and treated them for 11 weeks.[31] One group received cognitive therapy, and the other was given imipramine, a popular tricyclic antidepressant.

Based on instruments that measured degree of depression, hopelessness and self-concept, the patients receiving cognitive therapy were significantly more improved at the end of 11 weeks than were those given drugs. When the patients were followed up one year later, those who had been in cognitive therapy still had substantially fewer depressive symptoms.[31]

More recently, 236 persons who had moderate to severe depression were treated in clinical trials designed to test the effectiveness of cognitive therapy, interpersonal therapy and drug therapy.[32] Married patients with longer episodes of moderate depression did best with cognitive therapy. Men with good social functioning responded most to interpersonal therapy, which focuses on developing better ways to relate to family members, coworkers and others. Drug therapy (using imipramine) was most effective for married patients with severe depression and work stress.

Changing Chemistry with Talk

Although some drug-therapy patients seem to do as well as their cognitive counterparts, additional studies are needed to determine if correction of the biochemical imbalance in the brain leads to a correction in the distorted thinking of the person. In cognitive therapy, the prime focus is on the patient's distorted way of looking at self, the world and the future, with emphasis on changing the person's pervasive pessimism and little sense of control. Changing the thinking apparently helps to restore the biochemical balance.

Because talking to people can lead to their thinking differently, chemical changes seem to occur in the brain from psychotherapy. Steven Paul, chief of clinical neuroscience at the National Institute of Mental Health, has said flatly: "Talk therapy changes chemistry. It's perhaps the profoundest way to change it."[33]

When people change how they are looking at problems—as setbacks instead of catastrophes—or understand that they can at least control how they react, the neurotransmitter disturbance appears to be relieved. Some of the cognitive distortions characteristic of depression also improve. For instance, norepinephrine seems to be necessary for focusing properly on stimuli from the environment.[21] In depression, with a disturbance in the norepinephrine system, a person does not receive and process information without distortion. Misinterpretations are common and criticisms perceived. In therapy, with restoration of norepinephrine and other neurotransmitter balance, the person begins to perceive and process with less distortion. Once he starts to look at the world less negatively and changes his causal style of explaining problems, he begins to protect himself from the kind of thinking that made him vulnerable to depression in the first place.

Examples of cognitive distortions often found in people who end up getting depressed are: overpersonalizing (the individual sees himself as the cause of all negative events that happen to him); overgeneralizing (a single setback is seen as a never-ending pattern of defeat); catastrophizing (every goof-up and bad situation is regarded as the end of the world), and jumping to conclusions (concluding the worst without adequate evidence).[34]

Since depression may be the result of both a genetic predisposition and a learned, distorted way of looking at stressful situations, each of these contributing factors must be considered. Some depressed people, for instance, may have a defect in brain regulation of adrenal secretion, particularly corticosteroids, leaving them particularly vulnerable to excessive stress hormones.[35] Normally, a feedback switch in the brain keeps these hormones within limits. With some depressed persons, high concentrations of corticosteroids seem to be due to the brain switch's failing to suppress excessive adrenal secretion.

But without any genetic tendency present, a characteristic style of pessimistic and stressful thinking can lead to disregulation in a neurotransmitter, which then sets off a chain of disturbing events in other systems. An imbalance in neurochemicals released by the hypothalamus, which was in turn triggered by disregulated transmitters in other parts of the brain, can lead to an imbalance of pituitary hormones and an excess of cortisol from the adrenal cortex. A chronic stress reaction can thus result.

The fact that both drugs and cognitive therapy can help many people who are depressed affirms the two-way influence of biology and behavior—which includes the internal behavior of our minds as well as the external behavior of our bodies. Just as our biological processes—such as our hormone levels—affect our behavior, so do our thinking styles and learning experiences change cell structures within the central nervous system. While drugs directly affect brain chemistry and may help restore neurotransmitter balance, relapses may occur among people taking tricyclic antidepressants or MAO inhibitors. Drugs alone, without changes in how a person looks at the world and deals with it, are seldom the longterm solution.

Other Therapies

In addition to cognitive therapy and antidepressant drugs, other strategies have been used for depression. Aerobic exercise and long-distance running have been found to increase a sense of control and to elevate norepinephrine, which becomes depleted in depression.[36] Lower levels of depression and anxiety, fewer days sick and increased work satisfaction have all been reported for participants in aerobic fitness programs.[37]

As we mentioned in Chapter 5, some food containing certain amino acids may also have promise in the treatment of some forms of depression. Tyrosine, found in many foods, seems to increase norepinephrine and dopamine because it serves as a building block for these catecholamines in the brain.[38] L-phenylalanine, another amino acid found in popular drinks and food, is necessary for another neuroregulator that may be involved in depression—2-phenylethylamine (PEA).[39] PEA has been described as the brain's own amphetamine, and when it is deficient, we may get depressed. The effects of food on the brain, however, are complicated by a number of other factors. We cannot expect to relieve chronic depression simply by eating more food containing tyrosine and phenylalanine, as we noted in Chapter 5.

Although running and possibly diet may help to reduce depression, clinical trials sponsored by the National Institute of Mental Health have thus far been largely limited to antidepressants, cognitive therapy and interpersonal psychotherapy.[40] Some clinicians and researchers who have had success with aerobic fitness or dietary "precursor treatment" believe more support should be offered for these strategies.

When Having Little Control
Is No Problem

Although perceiving no control has been associated with disturbing the biochemical balance in our brains and bodies and increasing our chances of getting sick or depressed, not everyone has such negative effects. The degree to which we react to a no-solution situation depends on how important we consider it to be. If we are not particularly invested in a problem, it does not make much difference whether we can control it or not. For instance:

> Person A might consider the success of professional activities to be of singular importance and consider interpersonal relationships and home life of secondary concern. Hence an unexpected setback at work may cause Person A to respond with irrational cognitions and depressive symptoms, whereas disruptions in the interpersonal-affective realm would pose little threat. In contrast, Person B might cope with a sudden failure in the workplace, whereas threatened loss of a loved one might result in a depressive reaction.[41]

How much we believe we need to control a situation, then, is a key determinant of how distressed we will be if we start appraising it as beyond our control. Some people have high needs for power—that is, they must not only control the situation but impress and influence others.[42] Other people have strong affiliative needs—they want to be loved and accepted by everyone.[43] A third group is made up of those who need to perform perfectly in whatever they do.

If the problem we encounter falls into one of our high need categories, then we are likely to believe we absolutely must control it. If we conclude that it is beyond our control and we are helpless, then if the problem continues long enough we are likely to become vulnerable to illness or other distress. On the other hand, if we do not need power or acceptance or perfection—if these are things we can live without and be happy—then whether we control the problem is not a life-or-death issue with us. And we are not likely to keep our stress hormones high or go into an extreme state of conservation-withdrawal.

Power Needs and Impaired Immunity

The empirical evidence on the powerful effect of our personal needs comes from several sources. David McClelland, professor of psychology at Harvard University, and his associates have done a number of studies showing that "power stresses"—stresses that threaten someone's ability to impress, affect and influence—have negative effects only for people with high power needs and a tendency to inhibit expression of those needs.[44] Such people are found to have more high blood pressure, heart problems and illness in general. Because they perceive so many stresses to be a challenge to their power needs and their ability to control the situation, they have chronic activation of the sympathetic nervous system and lower levels of immune function.

Similarly, people who have high needs for love, acceptance and warm relationships with everyone are also at risk when affiliation stresses are encountered—rejection, losses, criticism. Psychologist Susan Burchfield of the University of Washington demonstrated that women with unfulfilled affiliative needs reported more symptoms of illness after experiencing interpersonal stress than did individuals whose needs were fulfilled.[43] Stress that was noninterpersonal—such as power stress or achievement stress—did not have effects on those with high affiliative needs.

McClelland, together with colleagues at Harvard and Tufts University School of Medicine in Boston, showed that individuals with a high need for power have significantly lower salivary IgA antibody levels after facing power stresses.[45] IgA antibodies provide a main line of defense against upper respiratory illnesses. In testing 46 college students, the researchers found that those higher in a need for affiliation and friendship showed hardly any drop in salivary IgA after the stress of their most important midterm examination. In contrast, those with strong needs for power had sharp rises in the stress chemical norepinephrine, followed by a marked decline in s-IgA an hour and three quarters later. The investigators suggested that people with high power needs, who are frequently confronted with exams and other power stresses, become more susceptible to illness because of greater output of stress hormones and neurotransmitters, which attach to receptors on B-lymphocytes and depress immune capacity.

In looking at the impact on the immune system of both power needs and affiliative needs, a group of Boston researchers headed by social psychologist John Jemmott III, a former student of McClelland's who is now at Princeton, studied 64 first-year dental students before, during and after examination periods.[46] Again, salivary secretion of immunoglobulin A—one of five classes of antibodies found in humans—was measured as an index of how much the immune system was being affected in the three periods. Before exam periods, secretion of salivary IgA was not substantially depressed for students who were high in either power or affiliative needs, although the former showed lower levels. During the three months when exams were held, however, students with high inhibited needs for power had a significant lowering of their s-IgA, meaning their immune system was being affected and their firstline defense against upper respiratory illness impaired. In the month after the exams, the secretion rate for students with strong power needs continued to decline instead of going back to normal levels as was the case with the other students.

These studies helped to confirm that not everything stressful results in distress. Much depends on our needs and expectations, which shape how we appraise the situation and whether we think we must control it to feel okay about our-selves. If our needs are not demanding or we do not insist on controlling every situation, then we are not as inclined to end up sick or depressed.

Looking at Life Less Stressfully

To help us become less vulnerable to stress and illness, car-diologist Robert Eliot of the National Center of Preventive and Stress Medicine in Phoenix recommends that we keep things in perspective by recognizing that much of what we disturb ourselves about is "small stuff."[2] We also usually have a number of options for coping with problems, including the traditional fighting and fleeing. As he points out, if we can do neither of these, we can always "flow"—which means looking at the problem in a less stressful way.

Reminding ourselves that "it's all small stuff" may be equivalent to recognizing that our "needs"—what we think we must have and cannot live without—are really wishes and preferences that we have arbitrarily made mandatory to our well-being.[47] In terms of effects on our mental and physical health, there is a world of difference between preferring to be loved or wishing to impress others and believing that these are necessary to life itself.

To flow includes accepting things we cannot change and moving on. A study by psychologists Jerry Suls and Brian Mullen of the State University of New York at Albany showed that "uncertain" uncontrollability places people at higher risk of illness than do situations seen as unequivocally beyond control.[48] The trick seems to be to distinguish between un-desirable events we can do something about and those we cannot fight or flee from. If there is nothing we can change—except our attitudes—then it may be best to accept and, as Eliot said, "go with the flow."

The truth in all this was recognized years ago by Alcoholics Anonymous, which adopted as its motto a prayer composed by theologian Reinhold Niebuhr in 1934:

> God, grant me the strength to change what I can, the courage to bear what I cannot and the wisdom to know the difference.[49]

PART 5
Self-repair

13. Love, Optimism and Healing

*It has been said
that love cures people,
both those who give it and
those who receive it. . . .*[1]

*If I told patients to raise
their blood levels of immune
globulins or killer T-cells, no
one would know how. But if I
can teach them to love
themselves
and others fully, the same
changes happen automatically.
The truth is: Love heals.*[2]

*A cheerful heart is good
medicine, but a downcast spirit
dries up the bones.*[3]

How positive thoughts and feelings can promote healing and help keep us well is a
question that mind-body researchers are now seriously exploring. The profound effect of faith, love and positive expectations on health and disease has long been acknowledged in clinical practice, but the way these forces work in
the body is just beginning to be unravelled.

We appear to have powerful healing systems in our
bodies that give us the potential to overcome much pain
and illness if we can learn to mobilize them.[4] The evidence
suggests that the systems respond to optimism, caring, intimacy, hope and other positive cognitions. Those who most
get sick may be the most out of touch with these self-healing
processes.

We have seen that when we tone down our negative
thoughts and beliefs, we seem to be less susceptible to illness. When we use cognitive control and restructuring, we
help restore an equilibrium to the mind and body through
effects on the nervous system, our hormones and immune
defenses. But being less negative is one thing, being positive
another. We have more evidence on the negative, but at last
some scientific attention is being given to the positive as it
affects our health. Just as we now know there is such a thing
as "mind-made disease"—illness largely triggered by our own
stressful thoughts and behavior—there is good reason to believe that "mind-made health" is also a reality.[4]

Body's Response to Love

Psychologist David McClelland of Harvard has found that
when students are shown a film designed to inspire feelings

of love and caring, an antibody—salivary IgA—increases that provides major protection against colds and upper respiratory infection.[5] The film they saw was on Mother Teresa, the nun who won a Nobel Peace Prize for her work in caring for the poor on the streets of Calcutta.

Even those who professed intense dislike for Mother Teresa—some said she was a fake and that her work did no good—showed immune function improvement.[6] Such a finding is consistent with McClelland's theory that deeper, unconscious beliefs and motives determine people's bodily reactions and their behavior more than do conscious cognitions. He thinks a figure like Mother Teresa reaches "the consciously disapproving people in a part of their brains that they were unaware of and that was still responding to the strength of her tender loving care."[7]

When the students were shown a film on Attila the Hun, their antibody levels dropped. Salivary IgA levels also decrease when people see a film that evokes feelings of helplessness, which suggests why a sense of control can help protect health.

Having as a trait the ability to love and care about others seems to result in lower levels of the stress hormone norepinephrine and a higher ratio of helper/suppressor T-cells, an important balance in a healthy immune system.[5] Less illness is associated with the caring trait. McClelland also has tested for the physiological effects of intimacy.[8] People with high scores on intimacy have higher levels of IgA antibodies and report less serious illness. In addition, he has found that people who seek friendship and affiliation with others are generally more healthy.[5]

In Topeka, Kansas, at the Menninger Clinic, tests showed that people who are romantically in love suffer fewer colds and have white blood cells that more actively fight infections.[9] The lovers also are reported to have lower levels of lactic acid in their blood, which means they are less likely to get tired, and higher levels of endorphins, which may contribute to a sense of euphoria and may reduce pain.

McClelland acknowledges that "we don't have any idea about how love aids the lymphocytes and improves immune function," but the evidence strongly suggests it does.[10] Bernie Siegel, an assistant clinical professor of surgery at Yale Medical School who has been a practicing surgeon for more than 30 years, predicts that "someday we will understand the physiological and psychological workings of love well enough to turn on its full force more reliably. Once it is scientific, it will be accepted."[11]

Effects of Caring

Other evidence also suggests that caring is a potent mediator of bodily responses. For instance, as noted in Chapter 6, persons who have pets to care for have been found to recover faster from illnesses. People with myocardial infarctions who own animals have been reported to have one half the mortality rate of those who do not have pets.[12] Among patients in hospitals who have had heart attacks, those with pets waiting for them live longer after returning home. Pets also seem to help us be more optimistic, another quality that contributes to better health.[13] Giving people something to care for can enhance their sense of control in life.

As we saw in Chapter 7, when a group of nursing home residents was given plants of their own to take care of and was urged to assume more responsibility for themselves as well, they reported a greater sense of control and showed significant improvement in their health and activity.[14] They also lived longer.

The effects of tender loving care on both animals and humans can be profound. Rabbits on a high-fat diet that were talked to and petted developed significantly less atherosclerosis than those that received only routine treatment in the laboratory.[15] Women surgical patients whose hand was held by a nurse while blood pressure and temperature were taken were able to leave the hospital sooner and recovered faster at home.[16]

Social support in general provides additional indirect evidence of the benefit of positive thoughts and feelings on health. As mentioned in Chapter 6, even people who smoke, overeat or practice other unhealthy habits seem to be at reduced risk of disease if they have strong support systems. There is even the suggestion that "love is more important than healthy living."[12] One effect of social contact and reduced loneliness may be a strengthening of the immune system.[17] As we have seen, loss of support leads to a decrease in immunity.

What Positive Stimulation Can Do

Because brain chemistry can be influenced by the kinds of perceptions we make and the thoughts we have, it is not surprising that the types of environment we experience can affect the cerebral cortex. When we view our environments as enriched and interesting, the very neurons in the cortex apparently enlarge.

There is much evidence from animal studies to suggest that when we feel stimulated from our lives, we are likely to increase our longevity and our mental sharpness. Neuroanatomist Marian Diamond of the University of California at Berkeley has spent more than 30 years of research demonstrating the plasticity of the brain—its "moldability."

She has shown that rats placed in stimulating environments live significantly longer and become smarter (they can run mazes better).[18] Their cerebral cortexes become larger, their neurons increase in size, their dendrite extensions lengthen and their glial (support) cells are more numerous. On the other hand, rats placed in impoverished environments (relative isolation and no stimulation) experience a decrease in thickness of the cerebral cortex and earlier death. A stimulating environment for rats consists of a spacious cage with "toys"—such as wheels and blocks—and other rats to play with. Rats in the impoverished setting were in smaller cages by themselves and without toys—a more standard laboratory treatment.

From doing interviews with elderly people who remain healthy, Diamond is convinced that her animal findings extend to humans.

> I found that the people who use their brains don't lose them. It was that simple. These people were interested in their professions even after retirement. They kept healthy bodies.[19]

With the rats, Diamond also reported that tender loving care—holding the animals and talking to them—contributed to their longevity and enlarging the cerebral cortex. With the old people, she found that "love of others and being loved" played a key role in a longer life. Diamond's laboratory experiments indicated that enjoying one's environment and the presence of others contributes to actual brain growth in the elderly.

Benefiting Others and Living Longer

Paul Rosch of the American Institute of Stress (see Chapter 2) has noted that "doing something you enjoy and take pride in, and doing something enjoyable that pleases others, appears to have health benefits."[20] He points to the "surprising longevity" of entertainers such as Bob Hope and George Burns and of "a host of symphony conductors and performing artists."

Hans Selye (also Chapter 2), the most quoted of stress researchers, argued that people with "altruistic egoism" lived longer and healthier lives. He described altruistic egoism as doing something that benefits others so that a person earns the goodwill and gratitude of others.[21]

The noted microbiologist René Dubos of Rockefeller University, who lived into his eighties, reviewed the literature on people who live to be 100 or more and found that they had certain key characteristics in common. He said: "All of them possessed a certain eagerness to live, a certain drive, a certain general happiness."[22] The centenarians did not have parents or ancestors who lived exceptionally long. Nor did they pursue particular lifestyles or occupations. Attitude and outlook on life were the common traits.

Memory and Learning Affected

The remarkable ability of the brain to undergo actual physical changes in response to our perceived environments is providing new insights also into memory and learning.[23] The synapses that connect each of our 100 billion neurons with as many as 50,000 other brain cells can be deactivated or enhanced based on our experiences. If we see ourselves trapped in a never-changing, gray environment, the synaptic connections may shut down and the release of neurotransmitters may diminish. Conversely, an experience of stimulation increases transmitter release and brings positive changes not only on the molecular but genetic level.

Eric Kandel, professor of physiology and psychiatry on Columbia University's Faculty of Medicine, and his colleagues have demonstrated that significant changes take place in the central nervous system of the marine snail *Aplysia* when different kinds of learning occur under different types of environmental situations.[24] Kandel's work, which earned him the prestigious Albert Lasker Basic Medical Research Award in 1983, may have important implications for Alzheimer's disease and may help explain how infants placed in socially deprived environments often suffer deficiencies in mental development. The plasticity of the brain may also lend itself to new approaches for rehabilitating those who suffer brain injuries.

On the down side, traumatic environments, as we saw in Chapter 4, may lead to changes in the brain associated with poor impulse control and violent behavior. Even offspring of animals subjected to such conditions have shown altered brain structure and higher levels of aggressive behavior.

Effects of Beauty on the Body

A number of years ago psychologist Abraham Maslow, in proposing that a hierarchy of needs motivates human behavior, suggested that beauty promotes health.[25] As we saw in Chapter 5, when we are moved by music, the beauty of nature or a work of art, we apparently "turn on" and release in the brain opioid substances—endorphins or similar peptides—that give us goose bumps, "thrills" or other sensations of pleasure.

Various studies have shown that nature scenes—views of water and vegetation, particularly—elicit positive feelings in people, reduce anxiety in those who are stressed and significantly increase the amplitude of alpha brain waves.[26] High alpha amplitude is associated with feelings of relaxation. When we experience beauty, then, we seem less likely to have stressful thoughts and physiological arousal.

Roger Ulrich, in the department of geography at the University of Delaware, tested the effects of hospital room views on the recovery of patients who had undergone gall bladder surgery.[27] Twenty-three patients were in rooms that overlooked a stand of trees with foliage. A matched group of 23 other patients who had gall bladder surgery in the same hospital had a view of a brick wall from their rooms.

Those with the tree view spent significantly less time in the hospital after surgery, required substantially less pain-killing medication and had fewer negative ratings from nurses on their recovery.

Smiling May Help

Just putting on a happy face may be beneficial. Some evidence suggests that smiling often may reset the autonomic nervous system so that it is less reactive to stress.[28] One study shows that if we assume facial expressions of happiness, we can increase blood flow to the brain and stimulate release of favorable neurotransmitters.[29] If we are anxious or depressed, according to this study, we may induce better feelings by putting positive looks on our faces.

Other conscious efforts to improve our demeanor may also encourage healthy responses in the body. For example, speaking softly and slowly brings heart rate down.[30] Being enthusiastic—as opposed to cynical or hostile—may help protect against the risk of heart disease.[31] As we will see in Chapter 16, thinking positively after an operation—such as focusing on better health, on the attention received in the hospital and a "vacation" from workaday pressures—reduces pain after surgery and promotes recovery.[32]

Acquiring the Hope Habit

Research on people who live longer shows that they characteristically have a sense of hope, order and control in their lives.[33] "The hope habit" seems to encourage longevity by reducing the effects of stress on the body and turning on self-healing systems.

Shlomo Breznitz, a researcher from the University

of Haifa in Israel who is at the National Institute of Mental Health studying hope, is convinced that hopeful patterns of thinking can be cultivated like any habit or discipline—brushing our teeth, for instance. Thinking hopefully is the opposite of being a doom-sayer or fatalist. Someone with the hope habit whose father died at 55 will say: "I'm going to live my life so I'll beat those odds," rather than, "My father died at 55, so I guess no matter what I do, I will too."[34]

Another hope researcher, psychiatrist Louis A. Gottschalk of the University of California at Irvine, believes that spiritual faith helps people lead more hopeful and less stressful lives. Gottschalk and his coworkers developed a way to measure how much hope people have by doing a content analysis of samples of their speech. They found that among 16 patients with various metastatic cancers, those with higher hope scores prior to treatment survived significantly longer.[35] A substantial correlation also was found between hope and survival in a group of 27 cancer patients undergoing radiation therapy at Cincinnati General Hospital.[36]

How Optimism Promotes Health

Although our outlook clearly affects the degree of stress we feel and our physiological reactions, the effects of being optimistic have only recently been researched.[37] Psychologists Michael Scheier of Carnegie-Mellon University in Pittsburgh and Charles Carver of the University of Miami found optimism was a predictor of physical well-being. Among some 140 undergraduates under the stress of deadlines and impending exams, those who were more optimistic reported being less bothered by physical symptoms than did the students who were inclined to be pessimistic.[37]

The psychologists decided that the optimistic students coped more effectively with problems and were thus less likely to experience physical symptoms of any magnitude from stress. In addition, an optimistic outlook may, in itself, activate protective healing systems.

Other research has indicated that an optimistic attitude is also a key factor in living longer and getting sick less often. For instance, people who are optimistic about their own health have been shown to be at reduced risk of dying. This is true even if "objective" measures—laboratory tests, doctor examinations—show them to be in poor health. In contrast, people who believe they are in poor health but objectively are in good or excellent health have an increased mortality risk.

Such findings were documented in a study of 3,128 people 65 years and older in Manitoba, Canada.[38] They were surveyed in 1971, and records were gathered from physicians and hospitals on their health status. The Canadians, none of whom were in institutions, were then tracked for the next six years. Even when differences in age, sex, income, residence and life satisfaction were controlled for, those who believed their health was excellent had one-third the risk of death of those who perceived their health was poor.

In the United States, even more dramatic findings came from the Alameda County, California, study of 6,928 adults, whose health was kept track of for nine years.[39] The mortality risk for the "health pessimists" among the men was some two times greater than that for the "health optimists" and a striking five times greater among women. Also, in a prospective study that monitored the health of Harvard College men over 40 years, the subjects' own perception of their health was significantly associated with later physical and mental illness.[40]

Although nobody knows for sure exactly how optimistic or pessimistic beliefs about the state of one's health may influence chances of dying, there is the possibility that such perceptions affect our resistance to disease. We have seen that through the central nervous system, beliefs and attitudes can influence the immune system and affect how susceptible we are to illness. A sense of optimism and control seems to protect against both impairment of immune defenses and damage to the cardiovascular system.

The effects of making "optimistic appraisals" when we are under stress have been documented.[41] As noted in Chapter 3, people who look at stressful situations with a sense of challenge, control and commitment have less illness than do those who moan and groan about events or who act helpless and feel alienated. Other evidence suggests, as we will see, that being optimistic is also a factor in promoting recovery from surgery.[42] Levels of personal optimism may be associated with activation of the left hemisphere of the brain (see also Chapter 4). Some research has indicated that when right-handed people turn their eyes and attention to the left and activate the opposite (right) cerebral hemisphere, personal optimism is reduced.[43]

Happiness and Health

The interdependence of happiness and health has been demonstrated in several longterm studies (see Chapters 3 and 9). In a study of 268 volunteers that controlled for the effects of age, work satisfaction and happiness were found to predict longevity better than any health or physical-activity factor.[44] A significant association between perceptions of life satisfaction and health was also reported among different groups of men and women whose illnesses were charted over 20 years.[45]

The quality of a person's marriage, as he or she perceives it, has been found to be a more powerful predictor of happiness than even satisfaction with work or relationships with friends.[46] Marital satisfaction is significantly associated with both level of immune functioning and psychological well-being.[44] As we saw in Chapter 6, a prospective study of 10,000 men in Israel showed that their risk of developing angina pectoris was nearly two times lower if they answered "yes" to the question: "Does your wife show you her love?"[47]

In a survey of 52,000 readers of *Psychology Today*, people were asked what happiness meant to them. From the replies, the survey authors concluded:

> Happiness, we found, comes from tending one's own garden instead of coveting one's neighbor's. . . . Happiness, in short, turns out to be more a matter of how you regard your circumstances than of what the circumstances are.[48]

Happiness, then, is related to attitude and how a person chooses to look at things. Four attitudes found to be particularly important to happiness were optimism, lack of cynicism, belief that life has meaning and feelings of control.[49]

Bruce Larson, Seattle clergyman-author (see Chapter 6 references), describes happiness as coming from being pleased with who we are and what we do.[50] In connecting happiness to health, he has noted that "doctors have been telling me for years that 'you can't kill a happy man.'"[51]

Even in the face of being old and in poor health, a number of people have a sense of happiness, and a study at Yale shows they live longer.[52] Among 400 elderly, poor residents in Connecticut, those in bad health who were rated as happy had a significantly reduced risk of mortality in the next two years. Another significant influence on mortality among the 400 was religiousness. For people in poor health who had "higher levels" of religiousness, there was also reduced risk of dying.

Although attitudes may help individuals rise above adversity, their circumstances and conditions cannot be ignored. When people grow up in poverty or are the victims of injustice, when they struggle day by day just to survive, their thoughts and beliefs cannot help but be deeply influenced by their environment. In the absence of love, support, minimum opportunity and security, faith and optimism are much harder to come by. By redressing wrongs and improving human conditions, we can give more people a decent chance to adopt less pessimistic views and contribute to their own health. We can make it easier for them to find love.

"Power of Positive Thinking"

For years Norman Vincent Peale, a leading New York minister, and many others after him have promoted the "power of positive thinking" as a remedy for spiritual, emotional and physical malaise.[53] The others include authors of best sellers, charismatic public speakers and TV personalities as well as preachers such as Robert Schuller, who has written extensively on "possibility thinking."[54] Peale followed in the footsteps of the French physician Émile Coué, who popularized a self-healing jingle for people to say to themselves each morning: "Day by day in every way, I am getting better and better."[55]

Little scientific notice was taken of these ideas, largely because no empirical tests demonstrated that thinking positively could be credited with reducing the risk of illness or promoting recovery. Both medical and behavioral sciences have traditionally paid little attention to anything other than pathological influences—microbes, defective genes, unhealthy habits and lifestyles—and their association with disease, so the role of positive forces in people's lives has been badly neglected.

Now, with better understanding of the mechanisms by which attitudes and appraisals may affect illness, scientists have been less inclined to dismiss "positive thinking" as supported only by anecdotal evidence. In contrast to Peale's approach, behavioral scientists have developed systematic techniques for people to change their cognitions, reduce their "catastrophizing" or "awfulizing" and live life with less pain, if not better health.

In 1976, the widely quoted *New England Journal of Medicine* published an account by Norman Cousins, long-time editor of the *Saturday Review*, of how he had used humor to promote recovery from a life-threatening and crippling collagen disease.[56] Cousins, who had once been a medical writer, reasoned that if negative thoughts and emotions produced negative reactions in the body, then positive thoughts and feelings should bring positive responses. He watched tapes and films of his favorite comedians to make himself laugh. He also took large doses of vitamin C to help overcome his disease.

Later, after accepting an invitation to become a lecturer at the UCLA School of Medicine, Cousins suffered a heart attack and wrote a book on *The Healing Heart*, again championing the effects of positive thoughts and feelings in promoting recovery from serious illness.[57] Although Cousins' accounts are also anecdotal, they have aided in stimulating serious research on the subject.

Humor As Medicine

When Cousins, painfully ill with the collagen disease, systematically used humor to improve his body chemistry, he observed that 10 minutes of belly laughter produced an anesthetic effect lasting at least two hours.[58] One possible explanation of the pain-relieving effects of hearty laughter is that it increases the levels of endorphins and enkephalins in the brain, which act as the body's own natural opiates (see Chapter 5).[59] Cousins also determined that the laughter episodes resulted in a drop of at least five points in his sedimentation rate, which is an indicator of the severity of inflammation or infection in the body.

Empirical research is confirming what Cousins found in his own case—that, indeed, humor and laughter have beneficial physiological effects. One study reports that finding something funny results in a significant increase in IgA antibodies.[60] People who customarily use humor as a coping method have been found to have higher concentrations of these antibodies. Pleasant moods, such as mirthful ones, are associated with changes in levels of stress hormones, such as epinephrine and norepinephrine.[61] Because beta-endorphins also seem to be stimulated by laughter, the "natural high" that runners say they experience may also be produced by laughing.[62] Other effects of mirth include stimulation of respiratory and muscular activity, oxygen exchange and heart rate.[63]

In a study by the Laughter Project at the University of California at Santa Barbara, researchers found that laughter was as effective as biofeedback training in reducing stress. And, they said, one advantage laughter has as a stress-reducer is that it "requires no special training, no special equipment, and no special laboratory. All it requires is a funny bone."[62]

Effect of Humor on Outlook

A sense of humor also seems to reduce the impact of negative life events in terms of how we look at bad situations and feel about them. Psychologists Rod Martin and Herbert Lefcourt of the University of Waterloo in Ontario, Canada, did three studies, involving 159 young men and women, on the relation between negative life events and mood disturbance.[59] They found that among the people experiencing many negative events, the effect on mood was less for those who had high humor scores than it was for subjects with little sense of humor. In general, humor was found to produce a significant moderating effect on the emotional impact of experiencing bad events.

Freud, who wrote extensively on the subject, concluded that through humor we can take the sting out of bad situations and let the "pleasure principle" rule even in the face of "adverse real circumstances."[64] The reason that a sense of humor can have such a saving effect on both our physical and psychological well-being is that it provides us with a way of looking at problems with less doom and gloom. It provides us with a cognitive shift and a change in perspective.[65] Bodily processes are thus less disturbed.

Helping People Laugh

Programs have been started in some hospitals to evoke humor and encourage positive thoughts and feelings in patients. After Norman Cousins wrote on the therapeutic value of laughter in his own illness, he began being asked by physicians to contact patients who needed humor and a new outlook in their lives to help them get well or relieve pain. Recognizing the importance of laughter and psychosocial factors in illness, St. Joseph Hospital in Houston opened a "Living Room" for cancer patients, and Cousins was invited to the dedication as keynote speaker. In the Living Room are videocassettes and stereos for patients to use as they watch and listen to their favorite comedians and music.

Oncologist John Stehlin, who started the program, has instructed his staff to tell patients a funny story each day. Although the specific effects of laughter and "good feelings" on cancer have yet to be quantified, there is much evidence to suggest that the course of the disease will be affected by whether the patient's attitudes are positive or negative.

Probably the most extensive anecdotal evidence on

the healing influence of humor—not only in cancer but in many other diseases—comes from Raymond Moody Jr., a physician in Charlottesville, Virginia. As a repressed humorist, Moody has long used humor to help people get well. He speculates it works because it diverts us from thinking about ourselves and our worries and because it marshals our will to live.[66]

14. What Faith Does for Patients and Doctors

The doctor who fails to have a placebo effect on his patients should become a pathologist or an anesthetist. . . . In simple English, if the patient does not feel better for your consultation, you are in the wrong game, call it placebo or what you like.[1]

Placebo is the doctor within.[2]

Placebos . . . surely must have a direct effect on the immune system. . . .[3]

When we strongly believe that a pill, procedure or any other intervention into our problems will help us, most of us experience physiological changes known as a placebo response. Because thoughts themselves are electrochemical events, capable of initiating physical effects, this response is not only real but also powerful. It plays a part in "miracle cures," control of pain and other symptoms, spontaneous remissions from disease, and the effect we get from drugs.[4] Much of what is known about the influence of "the positive" on the body comes from research on placebos, which depend on faith and positive expectations for their effect.

Placebos are a focus of renewed behavioral and biological studies now that researchers have some of the tools for investigating positive thoughts and feelings more scientifically.[5] When faith and hope elicit a placebo reaction, it produces both subjective and objective changes in the body—both psychological and physiological changes that are measurable.[6]

New Recognition of Placebos

A placebo refers to "any effect attributable to a pill, potion or procedure, but not to its pharmacodynamic or specific properties."[7] It describes the physical change that occurs from the thoughts we have about what the pill, potion or procedure will do. In other words, it is the effect we ourselves produce on our bodies through what we strongly hope, imagine or expect. A placebo gives people permission to heal through the strength of their own belief.

What is now new and promising is the recognition and realization that the placebo effect can occur in the absence of a pill or potion and requires no deception to produce results.

> . . . the same pathways and connections that come into play through the use of placebos can be activated without placebos. The main ingredient is the human belief system.[8]

To repeat, when people deeply believe they will be helped by something, bodily changes occur from the physiological impact of that cognition. The something may be prayer, love, a newly learned way of coping, a relationship or a doctor. If the something is only an inert "sugar pill" that has no inherent pharmacological action, the changes still take place.[9] If the pill is a drug with specific effects of its own, the resulting changes are a combination of belief and pharmacological action.[10] A pill that we feel will cure us is metabolized in a very different internal environment than is one we think will do us no good.[11] The results will also be different even if the two pills are actually the same.

Research on the power of the placebo response is now helping to explain why two people with the same illness who are given the same treatment can get quite different results. The results, we now know, do not depend solely on the treatment but are also influenced by the way it is given and our faith in it.

The Power Of Suggestion

Just about every contact a physician has with a patient carries some suggestion, implicit or otherwise. What the doctor says or does not say, what he or she does or does not do can have profound effects on the attitudes and beliefs of a patient and thus affect the course of illness or recovery. Mack

Lipkin of the University of North Carolina School of Medicine has emphasized that the very presence of a physician has the power of suggestion to the patient. He defines a suggestion as being "an idea which is then accepted without critical thought by the recipient, resulting in alteration of function, sensation, attitude or behavior. . . .The suggestion may be given intentionally or not and may do good or harm."[12]

For physicians, then, to make the statement that they never apply a placebo betrays a gross ignorance of what it is. The question is not whether the doctor does or does not use a placebo, but how he or she can best promote its ever-present effect beneficially.[13]

Misunderstanding of Placebos

In recent years medicine has treated placebos as a stepchild. Physicians have consciously reserved them for "crocks" and malingerers and as a test to see if pain is "imaginary."[14] Placebos, in the form of sugar pills and dummy tablets, were considered trivial in their effects.[15] The neglect and ignorance of the placebo's potential for positive effects have been so complete that a survey of recent medical school graduates and nurses found that the majority were unaware of its therapeutic value.[14] Traditionally, the placebo has been defined by doctors in negative terms and has been erroneously equated with trickery and deception.[16]

One of the early medical definitions (1811) of the placebo described it as "an epithet given to any medication adopted more to please than to benefit the patient."[17] In fact, the very word "placebo" is taken from the Latin, meaning "I will please" or placate. Only recently have researchers begun to recognize that "placebo" is a misnomer that has led physicians into thinking they must give patients something to please them or to take advantage of most patients' desire to please the doctor by getting well.[18] More correctly, what the placebo response represents is the person's power of belief, which can be mobilized without deceit or deception, as we will see.

In medical research, the placebo effect has been regarded as a nuisance factor and confounding variable that must be controlled rather than encouraged. The negative attitude toward the placebo response is similar to the treatment that penicillin originally received at the hands of researchers.[19] Penicillin was regarded as a contaminant until the lowly fungus was recognized as having therapeutic promise of its own. Now that new interest is being taken in the placebo, there is a growing sense that it offers a way to tap powerful self-healing processes.[20]

How Doctors Have Benefited

Across the centuries, the power of the placebo has kept physicians in business despite their attitude toward it.[7] Before the development of therapeutic drugs, doctors subjected patients to purging, puking, cutting, blistering, bleeding, freezing, heating, leeching and shocking. Physicians had no specific treatments for disease, yet patients got better. Their "medicine" included powders of precious stones, spider webs, wood lice, pigeon and turtle blood for hematomas, goose dung for baldness and sheep dung for gallstones.

Arthur Shapiro of Mount Sinai School of Medicine and Hospital in New York, an authority on placebos, has pointed out that "despite these useless, abhorrent, and often harmful drugs . . . the physician continued to be a useful, respected and highly honored member of society."[21] How was this possible? "Because placebos work." They produce indirect or nonspecific effects in the body that help many people overcome a variety of disorders. These effects may involve any system of the body—biochemical, musculoskel-etal, cardiovascular, gastrointestinal, neurological.

If a physician believes a patient can be helped by a particular pill or operation, that attitude rubs off and is often adopted by the patient.[22] The patient then believes that there is a way his illness can be controlled, and that positive expectation is likely to produce physiological effects—effects that are just as real and measurable as those resulting from a drug or surgery. The power of a placebo to affect the body is directly proportional to the power of cognitions to influence internal processes.

Although physicians relied almost exclusively on eliciting placebo responses in patients before the era of scientific medicine began in the early 1900s, such effects were not so powerful that they could overcome any illness or counteract the irreversible damage of extreme "therapeutic" measures. In fact, the public began rebelling against the bleedings and purgings in the mid-1800s, and doctors switched to "dispensing vast quantities of opiates and alcohol (and later, cocaine), drugs that affected patients' moods without altering underlying pathology."[23] While the drugs dispensed today do not generally lead to widespread addiction, which occurred in the last century, we will see that the most popular prescriptions do not have direct effects on specific illnesses but largely rely on arousing the nonspecific effects of a placebo response, which can be significant.

But what proof is there that placebos bring significant physiological changes?

Placebos as Good as Surgery?

Some of the most vivid evidence of the placebo effect comes from surgical procedures in which incisions are made under anesthesia but no operation is performed.[24] The patient, however, believes surgery was done. For example, a previously popular operation that was designed to increase circulation to the heart and reduce chest pain was tested in two double-blind studies against a sham surgical procedure.[25] In the fake operation, only a skin incision was made but the patient was taken to the operating room and thought he had undergone the full "internal mammary artery ligation."[24]

Regardless of which procedure patients underwent, the results were almost identical: less anginal pain, reduced need for nitroglycerin and increased tolerance for exercise. The studies "demonstrated that ligation of the internal mammary artery was no better than a skin incision, and that such an incision could lead to a dramatic, sustained placebo effect."[26]

Similarly, with the coronary bypass operation that has been in vogue, 60 percent of patients were found to be much improved even though their bypasses were not open and "the heart was getting no more blood than before the operation."[27] They had relief of anginal pain, improved quality of life and increased exercise tolerance as measured by electrocardiogram. Ninety percent of those with open bypasses from the operation had similar improvement.

Because of more stringent medical ethics and a requirement to inform patients ahead of time what treatment will or will not be administered, placebo surgery is now mostly a thing of the past. However, recently a study was completed in Denmark on 15 patients who underwent a prescribed "endolymphatic sac shunt" for Ménière's disease, a disorder of the inner ear characterized by deafness, dizziness and a buzzing in the head.[28]

Fifteen patients with the same disorder received a placebo operation. A three-year follow-up showed no significant difference between the surgery and placebo groups. About 70 percent in both groups had nearly complete relief of symptoms. The improvement "was most likely caused by a placebo effect," the Copenhagen specialists concluded.[29]

What all these studies indicate is that when we truly think that an operation or any other intervention will help us, our cognitions have the power to produce changes in the body that lead to relief of symptoms. Whether such effects occur depends primarily on our positive expectancy, which in turn can be influenced by the attitude of our physician or other health professional and the confidence inspired by the treatment setting and those in our support group.

Regardless of what form the intervention takes—a pill, surgery, suggestion, learning new coping skills—if people believe it will lead to control of their disorders, placebo effects and physiological changes are likely. The effects seem to involve a number of systems in the body—neural, hormonal, immune—and are not specific for any particular disease.

Given a better understanding of the placebo, some researchers are beginning to recognize, as we said, that a person need not be deceived for the placebo response to occur. The natural healing systems that are activated by placebos can be mobilized by enhancing our sense of control. Learning how cognitively to control pain or the aversiveness of a stressful experience seems to tap the same self-healing processes as does strong belief in a pill or an operation.[10]

Ulcers, Arthritis and Wounds

Because cognitions—electrochemical impulses from the cerebral cortex—can influence virtually every organ in the body, placebos have demonstrated effectiveness in a variety of disorders. Studies have shown that the placebo effect can reduce gastric acidity and improve peptic ulcers, it can be more beneficial than aspirin or cortisone in rheumatoid arthritis, it can lower blood pressure and be as potent as codeine in suppressing a cough.[4]

In one study of patients hospitalized with bleeding peptic ulcers, 70 percent showed "excellent results lasting over a period of one year" from being given a placebo.[30] Their physician said he had a new medicine that would cure them. What he gave them was an injection of distilled water. A control group received the same placebo but from a nurse who told the patients that it was an experimental medication of undetermined effectiveness. Only 25 percent in this group experienced a remission of symptoms.

The potent expectations on which the placebo effect depends were dramatically demonstrated in a study of pain among soldiers wounded in World War II on the Anzio beachhead.[31] Only 32 percent of the wounded required morphine. A comparison was made with a group of patients in civilian hospitals who had similarly serious wounds and injuries. Eighty-three percent of the civilians required morphine. Anesthesiologist Henry Beecher of Harvard Medical School and Massachusetts General Hospital, who conducted the study, concluded that the soldiers expected their wounds to "give them a ticket home." The belief that the war was over for them seemed to be enough to activate a placebo effect, which protected the majority of them against intense pain.

Stopping Nausea

When Internist Stewart Wolf was conducting clinical research at Cornell Medical Center, he showed that the placebo response can be so strong that it reverses the action of a pharmacologically potent drug.[32] Nausea was induced in a group of individuals by giving them syrup of ipecac, an emetic often used in emergency rooms to precipitate vomiting in persons who have overdosed. Later, when one of the patients in the experiment was nauseated from other causes, he was told that a new medicine was available that was sure to correct the trouble. The medicine that the patient was then given was syrup of ipecac, introduced through an intragastric tube in the same amount as in the earlier experiment. Within 15 minutes the nausea disappeared and normal gastric activity was restored. On another occasion, a 28-year-old woman who had been suffering from the nausea and vomiting of pregnancy was told there was a new drug that would control such symptoms. She also was given the ipecac syrup and within 20 minutes she stopped being nauseated.

Regulations on medical ethics fortunately no longer permit such experiments on humans. Patients must be informed as to what they are taking and freely give their consent. But the research was valuable in that it helped to confirm that the mechanisms responsible for controlling symptoms and many physiological processes are connected to circuits in the cerebral cortex. Through them, our beliefs and expectations exert profound influence on what occurs in our bodies.

Affecting Blood Pressure

To demonstrate to medical students how powerful their own expectations are, professors at the University of Cincinnati conducted an experiment on the psychological and physiological effects of placebos.[33] The students were asked to participate in a study on sedatives and stimulants. Each student was given either one or two pink or blue capsules. The students assumed they were being given medication that either stimulates or sedates. In an hour, 54 percent of the subjects reported feeling more drowsy, 38 percent said they were more relaxed or less jittery. Others reported feeling more talkative and less sluggish.

Pulse rate decreased in 61 percent of the students and increased in 15 percent. Systolic blood pressure dropped in 71 percent and increased in 18 percent. The students given the blue capsules thought they were sedatives and expected sedation effects. Those who got the pink expected stimulation. In reality, both types of capsules were inert substances having no pharmacological properties.

Expectations can also have physiological effects completely apart from pills and medical or surgical procedures.

Distant Healing and Prayer

A German physician reported a study of "absent healing" in which three patients with serious diseases improved dramatically.[34] One had inoperable cancer of the uterus, another chronic gallbladder disease and a third severe pancreatitis.

On his own, their physician contacted a local faith healer who had the reputation of "curing" people by sending powerful therapeutic energy in their direction from a distance. The healer agreed to use his power on the doctor's patients, unknown to any of them. But after 12 "sessions," they experienced no improvement. The healer then went out of town and stopped sending his energy. The physician approached his patients and told them that there was this "absent" healer in the community who could help them.

On an appointed day, they would receive powerful healing forces from the healer. The doctor talked up the "treatment" and the target date arrived. Almost immediately, all three patients began improving. The one with gallbladder disease became free of pain and fever and was sent home, where she remained symptom-free for a year. The woman with pancreatitis gained 30 pounds, got out of bed and recovered completely. The patient with cancer had such a remission of symptoms that she was able to become active again and resume being housewife and mother. Although she died three months later, which was about the time originally expected, she was much happier, active and free of pain.

Another form of "distant healing" has been reported by a California cardiologist, Randy Byrd, who arranged for a group of people around the country to pray daily for 192 coronary care unit patients at San Francisco General Hospital.[35] While an assistant professor of medicine at the University of California, San Francisco, and a staff cardiologist at the hospital, Byrd did a double-blind, randomized study of 393 coronary patients. Those in the "prayed-for" group had from five to seven people in the country praying for them each day. The 201 patients in the control group did not receive prayers from the network.

The study was conducted over a 10-month period. Patients in the two groups were comparable in age and severity of conditions. The people doing the praying were given the name of the patient, the diagnosis and the condition and were asked to pray for "beneficial healing and quick recovery" of each person.

When the results were analyzed, Byrd found that the prayed-for subjects had significantly fewer complications while in the coronary care unit. Only three required antibiotics, compared with 16 in the control group. Six prayed-for patients suffered pulmonary edema while 18 in the other group experienced that complication. None of those receiving prayers needed intubation, compared with 12 of the unprayed-for.

Other physicians, informed of the study, agreed on the efficacy of prayer. An assistant professor of medicine at Mayo Medical School in Rochester, Minnesota, said the study lent credibility to his own observations that prayers help. "I pray for my own patients, and I feel my prayers benefit them," said Arthur Kennel.[36] In Tulsa, John Merriman, chief of staff at Doctors Medical Center and former professor of medicine at the University of Saskatchewan School of Medicine, accepted the findings without surprise, saying, "I believe that patients who are named in prayer do better."

Expectations and Immunity

The ability of our expectations to produce profound effects on the immune system has been demonstrated in studies in both humans and animals. Psychologist Robert Ader and his colleagues at the University of Rochester School of Medicine—in experiments that became classics in the new field of psychoneuroimmunology—were able to condition mice into decreasing their production of antibodies that were attacking the animals' own tissue, causing a type of lupus, an autoimmune disease.[37]

They did this by injecting the mice with an immunosuppressive drug and pairing it with a drink of saccharin solution. Saccharin injections were then substituted for the drug, cyclophosphamide, which relieved symptoms by reducing the antibodies attacking the mice's tissue. The conditioned mice that got the saccharin, and associated it with the drug, showed greater survival and slower development of symptoms of lupus than did control groups of animals. The saccharin signaled the mice to suppress their immune system just as if they were receiving the drug.

In humans, University of Arkansas medical researchers showed that response to tuberculosis skin testing could be significantly altered when subjects expected their reaction to be negative.[38] Nine volunteers, all positive to the tuberculin skin test, were told they would be given a skin test on each arm once a month for six months. For five months the right arm of each person was administered a tuberculin solution and the left arm saline. A skin reaction would appear on the right arm only. On the sixth month, the procedure was reversed and the left arm got tuberculin and the right arm saline. Because the volunteers expected the left arm, as usual, to show no reaction, the response to tuberculin was significantly diminished.

Findings of expectations affecting our immune system provide additional evidence on how our thoughts and beliefs can influence our health. Our cognitions seem to play a role not only in whether we get sick but also in our responses to medicine once we are ill.

15. Effect of Attitudes on Drugs and Recovery

When the sick recover by the use of drugs, it is the law of a general belief, culminating in individual faith, which heals.[1]

A doctor who tells a patient that there's no hope . . . is making an enormous assumption in presuming his power is the only one that can restore . . . health. Telling a patient he or she is going to die is tantamount to a curse. The patient believes it, so it comes true.[2]

Although there is no scientific evidence that we can depend solely on our faith to heal ourselves, it is true that the attitudes of doctors and patients markedly influence the effects of drugs and surgery as well as our prospects of recovery. Our "mind sets" affect the reactions we get from both the substances we put in our bodies—including alcohol—and the internal repair system we have for combating illness.[3]

If a patient's doctor is enthusiastic about a new drug he or she is giving the person, the effects are almost always greater than if the physician were neutral or negative toward the medicine.[4] The influence of doctors' attitudes on patients' expectations and, thus, on physiological effects of a new drug or therapy has long been recognized.

In fact, the admonition to physicians that "you should treat as many patients as possible with the new drugs while they have the power to heal" has been handed down for so many generations that the quotation has been attributed to at least half dozen historical figures in medicine, including Osler and Trousseau.[3] Patients often do get better when they are given a new drug, but their response may have little to do with the agent's chemical contents.

Across the years, many new remedies have not undergone well-controlled studies that compare their pharmaceutical effectiveness with purely placebo responses. The federal Office of Technology Assessment estimated that only 10 percent of all drugs have received such testing, which is now more standard procedure.[5] When controlled studies were done on some of the drugs that became popular with physicians, the remedies were found no more beneficial than placebos were. Studies suggest that up to one-third of the drugs prescribed by physicians in the United States may depend on placebo action for their efficacy.[6]

Effect of Expectations on Valium

For example, one of the most widely prescribed drugs in the world has been Valium, given to more than 30,000,000 Americans a year. Some 30 double-blind studies have now concluded that Valium (diazepam) is no more clinically effective than a placebo is for anxiety, which is the complaint the drug is most prescribed to relieve.[7] In 1983, Shapiro and his colleagues in New York reported the results of a double-blind study in which 224 anxiety patients were given either Valium or a placebo, plus brief psychotherapy, over six weeks.[8] After the first week, those who were receiving the tranquilizer showed no greater improvements than did the patients who were taking a placebo.

Antibiotics, as well as tranquilizers, have mostly placebo effects for some conditions. Aureomycin was hailed as effective treatment of atypical pneumonia.[9] "Many hundreds of pounds" of the drug were prescribed for thousands of cases.[10] Four years later, when a controlled study was completed, aureomycin was found to be no more effective than placebos were.[11]

Vitamins for Angina

Other popular treatments for common disorders have met similar fates when tested rigorously. Methyl xanthines, for instance, were believed to dilate coronary arteries, improve circulation to the heart and relieve anginal pain. In nonblind studies—that is, both the doctor and patient knew what drug was being given—up to 80 percent of patients reported improvement.[12] Even exercise tolerance increased.

289

However, when the xanthines were later compared with placebo pills in single-blind studies—the patients were unaware of which agents they were receiving—greater benefit came from the placebos.[13]

Still later, vitamin E was touted as effective in relieving angina pectoris. Enthusiastic reports credited vitamin E therapy with bringing benefit in 90 percent of patients.[14] Advocates of the therapy continued to report results of effectiveness. Skeptics, meanwhile, did other studies finding no therapeutic benefit in vitamin E. A double-blind trial— neither the patient nor the doctor knew whether vitamin E or a placebo was being given—found in favor of the vitamin.[15] But larger, well-controlled trials later reported that vitamin E was no better than placebo pills were.[16] Cardiologist Herbert Benson, director of behavioral medicine at Harvard and Beth Israel Hospital in Boston who has long studied placebo effects, noted: "Again, the discrepancy between the results of advocates and skeptics may be attributed, in part, to the greater degree of placebo effect evoked by the enthusiasts.[17]

"Halo Effect" and Beta-Blockers

The enthusiasm that physicians bring to promising new drugs inspires faith in patients and encourages placebo responses, which is all to the good except it makes it impossible to determine how much pharmacological agents are contributing to the results. When a drug, or any other intervention, results in effects due to both the pharmacological action of the agent and the expectations of the patient, it qualifies as an "active placebo."[18] An "inactive" placebo is any inert agent that has no direct effects of its own and depends entirely on physiological reactions due to the person's belief and expectations.

As pointed out by Andrew Weil, Harvard psychopharmacologist who has written extensively on drugs and the mind, "as belief in a new drug fades, so does its potential to serve as active placebo."[19] In other words, as the "halo effect" around the drug wanes and new studies raise questions about effectiveness, doctors begin to have second thoughts and temper their enthusiasm. Their eroding faith is then transmitted to the patients, causing the drug to lose effectiveness due to a diminished placebo response. Double-blind, controlled studies cannot eliminate the effects that a placebo response adds to a new drug.

Weil points to the painkiller Darvon as an example of this process.[3] When it was introduced in 1957, it was promoted as a safe, nonaddicting analgesic that could not be abused. Later, it was discovered that heroin addicts liked to use it to inject intravenously. Questions then arose as to whether Darvon really relieved pain as well as older drugs. As belief in the drug receded, so did the percent of patients reporting satisfactory effects from it.

More recently, a new look has been taken at an even bigger favorite of physicians—beta-blockers. These drugs showed considerable promise for heart patients, who often have overactive sympathetic nervous systems. The beta-adrenergic blockers cause the heart to beat less intensely and require less oxygen. They were heralded as a way to reduce the amount of serious heart muscle damage in a myocardial infarction. But a six-year controlled study failed to confirm that propranolol, a popular beta-blocker, was any more effective than a placebo in decreasing the size of an infarct when administered from four to 18 hours after the start of a heart attack.[20]

Cancer, Krebiozen and Psychic Surgery

On their own, patients can become enthusiastic about a new cure and produce temporary relief of symptoms. A man with far-advanced lymph node cancer who had tumors in the neck, abdomen and groin, heard of Krebiozen, then a new "miracle cancer drug."[21] He insisted on being admitted to a clinical trial of the drug, although his doctors estimated he had only two weeks to live. The man was bedridden and his breathing was so labored, he had to gasp for air.

Within 10 days after receiving Krebiozen, his tumors had shrunk remarkably, and he was well enough to be discharged from the hospital. However, after two months, news reports began circulating carrying discouraging facts about Krebiozen, and the man returned to the hospital with tumors again enlarged. His physician announced to him that the first batches of Krebiozen had deteriorated with storage, and a new and more potent shipment was being received and would be given to the patient.

The doctor proceeded to give the man injections of plain water. In a short time, the tumors shrank again and the patient had nearly total remission of symptoms. He remained healthy until another news report came out in several months, this one declaring: "Nationwide AMA tests show Krebiozen to be worthless as a cancer treatment." The man died less than two days later.

The internal healing systems that apparently can be turned on by a profound belief in something have repeatedly demonstrated their power, but they rarely can reverse a case of advanced cancer. They may slow the disease or facilitate a remission, but there is little evidence that they "cure." Cruel deceptions are practiced on terminal cancer patients who desperately seek cures. No matter how much they believe in a Krebiozen or a Laetrile, any relief gained is not likely to last—if that is the only treatment they receive.

Andy Kaufman, a popular character in the hit television show, "Taxi," developed lung cancer and went to the Philippines to be cured by a "psychic surgeon."[22] For many years, psychic surgery has flourished in the Philippines and Brazil with claims that diseased organs and tissue—the "cause" of whatever illness a person has—can be removed by the "surgeon" entering the body with his bare hands. Photographs were taken of bloody tissue that supposedly came from Kaufman's lungs. The tissue and blood usually come from animals and are concealed before the operation, only to be produced by the "surgeon" after he has practiced his sleight-of-hand, knifeless operation. Kaufman died at 35 two months after the psychic surgery.[22]

Defeatist Physicians

In cancer, negative attitudes by doctors can be more of a problem than patients' becoming overly enthusiastic about unproved remedies. The attitude of the physician toward cancer is often similar to that of the patient, who frequently believes "that the disease comes from without, that it's synonymous with death, that the treatment is bad, and the patient has little or nothing that he can do to fight the disease."[23]

The pessimistic views of a doctor only exacerbate the helpless feelings of the patient. Physicians are obliged to be honest with those diagnosed as having cancer, but the way they do it can be devastating. Norman Cousins reviewed 300 cases of people with malignancies and was struck by how the disease often accelerated right after the patients got their diagnoses. "Is it possible," he asked, "that the diagnosis has the effect of . . . a pronouncement of doom?"[24]

Robert Mendelsohn of the University of Illinois School of Medicine, the self-described "medical heretic" quoted at the start of this chapter, notes:

> It's one thing to inform a patient that he or she suffers from a deadly disease and that the magic of the doctor doesn't go far enough to do any good. But it's another thing entirely to tell a patient that the end is inevitable.[25]

293

Along with the statistics on survival rates for particular kinds of cancer, doctors also need to give patients the findings on the effects that a "fighting spirit" and other powerful coping skills have on the disease. They need to inspire patients to adopt attitudes that will turn on, not suppress, self-healing systems. To do this, physicians must first become familiar with the evidence on the biological effects of attitudes in cancer and the connection between cognitions and intrinsic healing processes.

Pessimism in Surgery

Because the words and attitudes of a doctor can have profound effects on the physiological reactions of patients, physicians are being increasingly advised to watch what they say while a person is undergoing surgery.

Even under anesthesia, people can hear what is being said and carry the effect of the words for days after the operation.[26] Psychologist Henry Bennett, in the department of anesthesiology at the University of California at Davis, has found in his research that a person's autonomic nervous system, already aroused in surgery, is particularly sensitive to negative words spoken by medical personnel in the operating room. He observed:

> Clinical cases make clear that massive autonomic effects can follow pessimistic or insulting remarks made around the adequately anesthetized patient. These effects often are not apparent until the second or third postoperative day.[27]

A Dire Effect of Medical Jargon

Medical jargon heard by a patient, in or out of the operating room, can also be misinterpreted and produce severe physiological reactions. Bernard Lown, professor of cardiology at Harvard, recalls that early in his career his chief was making clinic rounds and examined a middle-aged woman, a librarian, with congestive heart failure and swelling in the ankles from an accumulation of fluid.[28] Her condition was not so serious that she could not work or attend to household chores. Lown's mentor turned to the entourage of physicians following him and announced, "This woman has TS." He had hardly gone out the the door before the woman began breathing rapidly, was drenched with perspiration and had a pulse of more than 150 beats a minute.

Lown quickly examined her and found that her lungs, which had been clear, now had an accumulation of fluid. He questioned the woman about why she seemed so upset and she responded that she had just been told by the visiting doctor that she had TS and she knew that meant "terminal situation." Lown tried to reassure her that it meant "tricuspid stenosis"—a narrowing of the tricuspid heart valve—and that she was not in a terminal condition. Despite his efforts, the woman soon developed massive lung congestion and later the same day died from heart failure. He said he will never forget the power—in this case, tragically negative—of a physician's words. As King Solomon observed: "The tongue has the power of life and death."[29] (For more on the power of words, see Chapter 16).

Being Told What to Expect

Since our physiological reactions can rapidly change depending on what we are told, who says it and where we hear it, the effects of alcohol, diet pills, "recreational" drugs and medical procedures in general will vary. Our physical responses, including how much pain and healing we experience, are markedly influenced by our cognitions—by what we expect to happen, by what we hope will happen or by what sense of control we perceive. This may be a sense of personal control or faith in an external power, such as God or a doctor, to take care of the situation.

The effects of any pill or intervention, then, regardless of whether it is an active drug or an inert substance, will vary depending on "set and setting"—our cognitive state and the circumstances under which we receive the agent. For instance, when people are given epinephrine (adrenaline), they have a greater response if they are also told to expect stimulant effects.[30] They have more of an increase in heart rate and greater response of free fatty acids and blood glucose.

Enhancing "Diet Pills"

At Cornell, tests were conducted to determine how expectations might influence the effects of an appetite depressant, phenmetrazine.[31] At first, subjects who received the drug were told nothing about it, and the total calories consumed per day were recorded. Then, they were told that appetite depression might occur. The number of calories eaten after this dropped considerably.

Interventions involving no drugs can also be enhanced when we expect a certain effect. For example, two matched groups of people who were given relaxation training got different effects on their blood pressure as a function of being told when to expect any change.[32] The first group was told that the relaxation exercises would have an immediate effect on reducing blood pressure, and those in the second were told the effects take time. Systolic pressure in the first group dropped 17 millimeters of mercury compared with 2.4 for the second group.

Just as the effects of diet pills and relaxation techniques may vary depending on what a person is told and believes, the same seems true of vitamin C. The value of

vitamin C in preventing the common cold—a subject of continued controversy—appears related to how convinced
someone is that it works. In clinical trials of the effectiveness of vitamin C, those who were given a placebo but
thought it was vitamin C had fewer colds than those given
vitamin C but thought it was a placebo.[33]

Expectations Change Alcohol, Marihuana Effects

Marihuana and alcohol provide possibly the most striking
examples of how physiological effects vary depending on
expectations and setting. Those who use marihuana can have
diametrically opposite reactions from the same dose.[3] Some
people smoke it as an aid to sleep while others use it for
stimulation and concentration. Some become extroverted on
it and others introverted. Some consider the drug to be an
aphrodisiac, others find it decreases their interest in sex.

Greater intoxication from marihuana occurs when it
is smoked among friends than strangers.[34] A social setting,
at least for Americans, facilitates an intoxicating effect from
marihuana.[35] In a laboratory setting, one experiment showed
that naive subjects taking marihuana will not get a "high"
when the staff refrains from encouraging them to have an
enjoyable experience.[36]

In Jamaica, another study found marihuana was used
as an all-purpose palliative and produced no intoxication or
hallucinations.[34] The effect depended on what they wanted
from cannabis. Some Jamaicans used it, for example, to
stimulate their appetite while others used it to suppress
hunger. There was no expectation of its enhancing sexual
responsiveness, fostering feelings of euphoria or producing
highs, which are outcomes reported by Americans.

The fact that the effects of marihuana vary so widely
has been attributed to the strong influence of different in-

dividual and cultural expectations toward the drug. These expectations result in physiological and psychological changes that largely overshadow changes due to the chemical content of marihuana.

With both marihuana and alcohol, when a person expects to have to contend with a stressor while using either drug, intoxication will be less.[37] Whether alcohol stimulates or calms depends considerably on the drinker's expectancy and setting. When people drink alone, alcohol tends to be a depressant, but when they drink in a social setting it usually acts as a stimulant.[38] Solitary drinkers talk more of the physical effects of alcohol, such as dizziness, and social drinkers of their psychological reactions, such as feeling more outgoing and friendly.

Men who believed they had been imbibing alcohol (regardless of whether they actually had or had been given a placebo drink) tended to have slower heart rates when trying to impress a woman. An opposite effect was found in women. Those who believed they had been drinking had greater arousal—faster heart rates, increased skin conductivity and more anxiety. In general, men expect a calming effect from alcohol in such situations, and women appear to expect the opposite.[38] Drinking can also have different effects on blood pressure, depending on what people expect. For instance, in a study of 32 young men who thought they were drinking alcohol but were actually consuming tonic, both systolic and diastolic blood pressure decreased.[39] They also became more elaborate in their speech.

Again, beliefs can produce intriguing effects from alcohol. In experiments where people do not know whether they are drinking vodka or tonic water, men become more aggressive—as they expect to be—when they think they have had alcohol even though they had tonic.[38] They become less aggressive when they believe they had tonic but actually drank alcohol. Men also become more sexually aroused when they believe they had alcohol, even though they received tonic.

Experts have thought that alcoholics have a physiological disorder that causes them to crave liquor if they have a single drink. Experiments have now shown, however, that alcoholics experience craving if they simply believe they had a drink when, in fact, they had been given tonic.[38] What is even more surprising is that when alcoholics were given vodka but believed it was tonic, they reported little or no craving. This is not to say that alcoholics have no genetic propensity for an addiction to alcohol; it suggests that, as with most disorders, people's perceptions strongly contribute to their biological reactions.

Same Drug, Different Effects

Because, as we have seen, expectations are present in every situation where we are aware that we are receiving a drug—or think we are—the effects that we experience are the combined results of both the chemical contents of the substance and our beliefs.[40] Our faith in the treatment, our physician and ourselves to control whatever problem we have can either contribute to the pharmacologic activity of the drug or—if we have no confidence—detract from it.

Two physicians can give two patients with the same illness the same antibiotic and get substantially different results.[41] The same patient may respond differently to the same drug at different times under different circumstances. If a physician or patient believes tetracycline will help a viral sore throat, rapid benefit may be experienced despite the inability of an antibiotic to work against viruses.[3] These paradoxes can largely be explained by the nonspecific effects that varying beliefs and expectations have on the human body. A cold, impersonal doctor is not likely to inspire the same degree of faith and expectancy in a patient as an equally competent physician who is warm and caring. When we are given a medication, our response depends not only on the properties of the drug but also on the attitude of our physician, on our beliefs about the treatment and the "karma" or relationship existing between us.[3] (Time of day and our circadian rhythms also can affect our drug responses).

In a typical clinical situation, 25 percent of those treated will not get relief from any medication.[42] Even the most potent of pain-killers, morphine, will not help most of these people. Five of every 12 patients will receive considerable relief from morphine but not much benefit from a placebo. About one-third of all people will get as much relief from a placebo as from morphine.[42]

Those who do respond to a placebo have an advantage over those who do not when both have to take active drugs. In one study, a standard dose of morphine was 95 percent effective for those who were sensitive to placebos but only 54 percent effective for those who were not.[42] Morphine is effective in 70 percent of all cases, with an estimated 30 percent of the effect due to a placebo response.[43]

Since, as we have seen, the effectiveness of a drug can vary depending on the belief in it of the physician who gives it, morphine is subject to the same influence. In one set of experiments, patients were administered morphine, a mild analgesic or a placebo. When the physicians thought they were giving morphine, the placebo was two times more effective than when they believed they were giving a mild analgesic.[44]

Placebos in Every Prescription

In many cases, our expectations and beliefs may be more responsible than the drug we take for any benefit received. Studies have estimated that from "35 to 45 percent of all prescriptions are for substances that are incapable of having an effect on the condition for which they are prescribed."[45]

For example, according to one study on treatment

of the common cold, 31 percent of patients received a pre-scription for an antibiotic, 22 percent got penicillin and 6 percent sulfanomides—"none of which could possibly have any beneficial specific pharmacological effect on the viral infection per se."[46] Whatever benefit received came from the nonspecific placebo effect, which can be considerable. The same applies to vitamin B-12 therapy, which has not demonstrated specific effects for any disease outside of per-nicious anemia, although thousands of doses have been ad-ministered each year for many other kinds of complaints. Halsted Holman, professor of medicine at Stanford Univer-sity School of Medicine, argues that "three of the four most commonly prescribed drugs treat no specific illness."[47]

Sir William Osler, who was considered the greatest clinician of the English-speaking world in the early 20th century, repeatedly said that the cures he brought about were due not to any remedies he applied but to the faith of the patients in the treatment.[48] Osler was convinced that psy-chological influences such as faith and positive expectations set in motion restorative mechanisms of "vis medicatrix na-turae"—the healing power of nature or what is now being called self-healing systems.

Faith Promotes Recovery

As with drugs, the success of surgery is partly dependent on our "expectant faith." A group of patients about to undergo an operation for detached retina was given a pa-per-and-pencil test to determine their "acceptance" of the surgery.[49] Those who scored highest on acceptance turned out to be the patients with the most rapid healing after the operation. Healing rate was judged independently by an ophthalmologist who had no knowledge of the test scores. Optimism and trust were two important attitudes of those who healed fastest.

The researchers who conducted the study concluded that "the person seeking to help the slow healer . . . should focus primarily on what variables enhance or destroy the patient's attitude of expectant faith."[50] As we saw in Chapter 10, people undergoing surgery who expect to die from the operation often do. It is important that surgeons spend time with patients before operations to give reassurance and promote positive feelings.

Side-effects of Placebos

Because negative expectations can contribute to negative effects from drugs as well as surgery, serious side-effects may result from "harmless" medication. Some people fear drugs and distrust doctors. Some may have had unfavorable treatment experiences in the past. When they are given a placebo, they may develop severe physiological reactions such as nausea, diarrhea or skin eruptions.[51]

Like active drugs, placebos can produce untoward side-effects. A placebo often may mimic the side-effects of whatever drug it is being substituted for or tested against. In a study of the effects that mephenesin had on anxiety, both the drug and a placebo proved to produce almost identical side-effects: sleepiness, sleeplessness, nausea, dizziness.[52] One person had a shock-like reaction—lowering of blood pressure, clammy white skin and fainting. The identical reaction occurred when the person was given either the drug or the placebo.

In double-blind studies, patients may complain of dry mouth, nausea, heaviness, headache, difficulty concentrating, drowsiness, rashes or sleep disturbance, but when the code is broken as to who received a drug and who a placebo, the complaints of side-effects have been found to come from those who received an inert substance. Reports of toxic reactions to a drug, then, may be due to a negative placebo effect rather than to the drug itself.[53] A negative cognitive "set"—a distrusting attitude or pessimistic outlook—may not always produce toxic reactions, but it is likely to keep a person from activating internal healing systems associated with a positive placebo effect.

Effects of Food We Believe We Ate

Just as the influence of drugs or placebos will depend to an important extent on our expectations and beliefs, so may the effects of a meal. Strong, toxic reactions can occur when we believe we have had something to eat or drink that was contaminated, even though later tests demonstrate that such was not the case. Negative placebo effects can closely mimic food poisoning and produce identical symptoms.

For example, at a football game in Monterey Park, California, four persons became severely nauseated and dizzy and had to leave their seats.[54] School officials determined that they had consumed soft drinks from a dispensing machine under the stands. The officials speculated that either the syrup used to mix with water for the drinks went bad or that copper sulfate from the pipes might have infiltrated the water itself. A public announcement was made asking that no one consume beverages from the dispensing machines until the cause of the illness affecting several persons could be established.

Immediately afterwards, the stadium was the scene of fainting and retching. A total of 191 people had to be taken to hospitals, all with symptoms of food poisoning. Laboratory tests, however, established that neither the syrup nor the water was contaminated, and the drinks were not responsible for the mass illness. Negative placebo effects were.

Proving Pain Is "Imaginary"

Because of the accumulating data demonstrating the potency of the placebo effect, we would expect that medical practitioners would treat placebos with respect. But the fact is, the opposite is more true. In a study of how much hospital doctors and nurses know about placebos and how they use the agents, researchers at the University of New Mexico School of Medicine found both ignorance and misuse prevailing.[55]

Based on a survey and interviews of 60 residents and interns, plus 39 registered nurses, the study found that (1) the majority of physicians and nurses grossly underestimated the percent of patients who gain relief from placebos; (2) only 16 percent of the doctors and 40 percent of the nurses recalled having received any formal instruction on placebos, and (3) placebos were typically given to disliked or difficult patients to "prove" their pain was only "imaginary" or exaggerated.

A senior resident on the medical service summed up his perception of placebo use this way: "Placebos are used with people you hate, not to make them suffer, but to prove them wrong."[56] The biggest misconception the doctors and nurses had was that if a placebo relieved the pain of a patient—often a patient who frequently complained and bothered the staff—this proved that the pain was imaginary.

As much research has shown, pain from indisputable tissue damage and "organic" disease—whether from a gunshot wound, tooth extraction or a myocardial infarction—often responds to placebos.[57] As we have noted, all pain has a subjective element, which largely determines its intensity. Pain may be pretended or exaggerated, but none is imaginary.[53]

Physicians who believe a patient is "faking" or who strongly dislike someone in their care may withhold active analgesics for that person's pain. As observed by the New Mexico researchers:

> The ordering of active narcotic analgesics seems to be viewed as a gift from the doctor to the patient; placebo is substituted when the physician feels too angry with the patient to bestow a "real" gift.[56]

The danger in the misconception that placebo relief means imaginary pain was illustrated by the case of a 47-year-old alcoholic man who loudly complained that nothing was being done to treat his nausea and vomiting, which the nursing notes described as "self-induced."[56] Finally, the patient was simultaneously given a saline placebo and Compazine, a drug used to treat psychotic disorders and anxiety. Relief of the vomiting resulted and was ascribed to the placebo. Alleviation of symptoms was taken as proof that the vomiting was indeed "self-induced." A week later, exploratory abdominal surgery was performed and the man was found to have a large pancreatic abscess.

Myths about Placebos

Empirical findings have exploded several other myths to which practitioners have subscribed. The summary that follows also includes some of the points we made earlier about placebos. The myths are:

Myth 1—The placebo effect is "all in a person's head" and any changes it brings are totally psychological. The fact is that placebos affect physiological processes, not just how people report they feel, and the changes can be objectively measured.[51]

Myth 2—Only neurotic or suggestible people respond to placebos. The fact is that there is no "placebo personality"; just about anyone is capable of responding under the right conditions—conditions that evoke positive expectations.[57] In a study involving patients with cancer pain who received a placebo several times, 90 percent reported a significant decrease in pain at least once.[58] Our state of mind and the situation we face, more than any particular trait, activates the placebo effect. Studies purporting to show that "placebo responders" are uneducated and naive have proved to be "nonsense."[58] Well-trained physicians often self-prescribe antibiotics for their sore throats and get relief. The relief is not due to the drugs, which have no effectiveness against viruses.

Myth 3—Placebos help only with pain or anxiety. The fact is that the placebo effect has been demonstrated in the relief of a variety of disorders and symptoms.[51]

Myth 4—If a drug or any other medical procedure does not bring any better results, in a double-blind controlled study, than a placebo does, then it is worthless.[59] The fact is that placebos are on the average 35 percent effective, and any drug or intervention that equals this cannot be considered useless.[60] Another unacknowledged fact about double-blind, controlled drug studies is that even if an agent shows greater effectiveness than a placebo does, not all the efficacy can be attributed to the drug itself. As we have seen, if people are aware they are receiving any substance, they normally have some expectations about it, and these contribute to whatever effects a drug has.[61] "In fact," Weil emphasizes, "the success of a new drug in double-blind trials, by convincing doctors of intrinsic efficacy, will give it a thicker coat of belief and so increase its potential to elicit placebo responses."[62] Examples are beta-blockers and Darvon.

As for interventions that involve no drugs, such as psychotherapy, some studies have suggested that it demonstrates no greater results than does the placebo effect.[63] Again, the implication is that the placebo effect is of little value. Such conclusions betray an ignorance of both the power of the placebo response and the contributions a competent psychotherapist can make in evoking specific effects in addition.

Myth 5—The placebo effect can be evoked only by deceiving people into believing that they are receiving something "real" and powerful when they actually are not.

The fact is that any intervention that enhances positive expectations and a sense of control can initiate the response, and no deceit is necessary.[64]

In one deceit-free study, patients were told that they would be given "sugar pills" and that these had helped a number of people and might also help them.[65] All but one of the patients showed improvement in a week. More recently, researchers have discovered that blood pressure can be controlled in some hypertensive patients simply by conveying to them the fact that the act of regular monitoring produces a lowering effect and then proceeding to check their pressure at frequent intervals.[66] By believing that such monitoring is beneficial, patients apparently have an enhanced sense of control over their hypertension, which results in a positive placebo effect.

Because researchers have discovered that the placebo response depends more on faith in the ability to control distress than in whatever pill may be taken, the trend now is toward teaching people how to tap intrinsic healing systems on their own—that is, without drugs, fake or otherwise.

Since placebos simply demonstrate that such systems can be activated by whatever we believe will give us some control over our problems, the more straightforward approach is to teach control outright. In other words, a placebo—in the form of sugar pills or sham surgery, for instance—is not necessary for the positive features of the placebo response to occur. As we will see, our internal repair systems apparently can be turned on in several ways, but each seems to depend either directly or indirectly on enhancing our sense of control.

16. Turning on Our Self-healer

*Healing does not
rest in the hands of a
selected few but in the hands
of every human being. . . .
No matter what physicians
do, they can only augment
the healing process of
the body itself.*[1]

*You carry with you
the most powerful medicine
that exists. . . . Each of us has
it if we choose to use it,
if we learn to use it.*[2]

Whatever gives us an increased sense of control—whether it is love, faith or cognitive coping—seems to mobilize our self-healing systems. Some people, told by their physicians they are going to die, appear to use courage, determination, even anger, to take control and turn on their healing systems. Others may do it by meditating, praying, restoring strained relationships, or giving their bodies love for the first time through exercise and good nutrition.

Regardless, then, of what leads us to believe it, if we become convinced that we can control our lives, our bodies or our health, we apparently gain access to our self-healer. Researchers are now identifying some of the ways that people can be taught to marshall a sense of control and to tap their potential for self-repair.

One way was recently demonstrated in a group of patients undergoing coronary bypass surgery. A common complication to such surgery is an alarming increase in blood pressure one to four hours after the operation. This complication was largely prevented by psychologists at the University of Iowa School of Medicine who told the patients what exercises they could do to reduce pain and promote recovery.[3]

A second group was simply given information, again before their bypass operations, on details of the surgery, tests they would have to undergo and other things they could expect from the time of admission to discharge. A third group received routine hospital treatment. All patients were randomly assigned to one of the three groups.

After surgery, patients in each of the three groups were required to do the exercises that only those in the first group were told about ahead of time. All patients were checked for the amount of anxiety and pain they had, how much control they perceived over their own recovery, how much postoperative hypertension they experienced and the rate of their physical recovery.

Patients in the first group fared significantly better on all counts. There was less hypertension, anxiety and pain. Although the exercises taught all the patients may have had specific effects on muscle tension and reduction of pain, those in the first group had a greater sense of control, and that proved to be the most powerful predictor of recovery without complication.[3]

Less Pain, Quicker Recovery

Learning cognitive reappraisal is another way to gain a sense of control and facilitate self-healing processes. Psychologists taught a group of patients at Yale-New Haven Hospital how to look at their surgery and hospitalization more positively, thus changing their appraisal of the experience and reducing physiological reactions to it.[4] It was explained that rarely do events cause stress, but rather the view that people take of them and the attention given to them. The patients were encouraged to consider such positive features to being in the hospital as a vacation from outside pressures, a chance to relax and take stock of oneself, an opportunity to lose weight and to be taken care of.

As part of learning cognitive control, the patients also were taught calming self-talk to deal with stresses. A comparable group of surgical patients in the same hospital was given information about their surgery and recovery. A third group received usual hospital treatment and were not taught coping skills or given information. The first group did significantly better after surgery, requiring few sedatives, reporting less anxiety, coping more effectively and recovering faster. All told, 60 patients were in the three groups.

Those who had been instructed in cognitive coping adopted a belief that they had the power to exercise some control over their situation. Such a belief is what activates the placebo response, which, along with the cognitive reappraisal and calming self-talk, produced positive physiological changes. The nonspecific, placebo effects were augmented by the specific effects of cognitive coping.

Teaching children how to cope with hospitalization and reduce fear has had similar effects in terms of promoting their recovery from surgery. When children are shown that they do have some control over how they feel while in the hospital, the placebo effect seems to result in less pain and fewer complications. The children also experience less fear and stress.

In a well-controlled study of children who were in the hospital for tonsillectomies, hernias and other surgical conditions, one group viewed a film showing a child coping with hospitalization and a second group was shown a film unrelated to the hospital experience.[5] On the evening before surgery and three to four weeks after, the first group of children had reduced fear, as measured by both subjective and physiological indexes. Fewer children in the first group received pain medication after surgery and were nauseated or vomited. More were able to eat solid food earlier.

The more relevant information is, the more likely a person will gain a sense of control and experience both positive placebo effects and milder stress reactions. Women undergoing gynecological operations had less pain and recovered faster if they were given information on how to deal with their fears and postoperative symptoms (see Chapter 7).[6] They did better than a group that had the same surgery but were given only reassuring statements. Relevant information, then, can not only tell us specific things to do to reduce pain but also increase our sense of control and enhance nonspecific effects in our bodies.

Effects of Self-efficacy

Any painful, chronic illness often leads people to believe that nothing can be done to help them and that their situation is hopeless. Dramatic changes in pain relief can occur, however, if such people can gain some sense of control or efficacy.

At the Stanford Arthritis Center, significant improvement occurred in patients who attended five weekly classes for an hour each time, and were taught relaxation techniques, physical activities and cognitive skills designed to reduce arthritis pain.[7] They were compared with a similar group of patients who did not take the classes.

Although there were no correlations between increased knowledge of relaxation or change in activity and reduction in pain, there was a significant association between greater self-efficacy—which the program participants experienced—and pain relief. In other words, no specific element of the program accounted for the improvement, but overall the classes gave the patients a better outlook and a greater sense of control, and these were associated with less pain. Increased self-efficacy was correlated not only with less pain but also with a decrease in swollen joints and a decline in depression.

People who believe they can be effective in managing problems, including their own arthritis, have also been reported to experience beneficial effects in their immune systems.[8] In addition to less pain and fewer swollen joints, they have higher levels of suppressor T-cells. Such cells seem to keep the body from producing antibodies against its own tissue—a problem that occurs in autoimmune diseases like rheumatoid arthritis.

Self-efficacy also is associated with reduction of other kinds of pain. For example, with pain of childbirth, a group of mothers-to-be was taught relaxation and breathing exercises to reduce discomfort. Those who believed the exercises would help them control pain scored higher on perceived self-efficacy.[8] In the hospital, they did not require as much pain medication and reported less discomfort than did the mothers who did not believe the exercises would help them and had lower self-efficacy.

Mobilizing Faith to Heal

At the University of California at Irvine, a group of people with chronic back pain was taught how to mobilize both their faith and their capacity for self-healing.[9] Psychologists Perry London and David Engstrom took 32 people who were receiving placebos and split them into two groups of 16 each. At the end of three weeks, after the patients' pain had been noticeably reduced, one group was told that they had been getting an inert substance.

The placebo had been used to help the people appreciate the power of their own minds. The researchers wanted to show the patients that they could control their pain and bodily processes through cognitions of faith and belief, which mobilize self-healing systems. Since placebos work through the power of belief, the psychologists explained that it should be possible to harness the body's internal healing capacity without depending on a sham drug.

London and Engstrom then proceeded to train the group in how to harness their inner resources through conscious effort, just as the patients had unknowingly done through belief in a placebo. They were taught coping strategies for controlling pain. These included systematic muscle relaxation and slow breathing, use of mental pictures incompatible with pain, imagery to transform pain sensations into positive sensations, and self-instruction that taught the patients how to talk to themselves in a positive way that reinforced pain-free feelings and gave them more optimistic outlooks.

The training continued for four weeks. Through before-and-after measures of locus of control, the researchers were able to show that the training not only increased relief of pain for the patients but also enhanced their sense of control. Meanwhile, the other group of 16 patients, who continued to be unaware that they were taking placebo pills, received beneficial effects for the first three weeks. After that, however, the relief slowly diminished. By the end of the seventh week, pain had returned and by the end of 10 weeks, the people in the uninformed group were suffering as much as they were before they began taking placebos.

In the informed group, which received the training, pain levels continued to decline from the third to seventh week. More importantly, the patients held these gains for the three weeks after training ended and testing continued.

London and Engstrom believe that their study demonstrates that people who benefit from placebos are also able to reproduce the effect on their own. The placebos work in the first place, the researchers said, to the extent that people have a "talent for faith" and a capacity for hopeful belief. When they invest this faith and belief in a healer, a pill or some other intervention, their bodies respond by mobilizing intrinsic healing systems—even when the remedy is just a placebo. The psychologists concluded:

> Our research shows that we can constructively harness this talent for faith by teaching people their capacity for internal control. The body's healing power does not have to be inspired by confidence in a doctor; we can develop it by learning greater confidence in ourselves.[10]

Self-healing from Hypnosis

Just as a "talent for faith" may be used to tap intrinsic healing systems, an "aptitude and attitude" for hypnotic suggestion also can produce beneficial effects in the body. In both cases, success seems to depend on the people's belief in something—such as in their own ability to use their thoughts to cope better or in the suggestions a doctor or hypnotist is giving them. Hypnosis seems to evoke specific effects that are apart from the placebo response. As with a drug or surgery, a person who believes in a hypnotic procedure may receive benefits from both the specific intervention and from placebo effects. People who are good hypnotic subjects and accept a suggestion in an uncritical manner have been able under hypnosis to stop excessive bleeding and to control asthma, migraines, pain and other disorders.[11]

One woman had become a chronic invalid from prolonged attacks of asthma and respiratory distress.[12] After 10 years of treatment with a variety of medicines, she began hypnosis and was given the suggestion she would have no difficulty with breathing, nasal problems, itching or sneezing. The suggestion was repeated a number of times during a 30-minute session. The result was that the woman obtained complete relief from her asthma even though the pollen season was just beginning. Another practitioner treated 121 asthma patients with hypnosis over a 10-year span.[13] Those who were cured—that is, they gained normal ventilation capacity—were highly hypnotizable while those who showed no improvement were unhypnotizable. Similarly, in a study of 100 people with frequent migraine headaches, 23 who became free of symptoms were all capable of deep or medium hypnotic depth.[14] Those who still had migraine symptoms were low in their responsiveness to hypnosis.

The Power of Words

Hypnosis demonstrates the power of words to change physiological processes in the body, to turn on self-healing systems. One of the most dramatic and well-documented cases of the influence of words on the body and self-healing came from a British anesthesiology resident who used hypnosis to treat a 16-year-old boy.[15] The youth had congenital "fish-skin disease" (ichthyosis erythrodermia), which had been present since birth and left his arm with a thickened, scaly, cracked surface. Using hypnosis, A.A. Mason, the anesthesiologist, suggested that the skin on the arm would gradually become normal. One week later, it was virtually normal with fresh pink skin replacing the "fishskin." Four years later, the skin still showed 60 to 70 percent improvement.

Exactly how suggestion can produce such graphic physiological responses is still unclear. One authority argues that hypnosis is not necessary, that success lies in a person believing the suggestion.[16] Hypnosis may simply add a context of believability. The physiological control that strong belief in suggestion produces seems to involve alterations in the blood flow.

Altering Immunity

Both hypnosis and relaxation techniques, as we have seen, have been reported capable of changing our immune responses. Four subjects known to show positive reactions to tuberculin skin tests were hypnotized and given the suggestion not to react any more.[17] When the skin test was then given, a diminished reaction occurred. In another study, increased immune defenses occurred in a group of people who were hypnotized and instructed to imagine their lymphocytes fighting cold viruses and other germs.[18] They were asked to visualize their white blood cells as being like powerful sharks attacking weak and confused germs. The subjects also were taught self-hypnosis to use at home for a week while continuing the imaging.

Among those under 50 years old, a significant increase in immune functioning was found. Reactivity of T-cells was greater at the end of the week. For those more than 50 years of age—the oldest was 85—there was an also an increase in immune functioning, but it was not statistically significant. One explanation might be that with age, immune activity is normally lower and not as responsive to stimulation.

Other studies have also found that hypnosis may be useful in lowering the level of stress hormones or countering specific viruses. For example, hypnotic suggestions to relax have been reported to result in reducing the level of circulating corticosteroids in the body, which may lead to increased resistance to disease.[19] Warts have been removed by suggestions given a person under hypnosis. Since warts are of a viral origin, one mechanism may be the increase or activation of interferon, an antiviral agent in the body.[20]

How Hypnosis May Work

Lewis Thomas, chancellor of Memorial Sloan-Kettering Cancer Center in New York, has suggested that understanding how warts can be "hypnotized away" is so important a basic question that it deserves a "National Institute of Warts" to study it.[21]

The power of the mind and body to hypnotize away any disorder assumes the existence, Thomas believes, of an inner "controller"—"a kind of superintelligence that exists in each of us."[21] Self-healing seems to involve the ability to make contact with this inner controller and superintelligence we all have. What happens on the biological level when we do this is the scientific question remaining to be answered.

Hypnotized persons have been reported to be able to produce voltage changes in target areas of the body on command.[22] If these alterations of voltage control chemical and cellular processes, then science may have an explanation for not only how hypnosis can cure warts but how placebos work.[22]

Ability to Be Hypnotized

Unlike responsiveness to placebos, whether a person is susceptible to hypnosis depends largely on a trait that seems to remain fairly stable from childhood on.[23] This trait seems to be most present in people who had intensive imaginative experiences as children. That is, they actively used their imaginations to build fantasies and provide themselves with experiences they found satisfying and pleasurable. Imaginative involvements also are associated with immersion in reading, adventuresomeness, listening to music and performing. All these suggest an ability to ignore distractions and become totally immersed in an experience or activity. The ability to "dissociate" and screen out distracting influences can contribute to a certain sense of control.

Although "there is no relationship between placebo responsiveness and hypnotic ability," a capacity for faith and belief or an aptitude for imagination or concentration seems central to both.[24] Since some people who fail to respond to placebos do respond to hypnosis, and vice versa, the two approaches appear to use different pathways to activate healing systems. Suggestions given in psychotherapy as well as hypnosis can also bring improvement in some somatic disorders.[10] The success that certain cancer patients have from imaging and visualization "may be due as much to . . . high hypnotic ability . . . as it is to the patients' positive and optimistic attitudes."[25]

Spontaneous Recoveries

Cancer patients who manage to adopt positive attitudes after getting sick may experience significant changes in their disease. In fact, when more than 400 reports of "spontaneous" recoveries from cancer were investigated, the experiences of patients ranged from "grape juice cures" to visits to Lourdes. The only common element across the cases was a shift to a more positive and hopeful attitude, which took place before remission of the disease.[26] The theory is that the strength of these cognitions succeeded in activating powerful self-healing systems, which had marked effects on their disease.

When people's attitudes become more positive and their belief in control increases, the way they picture their disease and the ability of their bodies to do battle may also change. Both the change in attitude and the imagery may produce benefits.

How Does Imagery Produce Effects?

Through the pictures and images—as well as the internal dialogue —we have in our minds, we let the body know what we expect. But exactly how do images produce physiological benefits?

Research over the years has suggested that when we mentally picture our bodies' doing something, internal changes occur accordingly.[27] For example, if we mentally rehearse running a marathon, we are likely to evoke muscular changes, our blood pressure will go up, our brain waves will alter and our sweat glands will become active. Biofeedback research has shown that if we turn on "hot thoughts"— imagine hot scenes, such as the sun, a beach, a desert—we can increase blood flow and the warmth of our hands and other parts of the body.[28]

Evidence now indicates that people may also be able to alter their immune systems and disease states by what they imagine and visualize. In effect, they may be able to turn on self-healing systems. But how does a mental picture or symbol get translated into an impact on white blood cells or self-repair mechanisms? The autonomic nervous system as well as the brain itself is thought to act on the immune system and our self-healers, but the steps in the process are still to be determined.

The process may begin with activation of the right cerebral hemisphere of the brain. Whether images are mental pictures or—as some authorities emphasize—are symbolic representations of various kinds, they seem to activate our right brains. One theory holds that if we engage in right hemisphere activity—that is, imagery—we may raise the level of serotonin, a neurotransmitter associated with a sense of calmness and pain relief.[29] On the other hand, when we engage in stressful thinking and carry on doom-and-gloom internal dialogues with ourselves, our left brains are activated and may produce depletion of norepinephrine and dopamine. As we have noted (see Chapters 4 and 12), depletion of these two neurotransmitters is implicated in depression and other disorders. The theory is that by engaging in positive imagery, we may encourage self-healing processes by elevating serotonin while protecting the left hemisphere from catecholamine depletion.

Regardless of what the mechanisms may be for triggering self-repair, imagery is a growing focus of clinical research. For instance, Jeanne Achterberg, associate professor and director of research in rehabilitation science at the University of Texas Health Science Center at Dallas, has found that how a group of cancer patients pictured their malignant cells and their immune systems was the most powerful factor in predicting their disease status two months later.[30] Sense of control was another predictive factor, though less significant. Achterberg, together with Carl and Stephanie Simonton of the Cancer Counseling and Research Center in Fort Worth and psychologist Frank Lawlis, reported that cancer patients with the best outcome were those who visualized their white blood cells as being like Vikings or other legendary figures who fought for God and country. Those with poor outcomes pictured their immune cells as weak or soft, like snowflakes or clouds.

Although well-controlled, longterm studies have yet to establish just how effective imagery may prove to be in influencing diseases such as cancer, emerging evidence strongly suggests that our mental pictures can indeed have an impact on our immune systems. At Michigan State University, investigators have demonstrated the effects of imagery on neutrophils, which are white, scavenger cells that are important in keeping us free of infections.[27] Biofeedback training, as well as imagery, relaxation and hypnosis, has also shown promise in helping people improve their immune defenses. What may remain as the key to turning on self-healing systems is a belief by the person that it can be done. With imagery, for instance, Achterberg noted that it seemed to have an impact for those who believed it would.[27]

The Nature of Our Internal Self-healing Systems

What are these internal healing systems, which seem to respond to our hopeful belief? Although the question is far from settled, Jon Levine of the departments of neurology and physiology at the University of California School of Medicine in San Francisco has identified gamma globulins, steroids, antibodies and endorphins as elements in the systems.[31] TNF (tumor-necrosis factor), interferon and interleukin-2 are also included in the healing mechanisms. Interferon and interleukin-2—proteins secreted in minute amounts by white blood cells—stimulate important parts of our immune defenses.

Each of these, according to Levine, is one link in multiple healing circuits and acts at numerous sites in the body. Ironically, he noted, people have been led to believe that these naturally occurring substances in the human body are "miracle drugs" that have been created and discovered by medicine, which neglects to tell patients that they are intrinsic parts of all of us. Given such a belief, people understandably look outside themselves to find a "cure" for what ails them. Medicine's current crisis, Levine argues, is largely due to its neglect of internal healing systems and its failure to research ways of mobilizing them.[31]

As we saw in Chapter 4, a central site for some of these intrinsic mechanisms is the brain, and when they are activated, they produce analgesia, relief of pain or other positive effects. The discovery that our bodies have a highly organized network for pain control built into the central nervous system is one of the most important recent advances in pain research.[32] The endorphins—morphine-like peptides found in the brain and other parts of the body—are a significant link in this endogenous analgesia system. Other neuroregulators, such as serotonin and substance P, also seem to be elements in the system.

Levine and his coworkers demonstrated that people with postoperative pain who respond to a placebo appear to increase their levels of endorphins.[33] Their pain goes down. But when they are given naloxone, a drug that blocks the action of endorphins, their pain goes up. With patients who did not respond to a placebo, naloxone did not increase their pain, presumably because they never activated the internal system that releases endorphins. Other studies indicate that endorphins are not responsible for all analgesia.[34] For example, pain relief induced by hypnosis is not blocked by naloxone, which suggests that endorphins are not involved. But endorphins do seem to be one physiological mechanism by which some placebos work.[35]

Turning on Without Poppies

Avram Goldstein of Stanford, a pioneer in the discovery of opioids in the brain, is pursuing exciting clues to the possible link between morphine that our bodies may make and dopamine, a key neurotransmitter that has been associated with a sense of reward and pleasure (see Chapters 4 and 5).[36] Although peptides like endorphin and dynorphin—the opioid Goldstein discovered—can clearly reduce pain by slowing the flow of nerve impulses, they activate cell receptors different from the one that the drug morphine itself uses. Since the receptor (called "mu") for that drug has been identified as being present on our cells, Goldstein is trying to determine just how the body makes its own morphine. He believes that humans—as well as poppies—use dopamine as a building block. If poppies can use a relatively simple molecule like dopamine to assemble the complicated rings of morphine, then Goldstein figures that we can too. Whether our cognitions, moods and perhaps diet affect that assembly remains to be seen. Meanwhile, the placebo response, tied to the intensity of our beliefs and faith, may help researchers understand how people may activate their own dopamine and morphine systems to relieve pain or induce pleasure.

Since pain relief is only one of many symptomatic or somatic changes associated with the placebo effect, other healing mechanisms are activated for problems of a different kind. Opioid peptides, as we noted in Chapter 5, are found all over the body. Their distribution not only tracks the routes of pain impulses to the brain but also leads to centers regulating mood and breathing. Our gut nerves use opioids as transmitters. Opioid pathways in one area of the brainstem, where breathing is controlled, have cell receptors ("kappa") for dynorphin while those in another area, where blood flow is regulated, use "delta" receptors, the target of enkephalins.[34] Finding ways to direct and selectively activate these systems—by mental, behavioral or other means—is likely to lead to effects far beyond just pain reduction.

But research on the mechanisms of self-healing is only in its infancy. Clearly, many transmitter systems besides the opioids are involved. Determining how specific systems may be turned on by positive thoughts and expectations, faith or suggestion is the focus of interdisciplinary efforts that have just started.

The Role of Checks and Balances

The adaptive mechanisms in the body's system of checks and balances have also been identified as part of the internal processes that promote healing.[37] An example is the autonomic nervous system with its complementary and opposing branches (the sympathetic and parasympathetic). The "relaxation response" is viewed as the balancing counterpart to the fight-flight response.[38] If hostility, cynicism or pessimism predispose a person toward heart disease and other illness, then some researchers reason that attitudes of affiliation and optimism must work in the opposite direction and facilitate health.[37]

Although everyone may not be able to learn affiliative and optimistic ways of thinking, just keeping our cognitions from chronically triggering our stress chemicals may be enough to reduce the risk of developing illness. We have already seen (Chapter 13) that having something we truly enjoy—particularly if it also benefits others—seems to have health rewards. Being invested in a hobby, volunteer work or friends and organizations is likely to give us something to fall back on when the going gets rough. At the least, such activities can be a diversion and help keep us from looking at stressful events as though the world is coming to an end. They can enhance our sense of balance.

Even when people have all the standard risk factors that predispose them to heart disease, only a small percent suffer a myocardial infarction or other cardiac trouble.[39] As we have suggested, a sense of support may offer powerful protection. Part of our healing mechanisms, then, appears to be strongly related to a feeling of being connected to others as well as being involved in a network of worthwhile activities or organizations. Given such social contact and support, the brain and body seem to turn on positive physiological responses.

Sense of Control the Key?

A greater sense of control appears to be the common denominator to cognitions that trigger the internal healing mechanisms or keep neuroendocrine and immune systems from turning against us. As we have pointed out, it is possible to teach people both cognitive and behavioral control—the ability to reduce the aversiveness of a situation by how we look at it and what we do about it.[40] If they can also can find love, laughter and beauty in their lives, these can only add to healing effects.

The advantage that cognitive control has over exhortations to think positively is that it is a skill that can be learned. Imploring people to adopt a positive attitude does not tell them how to do it. Cousins might be on the right track in proposing that people use joke books or whatever makes them laugh to induce more positive emotions in their lives during an illness.[41] Meichenbaum and other cognitive-behavioral psychologists give people a systematic list of positive statements to say to themselves as they confront pain or whatever distress they have.[42]

No mechanical recitation of positive statements, however, is likely to invoke intrinsic healing systems. The psychologists are first careful to provide an understanding of how the mind affects the body before teaching anyone a new internal dialogue. People who believe that the mind-body connection exists are then ready to learn how to influence physiological processes by using more positive self-statements and changing irrational ideas.

Our Body the Druggist

Faith, belief, a sense of control can come to people in a variety of ways. Cognitive-behavioral scientists may increase people's faith in themselves by teaching them control of bodily processes. Others may harness the power of the mind by faith in something external—God, a physician, hypnotist or a placebo pill.

When more is known about the psychobiological effects of love, laughter, visualization of strength and beauty, we may find that these alone—apart from what they may mean for our sense of control—are enough to inspire healing.

Whatever route is taken toward health, science may prove Cousins right when he said:

> . . . the human body is its own best apothecary and . . .
> the most successful prescriptions are those filled by the
> body itself.[43]

Perhaps those who most get sick have yet to invoke the healer in themselves that comes from the physical power of their own minds.

The good news is that—as Eliot (see Chapter 12) reminds us—we can teach our brains "to write healthy prescriptions for the body."[44] The heady revolution has now clearly demonstrated that "the brain writes prescriptions that spread to every portion of the body, producing health or illness."[44]

We have a choice, then, of teaching the brain to turn on healing systems or the opposite.

References

INTRODUCTION: THE HEADY REVOLUTION

1. Hamburg, D.A., as quoted in *Brain/Mind Bulletin* (1985, June 17). AAAS head: "Brain now top science category," p. 1. Hamburg, past president of the American Association for the Advancement of Science now with the Carnegie Corporation, was formerly a professor of psychiatry at Stanford University and head of the Institute of Medicine, National Academy of Sciences.

2. Public Health Service. (1979). *Healthy people: The surgeon general's report on health promotion and disease prevention* (DHEW Publication No. 79–55071). Washington, DC: U.S. Government Printing Office, p. 141.

3. King, L.S. (1982). *Medical thinking*. Princeton, NJ: Princeton University Press; Epstein, S. (1978). *The politics of cancer*. San Francisco: Sierra Club Books.

4. Cunningham, A.J. (1982). Should we investigate psychotherapy for physical disease, especially cancer? In S.M. Levy (Ed.), *Biological mediators of behavior and disease* (pp. 83–109). New York: Elsevier Biomedical.

5. Franklin, J. (1984, July 23–31). The mind fixers. *Baltimore Evening Sun* reprint series.

6. Eccles, J.C. (1985, October). *How mental events could cause neural events analogously to the probability fields of quantum mechanics*. Paper presented at the annual meeting of the Society for Neuroscience, Dallas.

7. Diamond, M.C., Connor, J.R., Orenberg, E.K., Bissell, M., Yost, M., & Krueger, A. (1980). Environmental influences on serotonin and cyclic nucleotides in rat cerebral cortex. *Science, 210*(4470), 652–654; Hopson, J.L. (1984, November). PT conversation with Marian Diamond: A love affair with the brain. *Psychology Today*, pp. 62–73.

8. Black, I.B., Adler, J.E., Dreyfus, C.F., Jonakait, G.M., Katz, D.M., LaGamma, E.F., & Markey, K.M. (1984). Neurotransmitter plasticity at the molecular level. *Science, 225*(4668), 1266– 1270; Kandel, E.R., & Schwartz, J.H. (1982). Molecular biology of learning: Modulation of transmitter release. *Science, 218*(4571), 433–443; Lavigne, M. (1983, December). The secret mind of the brain. *Columbia Magazine*, pp. 12–17.

9. Wagner, H.N. Jr., Burns, H.D., Dannals, R.B., Wong, D.F., Langstrom, B., Duelfer, T., Frost, J.J., Ravert, H.T., Links, J.M., Rosenbloom, S.B., Lukas, S.E., Kramer, A.V., & Kuhar, M.J. (1983). Im-

aging dopamine receptors in the human brain by positron tomography. *Science, 221*(4617), 1264–1266.

10. Franklin, J. (1984, July 23–31), p. 13.

11. Angell, M. (1985). Disease as a reflection of the psyche. *New England Journal of Medicine, 312*(24), 1570–1572.

12. Borysenko, J.Z. (1985). Healing motives: An interview with David C. McClelland. *Advances, 2*(2), pp. 29–41; McClelland, D.C., Alexander, C., & Marks, E. (1982). The need for power, stress, immune function, and illness among male prisoners. *Journal of Abnormal Psychology, 91*(1), 61–70.

13. McClelland, D.C. (1985, March). *Motivation and immune function in health and disease*. Presentation at the meeting of the Society of Behavioral Medicine, New Orleans.

14. Pert, C., as quoted by Baskin, Y. (1985, November). The way we act. *Science 85*, p. 96.

15. Ibid., p. 100.

16. Pert, as quoted in *Brain*/Mind *Bulletin* (1986, January 20). Pert "closet" interest in consciousness led her to opiate findings; Pursuit of peptides opens doors, p. 2.

17. Levy, S.M. (1985). Behavior as a biological response modifier: The psychoimmunoendocrine network and tumor immunology. *Behavioral Medicine Abstracts, 6*(1), 1–4.

18. Smith, E.M., & Blalock, J.E. (1981). Human lymphocyte production of corticotropin and endorphin-like substances: association with leukocyte interferon. *Proceedings of the National Academy of Sciences, 78*(12), 7530–7534; Locke, S., & Colligan, D. (1986), *The healer within*. New York: E.P. Dutton.

19. Kiecolt-Glaser, J.K., Stephens, R.E., Lipetz, P.D., Speicher, C.E., & Glaser, R. (1985). Distress and DNA repair in human lymphocytes. *Journal of Behavioral Medicine, 8*(4), 311–319; Glaser, R., Thorn, B.E., Tarr, K.L., Kiecolt-Glaser, J.K., & D'Ambrosio, S.M. (1985). Effects of stress on methyltransferase synthesis: An important DNA repair enzyme. *Health Psychology, 4*(5), 403–412.

20. Ingelfinger, F.J. (1977). Health: A matter of statistics or feeling? *New England Journal of Medicine, 296*(8), 448–449.

21. Bailar, J.C., & Smith, E.M. (1986). Progress against cancer? *New England Journal of Medicine, 314*(19), 1226–1232; Bush, H. (1984, September). Cancer, the new synthesis: Cure. *Science 84*, pp. 34–35; Kolata, G. (1985). Is the war on cancer being won? *Science, 229*(4713), 543–544.

22. Hammer, S., Dorfman, A., & Wilbur, A. (1985, August). Zeroing in on the molecular level to conquer cancer. *Science Digest*, p. 31.

23. Thomas, L. (1984). Foreword. In L. Roberts, *Cancer today: Origins, prevention, and treatment*. Washington, DC: Institute of Medicine/National Academy Press, p. ix.

24. Thomas, L. (1986, March). Getting at the roots of a deep puzzle. *Discover*, p. 65.

25. Simone, C.B. (1983). *Cancer & nutrition*. New York: McGraw-Hill, p. xiii.

26. Spring, B.J., Chiodo, J., & Bowen, D.J. (1986, March). *Behavioral effects of foods: Are we ready to use them for symptomatic relief?* Presentation at the annual meeting of the Society of Behavioral Medicine, San Francisco.

27. Borysenko, J.Z. (1982). Higher cortical function and neoplasia: Psychoneuroimmunology. In S.M. Levy (Ed.), *Biological mediators of behavior and disease: Neoplasia* (pp. 29–53). New York: Elsevier Biomedical.

28. Holden, C. (1978). Cancer and the mind: How are they connected? *Science*, *200*(4348), 1363–1369.

CHAPTER 1. IT TAKES MORE THAN GERMS

1. Rosch, P., as quoted by Newman, D.J. (1981, May 8). Stress causes cancer. *Daily Camera*, Boulder, CO, p. 26. Rosch, a clinical professor of medicine at New York Medical College, is president of the American Institute of Stress in Yonkers, NY.

2. Borysenko, J. (Speaker). (1984). *Psychoimmunology* (Healing Brain Series Cassette Recording No. T5–6). Los Altos, CA: Institute for the Study of Human Knowledge. Borysenko, trained in both psychology and immunology, teaches and does research in the division of behavioral medicine at Harvard Medical School.

3. Cunningham, A.J. (1981). Mind, body, and immune response. In R. Ader (Ed.), *Psychoneuroimmunology* (pp. 609–617). New York: Academic Press; Borysenko, M., & Borysenko, J. (1982). Stress, behavior, and immunity: Animal models and mediating mechanisms. *General Hospital Psychiatry*, *4*, 59–67.

4. Plaut, S.M., & Friedman, S.B. (1985). Biological mechanisms in the relationship of stress to illness. *Pediatric Annals*, *14*(8), 563–567.

5. Engel, G.L. (1977). The need for a new medical model: A challenge for biomedicine. *Science*, *196*(4286), 129–136.

6. Hinkle, L.E. (1974). The concept of "stress" in the biological and social sciences. *International Journal of Psychiatry in Medicine*, *5*(4), 335–357; Dubos, R. (1965). *Man adapting*. New Haven: Yale University Press; Wolf, S. (1961). Disease as a way of life: Neural integration in systematic pathology. *Perspectives in Biology and Medicine*, *4*, 288–305.

7. Wolf, S., & Goodell, H. (1976). *Behavioral science in clinical medicine*. Springfield, IL: Charles C Thomas.

8. Mason, J.W. (1975). A historical view of the stress field: II. *Journal of Human Stress*, *1*(2), 22–36.

9. Weil, A. (1983). *Health and healing*. Boston: Houghton Mifflin, p. 56.

10. Chesney, A.P., & Gentry, W.D. (1982). Psychosocial factors mediating health risk: A balanced perspective. *Preventive Medicine*, *11*, 612–617.

11. Centers for Disease Control. (1984). Smoking and cardiovascular disease. *Morbidity and Mortality Weekly Report, 32*(52), 677–679.

12. Thomas, C.B. (1981). Stamina: The thread of human life. *Journal of Chronic Diseases, 34*, p. 41.

13. Engel, G.L. (1960). A unified concept of health and disease. *Perspectives in Biology and Medicine, 3*, 459–485.

14. Price, V.A. (1982). *Type A behavior pattern: A model for research and practice.* New York: Academic Press.

15. Jemmott, J.B., Borysenko, M., Chapman, R., Borysenko, J.Z., McClelland, D., Meyer, D., & Benson, H. (1983). Academic stress, power motivation, and decrease in secretion rate of salivary immunoglobulin. *Lancet, 1*(8339), 1400–1402; Locke, S.E., Hurst, M.W., Heisel, S.J., Kraus, L., & Williams, M. (1979, March). *The influence of stress and other psychosocial factors on human immunity.* Paper presented at the annual meeting of the American Psychosomatic Society, Dallas, TX.

16. Solomon, G.F., & Moos, R.H. (1964). Emotions, immunity and disease. *Archives of General Psychiatry, 11*, 657–674; Talal, N., Frye, K., & Moutsopoulos, H. (1976). Autoimmunity. In H.H. Fundenberg, D.P. Stites, J.L. Caldwell, & J.V. Wells (Eds.), *Basic and clinical immunology.* Los Altos, CA: Lange.

17. Engel, G.L. (1971). Sudden and rapid death during psychological stress. *Annals of Internal Medicine, 74*(5), 771–782.

18. Friedman, M., & Ulmer, D. (1984). *Treating Type A behavior—and your heart.* New York: Knopf.

19. Wolf, S. (1967). The end of the rope: The role of the brain in cardiac death. *Canadian Medical Association Journal, 97*, 1022–1025.

20. Wolf, 1961.

21. Hinkle, L.E., & Wolff, H.G. (1958). Ecologic investigations of the relationship between illness, life experiences and the social environment. *Annals of Internal Medicine, 49*, 1373–1388.

22. Hinkle, L.E.,& Plummer, N. (1952). Life stress and industrial absenteeism. *Industrial Medicine and Surgery, 21*(8), 363–374.

23. Hinkle, L.E., Plummer, N., Metraux, R., Richter, P., Gittinger, J.W., Thetford, W.N., Ostfeld, A.M., Kane, F.D., Goldberger, L., Mitchell, W.E., Leichter, H., Pinsky, R., Goebel, D., Bross, I.D.J., & Wolff, H.G. (1957). Studies in human ecology. *American Journal of Psychiatry, 114*, p. 218.

24. Christenson, W.N., & Hinkle, L.E. (1961). Differences in illness and prognostic signs in two groups of young men. *Journal of the American Medical Association, 177*(4), 247–253.

25. Rose, R.M., Jenkins, C.D., & Hurst, M.W. (1978). *Air traffic controller health change study: A prospective investigation of physical, psychological and work-related changes* (Contract No. DOT-FA737WA-3211). Boston: Boston University School of Medicine.

26. Dubos, 1965, p. 164.

27. Mason, 1975, p. 33.

28. Meyer, R.J., & Haggerty, R.J. (1962). Streptococcal infections in families: Factors altering individual susceptibility. *Pediatrics, 29*, p. 539.

29. Ibid., 539–549.

30. Grade, M., & Zegans, L.S. (1986). Exploring systemic lupus erythematosus: Autoimmunity, self-destruction, and psychoneuroimmunology. *Advances, 3*(2), pp. 16–45.

31. Cohen, F., Horowitz, M.J., Lazarus, R.S., Moos, R.H., Robins, L.N., Rose, R.M., & Rutter, M. (1982). Panel report on psychosocial assets and modifiers of stress. In G.R. Elliott & C. Eisdorfer (Eds.), *Stress and human health* (pp. 149–188). New York: Springer.

32. Rabkin, J.G., & Struening, E.L. (1976). Life events, stress, and illness. *Science, 194*(4269), 1013–1020.

33. Funch, D.P., & Marshall, J. (1983). The role of stress, social support and age in survival from breast cancer. *Journal of Psychosomatic Research, 27*(1), 77–83.

34. Chesney, M.A., & Rosenman, R.H. (1983). Specificity in stress models: Examples drawn from Type A behaviour. In C.L. Cooper (Ed.), *Stress research*. Chichester, Eng.: Wiley, p. 23.

35. Solomon, G.F. (Speaker). (1982). *Emotions, stress and immunity* (Healing Brain Series Cassette Recording No. 5). Los Altos, CA: Institute for the Study of Human Knowledge.

36. Weiner, H., Thaler, M., Reiser, M.F., & Mirsky, I.A. (1957). Etiology of duodenal ulcer: I. Relation of specific psychological characteristics to rate of gastric secretion (serum pepsinogen). *Psychosomatic Medicine, 19*, 1–10.

CHAPTER 2. THE FUTURE
THAT FAILED TO SHOCK

1. Kobasa, S.O. (1984, September). Test for hardiness: How much stress can you survive? *American Health,* p. 64. Psychologist Kobasa, formerly of the University of Chicago, is now on the graduate faculty of the City University of New York.

2. Kobasa, S. (1979). Stressful life events, personality, and health: An inquiry into hardiness. *Journal of Personality and Social Psychology, 37*(1), 1–11.

3. Toffler, A. (1970). *Future shock*. New York: Random House, p. 325.

4. Kannel, W.B. (1982). Meaning of the downward trend in cardiovascular mortality. *Journal of the American Medical Association, 247*(6), 877–880; National Center for Health Statistics. (1980). *Health: United States, 1980* (DHHS Publication No. PHS 81–1232). Washington, DC: U.S. Government Printing Office; Knowles, J.H. (1977). *Doing better and feeling worse*. New York: Norton.

5. President's Commission on Mental Health (1978). *Task panel reports, Volume III*. Washington, DC: U.S. Government Printing Office.

6. Langner, T.S., & Michael, S.T. (1963). *Life stresses and mental health: The Midtown Manhattan study.* Thomas A.C. Rennie Series in Social Psychiatry, Volume II. New York: Free Press of Glencoe.

7. Regier, D.A., Myers, J.K., Kramer, M., Robins, L.N., Blazer, D.G., Hough, R.L., Eaton, W.W., & Locke, B.Z. (1984). The NIMH epidemiologic catchment area program: Historical context, major objectives, and study population characteristics. *Archives of General Psychiatry, 41*(10), 934–941.

8. Srole, L. (1975). Measurement and classification in sociopsychiatric epidemiology: Midtown Manhattan study (1954) and Midtown Manhattan restudy (1974). *Journal of Health and Social Behavior, 16*(4), 347–364.

9. Adams, W.F. (1932). *Ireland and Irish emigration to the New World.* New Haven: Yale University Press; Drolet, G.J. (1946). Epidemiology of tuberculosis. In B. Goldberg (Ed.), *Clinical tuberculosis.* Philadelphia: Davis.

10. Moorman, L.J. (1950). Tuberculosis on the Navaho reservation. *American Review of Tuberculosis, 61,* 586.

11. McDougal, J.B. (1949). *Tuberculosis—A global study in social pathology.* Baltimore: Williams & Wilkins.

12. M'Gonigle, G.C.M., & Kirb, X. (1936). *Poverty and public health.* London: Victor Gollanez.

13. Selye, H. (1976). *Stress of life* (rev. ed.). New York: McGraw-Hill.

14. Roskies, E., Iida-Miranda, M., & Strobel, M.G. (1977). Life changes as predictors of illness in immigrants. In C.D. Spielberger & I.G. Sarason (Eds.), *Stress and anxiety* (Vol. 4, pp. 3–21). Washington: Hemisphere.

15. Hinkle, L.E. (1974). The effect of exposure to culture change, social change, and changes in interpersonal relationships on health. In B.S. Dohrenwend & B.P. Dohrenwend (Eds.), *Stressful life events: Their nature and effects* (pp. 9–44). New York: Wiley.

16. Ford, A.B. (1970). Casualties of our time. *Science, 167*(3916), 256–263.

17. Hippocrates. (1938). *Works* of *Hippocrates* (Vol. 3). New York: Medical Classics.

18. Lief, A. (Ed.). (1948). *The commonsense psychiatry of Dr. Adolf Meyer* (pp. 419–420). New York: McGraw-Hill.

19. Levi, L. (1974). Psychosocial stress and disease: A conceptual model. In E.K.E. Gunderson and R.H. Rahe (Eds.), *Life stress and illness.* Springfield, IL: Charles C Thomas.

20. Selye, H. (1946). The General Adaptation Syndrome and the diseases of adaptation. *Journal of Clinical Endocrinology, 6*(2), 117–230.

21. Mason, J.W. (1974). Specificity in the organization of neuroendocrine response profiles. In P. Seeman & G.M. Brown (Eds.), *Frontiers in neurology and neuroscience research: First International Symposium of the Neuroscience Institute* (pp. 68–80). Toronto: University of Toronto Press; Lazarus, R.S. (1966). *Psychological stress and the coping process.* New York: McGraw-Hill.

22. Holmes, T.H., & Rahe, R.H. (1967). The social readjustment rating scale. *Journal of Psychosomatic Research, 11*, 213–218; Holmes & Masuda, M. (1974). Life change and illness susceptibility. In Dohrenwend & Dohrenwend, pp. 45–72.

23. Dohrenwend, B.S., & Dohrenwend, B.P. (1981). Life stress and illness: Formulation of the issues. In Dohrenwend & Dohrenwend (Eds.), *Stressful life events and their contexts* (pp. 1–27). New York: Prodist; Rabkin, J.G., & Struening, E.L. (1976). Life events, stress, and illness. *Science, 194*(4269), 1013–1020.

24. Roskies, Iida-Miranda, & Strobel, 1977, p. 17.

25. Engel, G.L. (1971). Sudden and rapid death during psychological stress. *Annals of Internal Medicine, 74*, 771–782.

26. Tuke, D.H. (1878). *Insanity in ancient and modern life.* London: Macmillan.

27. Esquirol, J.E. (1967). A treatise on insanity (1845). In C.E. Goshen (Ed.), *Documentary history of psychiatry: A source book on historical principles* (pp. 350–351). New York: Philosophical Library.

28. Osler, W. (1910). The Lumleian lectures on angina pectoris. *Lancet, 1*, 696–700, 839–844, 974–977.

29. Halliday, J.L. (1948). *Psychosocial medicine: A study of the sick society.* New York: Norton.

30. Ogburn, W.F. (1964). *William F. Ogburn on culture and social change: Selected pap*ers. Chicago: University of Chicago Press.

31. Henry, J. (1965). *Culture against man.* New York: Vintage Books.

32. Selye, 1976; Frankenhaeuser, M. (1979). Psychobiological aspects of life stress. In S. Levine & U. Holger (Eds.), *Coping and health* (pp. 202–223). New York: Plenum.

33. Selye, 1976, p. 392.

34. Kenniston, K. (1963). Social change and youth in America. In E.H. Erikson (Ed.), *Youth: Change and challenge.* New York: Basic Books.

35. Alaton, S. (1984, August 23). A comfortable jungle. *Toronto Globe and Mail*, pp. L1,L3.

36. Calhoun, J.B. (1962). Population density and social pathology. *Scientific American, 206*(2), pp. 139–150.

37. Coleman, J.C. (1973). Life stress and maladaptive behavior. *American Journal of Occupational Therapy, 27*(4), 169–180.

38. Rosch, P.J. (1979). Stress and illness. *Journal of the American Medical Association, 242*(5), p. 427.

39. Associated Press. (1983, August 5). 5-count indictment against Lavelle alleges perjury. *Houston Post*, p. 17A.

40. Sutton, L. (1978, March 2). Worker's stress claim setback for employers. *Austin American-Statesman.*

41. United Press International. (1983, June 18). Hare Krishnas ordered to pay $32.3 million in damages to women. *Houston Post*, p. 9C.

42. Beaber, R.J. (1983, April 4). Stress--and other scapegoats. *Newsweek*, p. 13.

43. Dubos, R. (1965). *Man adapting*. New Haven: Yale University Press, p. 323.

44. Borysenko, J. (Speaker). (1983). *Psychoimmunology* (Healing Brain Series Cassette Recording No. T5–6). Los Altos, CA: Institute for the Study of Human Knowledge.

45. Hamburg, D.A. (1982). An outlook on stress research and health. In G.R. Elliott & C. Eisdorfer (Eds.), *Stress and human health* (pp. ix–xxii). New York: Springer.

46. Frankenhaeuser, 1979.

47. Maddi, S.R., & Kobasa, S.C. (1984). *The hardy executive: Health under stress*. Homewood, IL: Dow Jones-Irwin.

48. Borysenko, M., & Borysenko, J. (1982). Stress, behavior and immunity: Animal models and mediating mechanisms. *General Hospital Psychiatry, 4*, 59–67.

49. McClelland, D.C., Floor, E., Davidson, R.J., & Saron, C. (1980). Stressed power motivation, sympathetic activation, immune function, and illness. *Journal of Human Stress, 6*(2) 11–19.

50. Engel, G.L. (1968). A life setting conducive to illness: The giving up-given up complex. *Bulletin of the Menninger Clinic, 32*, 355–365.

51. Williams, R.B. Jr., Haney, T.L., Lee, K.L., Kong, Y-H., Blumenthal, J.A., & Whalen, R.E. (1980). Type A behavior, hostility, and coronary atherosclerosis. *Psychosomatic Medicine, 42*(6), 539–549.

52. Hamburg, D.A., Elliott, G.R., & Parron, D.L. (Eds.). (1982). *Health and behavior: Frontiers of research in the biobehavioral sciences*. Washington: National Academy Press, p. 65.

53. Scharrer, E., & Scharrer, B. (1963). *Neuroendocrinology*. New York: Columbia University Press.

54. Guillemin, R. (1978). Peptides in the brain: The new endocrinology of the neuron. *Science, 202*(4366), 390–402.

55. Schally, A.V. (1978). Aspects of hypothalamic regulation of the pituitary gland. *Science, 202*(4363), 18–28.

56. Pert, C.B., Pasternak, G., & Snyder, S.H. (1973). Opiate agonists and antagonists discriminated by receptor binding in brain. *Science, 182*(4119), 1359–1361.

57. Franklin, J. (1984, July 23–31). The mind fixers. *Baltimore Evening Sun* reprint series.

58. Melnechuk, T. (1985). Reports on selected conferences and workshops. *Advances, 2*(3), pp. 54–58.

59. Pert, C.B., Ruff, M.R., Weber, R.J., and Herkenham, M. (1985). Neuropeptides and their receptors: A psychosomatic network. *Journal of Immunology, 135*(2), 820s-826s.

60. Franklin, 1984, p. 7.

61. Robinson, D.N., & Uttal, W.R. (1983). *Foundations of psychobiology*. New York: Macmillan.

62. Coyne, J.C., & Lazarus, R.S. (1980). Cognitive style, stress, perception, and coping. In I.L. Kutash, L.B. Schlesinger and associates (Eds.),

Handbook on stress and anxiety (pp. 144– 158). San Francisco: Jossey-Bass; Hamburg, Elliott, & Parron, 1982.

63. Selye, 1976, p. 450.

CHAPTER 3. THOSE WHO STAY HEALTHY

1. Kobasa, S. (1984, September). Test for hardiness: How much stress can you survive? *American Health*, p. 64.

2. Kobasa, S.C. (1979). Stressful life events, personality and health: An inquiry into hardiness. *Journal of Personality and Social Psychology, 37*(1), 1–11; Kobasa, 1984.

3. Kobasa, S.C., Maddi, S.R., & Courington, S. (1981). Personality and constitution as mediators in the stress-illness relationship. *Journal of Health and Social Behavior, 22*, p. 368.

4. Kobasa, S.C. (1982a). Commitment and coping in stress resistance among lawyers. *Journal of Personality and Social Psychology, 42*(4), 707–717.

5. Kobasa, S.C. (1982b). The hardy personality: Toward a social psychology of stress and health. In J. Suls & G. Sanders (Eds.), *Social psychology of health and illness*. Hillsdale, NJ: Erlbaum, p. 27.

6. Kobasa, 1982b.

7. Maddi, S.R. & Kobasa, S.C. (1984). *The hardy executive: Health under stress*. Homewood, IL: Dow Jones-Irwin.

8. Kobasa, S.C., Maddi, S.R., & Kahn, S. (1982c). Hardiness and health: A prospective study. *Journal of Personality and Social Psychology, 42*(1), 168–177.

9. Maddi & Kobasa, 1984.

10. Thompson, S.C. (1981). Will it hurt less if I can control it? A complex answer to a simple question. *Psychological Bulletin, 90*(1), p. 89.

11. McClelland, D.C., Ross, G., & Patel, V. (1985). The effect of an academic examination on salivary norepinephrine and immunoglobulin levels. *Journal of Human Stress, 11*(2), 52–59; McClelland, D.C., Alexander, C., & Marks, E. (1982). The need for power, stress, immune function, and illness among male prisoners. *Journal of Abnormal Psychology, 91*(1), 61–70.

12. Antonovsky, A. (1979). *Health, stress, and coping*. San Francisco: Jossey-Bass.

13. Boyce, W.T., Schaefer, C., & Uitti, C. (1985). Permanence and change: Psychological factors in the outcome of adolescent pregnancy. *Social Science & Medicine, 21*(1), 1279–1287.

14. Averill, J.P. (1973). Personal control over aversive stimuli and its relationship to stress. *Psychological Bulletin, 80*, 286– 303.

15. Maddi & Kobasa, 1984, p. 28.

16. Ibid.

17. Justice, B. (In press). Stress, coping and health outcomes. In M. Russell (Ed.), *Clinical management of stress in medicine*. Elmsford, NY: Pergamon.

18. Blotcky, A.D., & Tittler, B.I. (1982). Psychosocial predictors of physical illness: Toward a holistic model of health. *Preventive Medicine, 11*, 602–611.

19. Elliott, G.R., & Eisdorfer, C. (Eds.). (1982). *Stress and human health*. New York: Springer.

20. Wolff, H.G. (1968). *Stress and disease*. Springfield, IL: Charles C Thomas.

21. Borysenko, M., & Borysenko, J. (1982). Stress, behavior, and immunity: Animal models and mediating mechanisms. *General Hospital Psychiatry, 4*, 59–67.

22. Glass, D.C. (1977). Stress, behavior patterns, & coronary disease. *American Scientist, 65*, 177–187.

23. Hinkle, L.E., & Wolff, H.G. (1957). Health and the social environment: Experimental investigations. In A.H. Leighton, J.A. Clausen, & R.N. Wilson (Eds.). *Explorations in Social Psychiatry* (pp. 105–132). New York: Basic Books.

24. Hinkle, L.E., Christenson, W.N., Kane, F.D., Ostfeld, A., Thetford, W.N., & Wolff, H.G. (1958). An investigation of the relation between life experience, personality characteristics, and general susceptibility to illness. *Psychosomatic Medicine, 20*(4), 278–295.

25. Hinkle, L.E., Christenson, W.N., & Wolff, H.G. (1959). Hungarian refugees: Life experiences and features influencing participation in the revolution and subsequent flight. *American Journal of Psychiatry, 116*, 16–19.

26. Hinkle, L.E. (1965, August). Studies of human ecology in relation to health and behavior. *BioScience*, 517–520.

27. Roskies, E., Iida-Miranda, M., & Strobel, M.G. (1977). Life changes as predictors of illness in immigrants. In C.D. Spielberger & I.G. Sarason (Eds.), *Stress and anxiety* (Vol. 4, pp. 3–21). Washington: Hemisphere.

28. Reed, D., McGee, D., & Yano, K. (1984). Psychosocial processes and general susceptibility to chronic disease. *American Journal of Epidemiology, 119*(3), 356–370.

29. Hamburg, D.A. (1982). Foreword: An outlook on stress research and health. In G.R. Elliott & C. Eisdorfer (Eds.), *Stress and human health*. New York: Springer, p. xi.

30. Folkman, S., Schaefer, C., & Lazarus, R.S. (1979). Cognitive processes as mediators of stress and coping. In V. Hamilton & D. Warburton (Eds.), *Human stress and cognition* (p. 268). Chichester, Eng.: Wiley; Coyne, J.C., & Lazarus, R.S. (1980). Cognitive style, stress, perception, and coping. In I.L. Kutash, L.B. Schlesinger and associates (Eds.), *Handbook on stress and anxiety* (p. 153). San Francisco: Jossey-Bass.

31. Wolf, S., & Shepard, E.M. (1950). An appraisal of factors that evoke and modify the hypertensive reaction pattern. In *Life stress and bodily*

disease: Volume XXIX of the Proceedings of the Association for Research in Nervous and Mental Disease. Baltimore: Williams & Wilkins, p. 983.

32. Selye, H. (1976). *Stress in health and disease.* Boston: Butterworths.

33. Katz, J.L., Weiner, H., Gallagher, T.F., & Hellman, L. (1970). Stress, distress, and ego defenses. *Archives of General Psychiatry, 23,* 131–142.

34. Rahe, R.H., & Arthur, R.J. (1978). Life change and illness studies: Past history and future directions. *Journal of Human Stress, 5*(1), 3–15.

35. Ursano, R.J., Boydstun, J., & Wheatley, R. (1981). Psychiatric illness in U.S. Air Force Viet Nam prisoners of war. *American Journal of Psychiatry, 138*(3), 310–314.

36. Singer, M.T. (1981). Viet'Nam prisoners of war, stress, and personality resiliency. *American Journal of Psychiatry, 138* (3), pp. 345–346.

37. Dimsdale, J.E. (1974). The coping behavior of Nazi concentration camp survivors. *American Journal of Psychiatry, 131*(7), p.792.

38. Ibid., p. 793.

39. Antonovsky, A., Maoz, B., Dowty, N., & Wijsenbeek, H. (1971). Twenty-five years later: A limited study of the sequelae of the concentration camp experience. *Social Psychiatry, 6*(4), 186–193.

40. Ibid., p. 186.

41. Mahl, G.F. (1949). Effects of chronic fear in the gastric secretion of HCl in dogs. *Psychosomatic Medicine, 11*(1), 30–44.

42. Gröen, J.J. (1957). *De psychopathogenese van het ulcus ventriculi et duodeni; karakterstructuren en emotioneele believenissen en hun beteekenis voor aetiologie en therapie.* Amsterdam: Scheltema & Holkema's Boekhandel.

43. Svendsen, B. (1953). Fluctuations of Danish psychiatric admission rates in World War II: Initial decrease and subsequent increase (1939–1948). *Psychiatry, 27*(1), 19–37.

44. Schwab, J.J., & Schwab, M.E. (1978). *Sociocultural roots of mental illness: An epidemiologic survey.* New York: Plenum.

45. Middleton, W. (1947). Medicine in the European Theater of Operations. *Annals of Internal Medicine, 26,* 191.

46. Davis, S. (1956). Stress in combat. *Scientific American, 194*(3), pp. 31-35.

47. Gal, R., & Lazarus, R.S. (1975). The role of activity in anticipating and confronting stressful situations. *Journal of Human Stress, 1*(4), p. 7.

48. Bourne, P.G., Rose, R.M., & Mason, J.W. (1968). 17–OHCS levels in combat: Special forces "A" team under threat of attack. *Archives of General Psychiatry, 19,* 135–140.

49. Bourne, P.G., Rose, R.M., & Mason, J.W. (1967). Urinary 17–OHCS levels: Data on seven helicopter ambulance medics in combat. *Archives of General Psychiatry, 17,* 104–110.

50. Locke, S.E., & Heisel, J.E. (1977). The influence of stress and emotions on human immunity. (Abstract). *Biofeedback Self-Regulation, 2,* 320.

51. Locke, S.E. (1982). Stress, adaptation, and immunity. *General Hospital Psychiatry, 4,* 49–58.

52. Locke, S.E., Kraus, L., Leserman, J., Hurst, M.W., Heisel, J.S., & Williams, R.M. (1984). Life change stress, psychiatric symptoms and natural killer cells activity. *Psychosomatic Medicine, 46*(5), 441–453.

53. Miller, J.A. (1986, May 31). Immunity and crises, large and small. *Science News,* p. 340.

54. McClelland, D.C., Floor, E., Davidson, R.J., & Saron, C. (1980). Stressed power motivation, sympathetic activation, immune function, and illness. *Journal of Human Stress, 6*(2), 11–19.

55. Kemeny, M. (1984, August). *Psychological and immunological prediction of recurrence in Herpes Simplex II.* Paper presented at the annual meeting of the American Psychological Association, Toronto, Canada.

56. Baker, G.H.B., Byrom, N.A., Irani, M.S., Brewerton, D.A., Hobbs, J.R., Wood, R.J., & Nagvekar, N.M. (1984). Stress, cortisol, and lymphocyte subpopulations. *Lancet, 1*(8376), 574.

57. Good, R.A. (1981). Foreword: Interactions of the body's major networks. In R. Ader (Ed.), *Psychoneuroimmunology* (p. xvi). New York: Academic Press.

58. Borysenko, J. (1984). Psychoneuroimmunology: Behavioral factors and the immune response. *ReVision, 7*(1), 56–65.

59. Marx, J.L. (1985). The immune system "belongs in the body." *Science, 227*(4691), 1190–1192.

60. Miller, J.A. (1984, Dec. 8). Immunity: Two sides of the brain, *Science News,* p. 357.

61. Koff, W.C., & Dunegan, M.A. (1985). Modulation of macrophage-mediated tumoricidal activity by neuropeptides and neurohormones. *Journal of Immunology, 135*(1), 350–354.

62. Williams, R.B. Jr., Haney, T.L., Lee, K.L., Kong, Y-H., Blumenthal, J.A., & Whalen, R.E. (1980). Type A behavior, hostility, and coronary atherosclerosis. *Psychosomatic Medicine, 42*(6), 539–549.

63. Barefoot, J.C., Dahlstrom, W.G., & Williams, R.B. (1983). Hostility, coronary heart disease incidence, and total mortality: A 25-year follow-up study of 255 physicians. *Psychosomatic Medicine, 45*(1), 59–63.

64. Glass, D.C. (1977). Stress, behavior patterns, and coronary disease. *American Scientist, 65,* 177–187; Friedman, M., & Rosenman, R.H. (1975). *Type A behavior and your heart.* Greenwich, CT: Fawcett Crest.

65. Price, V.A. (1982). *Type A behavior pattern: A model for research and practice.* New York: Academic Press.

66. Marx, J.L. (1980). Coronary artery spasms and heart disease. *Science, 208*(4448), 1127–1130; Braunwald, E. (1981). Coronary artery spasm. *Journal of the American Medical Association, 244*(17), 1957–1959.

67. Kannel, W.B., Castelli, W.P., Gordon, T., & McNamara, P.M. (1971). Serum cholesterol, lipoproteins, and the risk of coronary heart disease: The Framingham study. *Annals of Internal Medicine, 74*(1), 1–12; Fessel, W.J. (1980). High uric acid as an indicator of cardiovascular disease: Independence from obesity. *American Journal of Medi-*

cine, 68(3), 401–404; Thomas, P.D., Goodwin, J.M., & Goodwin, J.S. (1985). Effect of social support on stress-related changes in cholesterol level, uric acid level, and immune function in an elderly sample. *American Journal of Psychiatry, 142*(6), 735–737.

68. Kiecolt-Glaser, J.K., Stephens, R.E., Lipetz, P.D., Speicher, C.E., & Glaser, R. (1985). Distress and DNA repair in human lymphocytes. *Journal of Behavioral Medicine, 8*(4), 311–319; Glaser, R., Thorn, B.E., Tarr, K.L., Kiecolt-Glaser, J.K., & D'Ambrosio, S.M. (1985). Effects of stress on methyltransferase synthesis: An important DNA repair enzyme. *Health Psychology, 4*(5), 403– 412.

69. Research on stress hormones: Powerful agents in health and disease. (1986, Summer). *The Salk Institute Newsletter*, pp. 2–3.

CHAPTER 4. BRAIN MESSENGERS AND
WHAT THEY MEAN TO HEALTH

1. Rush, J., as quoted by Harrell, A. (1984, August 31). UTHSCD researchers look at brain blood flow and mental illness. University of Texas Health Science Center at Dallas *News*, p. 2. Rush is a research psychiatrist at UTHSC, Dallas.

2. Ornstein, R. (Speaker). (1984). *The amazing brain* (Series on the Healing Brain Cassette Recording No. AMBR1). Los Altos, CA: Institute for the Study of Human Knowledge. Ornstein is a professor of human biology at Stanford University in Palo Alto, CA.

3. Restak, R.M. (1979). *The brain: The last frontier*. New York: Warner Books, p. 324. Restak, a specialist in both neurology and psychiatry, is on the clinical faculty of Georgetown University School of Medicine in Washington, DC.

4. Hamburg, D.A., Elliott, G.R., & Parron, D.L. (Eds.). (1982). *Health and behavior: Frontiers of research in the biobehavioral sciences*. Washington, DC: National Academy Press.

5. Price, V.A. (1982). *Type A behavior pattern: A model for research and practice*. New York: Academic Press; Ornish, D. (1982). *Stress, diet and your heart*. New York: Signet; Williams, R.B. Jr., Lane, J.D., Kuhn, C.M., Melosh, W., White, A.D., & Schanberg, S.M. (1982). Type A behavior and elevated physiological and neuroendocrine responses to cognitive tasks. *Science, 218*(4571), 483–485.

6. Borysenko, J. (1982). Behavioral-physiological factors in the development and management of cancer. *General Hospital Psychi*atry, *4*, 69–74.

7. Ahluwalia, P., Zacharko, R.M., & Anisman, H. (1985, October). *Dopamine variations associated with acute and chronic stressors*. Presentation at the annual meeting of the Society for Neuroscience, Dallas.

8. Bandura, A. (1985). Catecholamine secretion as a function of perceived self-efficacy. *Journal of Consulting and Clinical Psychology, 53*(3), 406–414; Rodin, J. (1979). Managing the stress of aging: The role

of control and coping. In S. Levine and U. Holger (Eds.), *Coping and health* (pp. 171–202). New York: Plenum.

9. Melnechuk, T. (1985). Reports on selected conferences and workshops. *Advances, 2*(3), pp. 54–58; Bloom, F.E. (1981). Neuropeptides. *Scientific American, 245*(4), pp. 148–168.

10. Baskin, Y. (1985, November). The way we act. *Science 85*, pp. 94–100.

11. Siever, L.J., & Davis, K.L. (1985). Overview: Toward a dysregulation hypothesis of depression. *American Journal of Psychiatry, 142*(9), 1017–1031.

12. Pert, C.B., Ruff, M.R., Weber, R.J., & Herkenham, M. (1985). Neuropeptides and their receptors: A psychosomatic network. *Journal of Immunology, 135*(2), 820s-826s.

13. Martinez, J.L. (1985, August). *Enkephalins: Hormonal modulators of learning and memory*. Paper presented at the annual meeting of the American Psychological Association, Los Angeles.

14. Weisburd, S. (1984, April 7). Food for mind and mood. *Science News*, pp. 216–219.

15. Restak, 1979.

16. Weiss, J.M., Glazer, H.I., Pohorecky, L.A., Bailey, W.H., & Schneider, L.H. (1979). Coping behavior and stress-induced behavioral depression: Studies of the role of brain catecholamines. In R.A. Depue (Ed.), *The psychology of the depressive disorders* (pp. 125–160). New York: Academic Press.

17. Vale, W., Spiess, J., Rivier, C., & Rivier, J. (1981). Characterization of a 41-residue ovine hypothalamic peptide that stimulates secretion of corticotropin and beta-endorphin. *Science, 213*(4514), 1394–1397.

18. Corticotropin releasing factor: A brain peptide hormone with multiple effects. (1982, Spring). *The Salk Institute Newsletter*, pp. 1–3.

19. Koob, G.F. (1983, March). *Behavioral effects of central nervous system peptides*. Presentation at seminar on Frontiers of Research in the Neurosciences, Cornell University Medical College, New York.

20. Brain peptides: The molecular key to stress. (1985, Spring). *The Salk Institute Newsletter*, pp. 1,4.

21. Shekelle, R.B., Raynor, W.J., Ostfeld, A.M., Garron, D.C., Bieliauskas, L.A., Liu, S.C., Maliza, C., & Paul, O. (1981). Psychological depression and 17-year risk of death from cancer. *Psychosomatic Medicine, 43*(2), 117–125.

22. Rubenstein, E. (1980). Diseases caused by impaired communication among cells. *Scientific American, 242*(3), pp. 102–121.

23. Hedrick, S.M., Nielsen, E.A., Kavaler, J., Cohen, D.I., & Davis, M.M. (1984). Isolation of cDNA clones encoding T cell-specific membrane-associated proteins. *Nature, 308*, 149–153; Yanagi, Y., Yoshikai, Y., Leggett, K., Clark, S.P., Aleksander, I., & Mak, T.W. (1984). A human T-cell-specific cDNA clone encodes a protein having extensive homology to immunoglobulin chains. *Nature, 308*, 145–149.

24. Saito, H., Krantz, D.M., Takagaki, Y., Hayday, A.C., Eisen, H.N., &

Tonegawa, S. (1984). Complete primary structure of a heterodimeric T-cell receptor deduced from cDNA sequences. *Nature, 309,* 757–762.

25. Reis, D.J. (1983, March). *The brain, emotion, and the control of circulation: The neurobiology of hypertension.* Presentation at a seminar on Frontiers of Research in the Neurosciences, Cornell University Medical College, New York.

26. Dreher, H. (1985). American Heart Association considers stress. *Advances, 2*(3), pp. 47–52.

27. Levine, J.D., Clark, R., Devor, M., Helms, C., Moskowitz, M.A., & Basbaum, A.I. (1984). Intraneuronal substance P contributes to the severity of experimental arthritis. *Science, 226* (4674), 547–548.

28. Olson, S. (1985, April). Following aspirin's trail. *Science 85,* p. 20; Escoubet, B., Amsallem, P., Ferrary, E., & Huy, T.B. (1985). Prostaglandin synthesis by the cochlea of the guinea pig. Influence of aspirin, gentamicin, and acoustic stimulation. *Prostaglandins, 29*(4), 589–599.

29. Ziporyn, T. (1985). PET scans "relate clinical picture to more specific nerve function." *Journal of the American Medical Association, 253*(7), 943–949.

30. Lewin, R. (1985). Parkinson's disease: An environmental cause? *Science, 229*(4710), 257–258.

31. Miller, J.A. (1985, November 2). Cell transplants into monkeys and human brains. *Science News,* p. 276.

32. Björklund, A., Stenevi, U., Dunnett, S.B., & Gage, F.H. (1982). Cross-species neural grafting in a rat model of Parkinson's disease. *Nature, 298*(5875), 652–654; Kolata, G. (1983). Brain grafting work shows promise. *Science, 221*(4617), 1277.

33. Phelps, M.E., & Mazziotta, J.C. (1985). Positron emission tomography: Human brain function and biochemistry. *Science, 228*(4701), 799–809.

34. PET projects with psychiatric drugs. (1986, May 10). *Science News,* p. 296.

35. Wagner, H.N. Jr., Burns, H.D., Dannals, R.F., Wong, D.F., Langstrom, B., Duelfer, T., Frost, J.J., Ravert, H.T., Links, J.M., Rosenbloom, S.B., Lukas, S.E., Kramer, A.V., & Kuhar, M.J. (1983). Imaging dopamine receptors in the human brain by positron tomography. *Science, 221*(4617), 1264–1266.

36. Wong, D.F., Wagner, H.N. Jr., Dannals, R.F., Links, J.M., Frost, J.J., Ravert, H.T., Wilson, A.A., Rosenbaum, A.E., Gjedde, A., Douglass, K.H., Petronis, J.D., Folstein, M.F., Toung, J.K., Burns, H.D., & Kuhar, M.J. (1984). Effects of age on dopamine and serotonin receptors measured by positron tomography in the living human brain. *Science, 226*(4681), 1393–1396.

37. Parkinson, D., & Daw, N.W. (1985, October). *Muscarinic receptors in visual cortex in cat, macaque and human.* Presentation at the annual meeting of the Society for Neuroscience, Dallas.

343

38. Gash, D., & Sladek, J. (Eds.). (1984). *Neural transplants development and function.* New York: Plenum.

39. Harbaugh, R.E., Roberts, D.W., Coombs, D.W., Saunders, R.L., & Reeder, T.M. (1984). Preliminary report: Intracranial cholinergic drug infusion in patients with Alzheimer's disease. *Neurosurgery, 15*(4), 514–518.

40. Iversen, S.D. (1981). Neuropeptides: Do they integrate body and brain? *Nature, 291,* 454.

41. Krieger, D.T., & Martin, J.B. Brain peptides II. (1981). *New England Journal of Medicine, 304*(16), 944–951.

42. Wender, P.H., & Klein, D.F. (1981). *Mind, mood, and medicine.* New York: Meridian.

43. Wilbur, R. (1986, March). A drug to fight cocaine. *Science 86,* pp. 42–46.

44. Franklin, J. (1984, July). The mind fixers. *Baltimore Evening Sun* reprint series.

45. Waldmeier, P.C. (1981). Noradrenergic transmission in depression: Under or overfunction? *Pharmacopsychiatry, 14,* 3–9.

46. Gold, P.W., Loriaux, D.L., Roy, A., Kling, M.A., Calabrese, J.R., Kellner, C.H., Nieman, L.K., Post, R.M., Pickar, D., Gallucci, W., Avgerinos, P., Paul, S., Oldfield, E.H., Cutler, G.B., & Chrousos, G.P. (1986). Responses to corticotropin-releasing hormone in the hypercortisolism of depression and Cushing's disease. *New England Journal of Medicine, 314*(21), 1329–1335.

47. Barnes, D.M. (1986). Steroids may influence changes in mood. *Science, 232*(4756), 2344–1345.

48. Turkington, C. (1985, September). Endorphins: Natural opiates confer pain, pleasure, immunity. *APA Monitor,* p. 19.

49. Träskman, L., Asberg, M., Bertilsson, L., & Sjöstrand, L. (1981). Monoamine metabolites in CSF and suicidal behavior. *Archives of General Psychiatry, 38,* 631–636.

50. Ballenger, J.C., Goodwin, F.K., Major, L.F., & Brown, G.L. (1979). Alcohol and central serotonin metabolism in man. *Archives of General Psychiatry, 36,* 224–227.

51. Rosenthal, N.E., Davenport, Y., Cowdry, R.W., Webster, M.H., & Goodwin, F.K. (1980). Monoamine metabolites in cerebrospinal fluid of depressive subgroups. *Psychiatry Research, 2,* 113–119.

52. Neimark, J. (1986, March). Mood and health: Right brain blues. *American Health,* p. 18.

53. Drake, R., as quoted in *Brain/Mind Bulletin* (1984, November 19). Power of beliefs, optimism tied to hemispheres, p. 1; Drake, R.A. (1984). Familiarity-and-liking relationship under conditions of induced lateral orientation. *International Journal of Neuroscience, 23,* 195–198.

54. Torrey, E.F. (1983). *Surviving schizophrenia.* New York: Harper & Row.

55. Ornstein, R., & Thompson, R.F. (1984). *The amazing brain.* Boston: Houghton Mifflin.

1. Rosenthal, N., as quoted in The food-mood link (1985, October 14). *Newsweek*, p. 94. Rosenthal, with the National Institute of Mental Health, has also found that people who get the "winter blues" crave carbohydrates and seem to try to self-medicate by increasing their levels of serotonin in the brain.

2. Revkin, A.C. (1985, April). Lunching to win. *Science Digest*, p. 36. Revkin is a writer for *Science Digest* and interviewed Wurtman and other leading authorities on food acting like drugs in the brain.

3. Gelman, D., King, P., Hager, M., Raine, G., & Pratt, J. (1985, October 14). The food-mood link. *Newsweek*, pp. 93–94.

4. Weisburd, S. (1984, April 7). Food for mind and mood. *Science News*, pp. 216–219.

5. Wurtman, J.J. (1984). The involvement of brain serotonin in excessive carbohydrate snacking by obese carbohydrate cravers. *Journal of the American Dietetics Association, 84*(9), 1004–1007.

6. Chiodo, J. (1986, March). *Psychological and expectancy effects in diet and behavior*. Presentation at the annual meeting of the Society of Behavioral Medicine, San Francisco.

7. Wurtman, R.J. (1983). Behavioural effects of nutrients. *Lancet, 1*(8334), 1145–1147.

8. Glassman, A.H., Jackson, W.K., Walsh, B.T., Roose, S.P., & Rosenfeld, B. (1984). Cigarette craving, smoking withdrawal, and clonidine. *Science, 226*(4676), 864–866.

9. Wurtman, R.J., as quoted by Weisburd, 1984, p. 216.

10. Revkin, 1985, pp. 36–37.

11. Wurtman, R.J. (1982/1983). Introduction [to papers on the effect of nutrients on mood and behavior]. *Journal of Psychiatric Research, 17*(2), p. 102.

12. Leathwood, P.D., & Pollet, P. (1982/1983). Diet-induced mood changes in normal populations. *Journal of Psychiatric Research, 17*(2), 147–154.

13. Wright, J.V. (1979). *Dr. Wright's book of nutritional therapy*. Emmaus, PA: Rodale Press.

14. Wurtman, R.J. (1982). Nutrients that modify brain function. *Scientific American, 246*(4), pp. 50–59.

15. Gelenberg, A.J., Wojcik, J.D., Gibson, C.J., & Wurtman, R.J. (1982/1983). Tyrosine for depression. *Journal of Psychiatric Research, 17*(2), 175–180.

16. Spring, B., Maller, O., Wurtman, J., Digman, L., & Cozolino, L. (1982/1983). Effects of protein and carbohydrate meals on mood and performance: Interactions with sex and age. *Journal of Psychiatric Research, 17*(2), 155–167.

17. Spring, B. (1986, March). *Possible mechanisms underlying diet-behavior effects*. Presentation at the annual meeting of the Society of Behavioral Medicine, San Francisco.

18. Sabelli, H.C., Fawcett, J., Gusovsky, F., Javaid, J., Edwards, J., & Jeffriess, H. (1983). Urinary phenyl acetate: A diagnostic test for depression? *Science, 220*(4602), 1187–1188.

19. Pollner, F., Alsofrom, J., Green, R., & Gonzalez, L. (1983, October 24). Phenylalanine: A psychoactive nutrient for some depressives? *Medical World News*, pp. 21–22.

20. Koehler, S.M., & Hartje, J.C. (1985, March). *Migraine headache and phenylalanine.* Poster presentation at the meeting of the Society of Behavioral Medicine, New Orleans.

21. Wurtman, R.J. (1983). Neurochemical changes following high-dose aspartame with dietary carbohydrates. *New England Journal of Medicine, 309*(7), 429–430.

22. Lieberman, H.R., Corkin, S., Spring, B.J., Growdon, J.H., & Wurtman, R.J. (1982/1983). Mood, performance, and pain sensitivity: Changes induced by food constituents. *Journal of Psychiatric Research, 17*(2), 135–145.

23. Weisburd, 1984, p. 219.

24. Wilbur, R. (1986, March). A drug to fight cocaine. *Science 86*, pp. 42–46.

25. Shamoon, A. (1986, May). Tryptophan turn-on turns off pain. *American Health*, p. 22.

26. Bowen, D.J. (1986, March). *Overview of food selection: Physiological, behavioral, psychological and social influences.* Presentation at the annual meeting of the Society of Behavioral Medicine, San Francisco.

27. Nadi, N.S., Nurnberger, J.I. Jr., & Gershon, E.S. (1984). Muscarinic cholinergic receptors on skin fibroblasts in familial affective disorder. *New England Journal of Medicine, 311*(4), 225–230.

28. Manic-depressive disorder: Can a skin test predict who will have it? (1984, Sept. 10). *Medical World News*, p. 88.

29. Bandura, A. (1986, March). *Perceived self-efficacy and health functioning.* Paper presented at the annual meeting of the Society of Behavioral Medicine, San Francisco.

30. Simone, C.B. (1983). *Cancer & nutrition.* New York: McGraw-Hill.

31. Jose, D.G., & Good, R.A. (1971). Absence of enhancing antibody in cell mediated immunity to tumor heterografts in protein deficient rats. *Nature, 231*, 323–325; Aschkenasy, A. (1975). Dietary proteins and amino acids in leucopoiesis: Recent hematological and immunological data. *World Review of Nutrition and Dietetics, 21*, 151–197.

32. Krieger, D.T., & Martin, J.B. (1981). Brain peptides I. *New England Journal of Medicine, 304*(15), 876–885; Sasek, C.A., & Elde, R.P. (1985, October). *Coexistence of enkephalin and dynorphin immunoreactivity in neurons in the dorsal gray commissure of the lumbosacral spinal cord in rat.* Presentation at the meeting of the Society of Neuroscience, Dallas.

33. Pert, C.B., & Snyder, S.H. (1973). Opiate receptor: Demonstration in nervous tissue. *Science, 179*(4077), 1011–1014.

34. Shamoon, A. (1986, March). Switched-on pain relief: Shocking alternative to novocaine needs no needles. *American Health*, p. 20.

35. Berger, P.A. (Speaker). (1982). *Endorphins and mental health* (Series on the Healing Brain Cassette Recording). Los Altos, CA: Institute for the Study of Human Knowledge.

36. Goldstein, A. (1976). Opioid peptides (endorphins) in pituitary and brain. *Science, 193*(4258), 1081–1086.

37. Foley, K.M. (1983, March). Current concepts of pain. Presentation at a seminar on Frontiers of Research in the Neurosciences, Cornell University Medical College, New York.

38. Johnson, H.M., Smith, E.M., Torres, B.A., & Blalock, J.E. (1982). Regulation of the in vitro antibody response by neuroendocrine hormones. *Proceedings of the National Academy of Sciences, 79*, 4171–4174.

39. Turkington, C. (1985, September). Endorphins: Natural opiates confer pain, pleasure, immunity. *APA Monitor*, pp. 17–19.

40. Gilman, S.C., Schwartz, J.M., Milner, R.J., Bloom, F.E., & Feldman, J.D. (1981). Beta-endorphin enhances lymphocyte proliferative responses. *Proceedings of the National Academy of Sciences, 79*, 4226–4230; Mathews, P.M., Froelich, C.J., Sibbitt, W.L., & Bankhurst, A.D. (1983). Enhancement of natural cytotoxicity by beta-endorphin. *Journal of Immunology, 130*, 1658–1662.

41. Shavit, Y., Lewis, J.W., Terman, G.W., Gale, R.P., & Liebeskind, J.C. (1984). Opioid peptides mediate the suppressive effect of stress on natural killer cell cytotoxicity. *Science, 223*(4632), 188–190.

42. Roundup. (1984, Oct. 22). *Brain/Mind Bulletin*, p. 2.

43. Van Epps, D. & Saland, L. (1984). Beta-endorphin and met-enkephalin stimulate human peripheral blood mononuclear cell chemotaxis. *Journal of Immunology, 132*, 3046–3053.

44. Levy, S.M. (1985). Behavior as a biological response modifier: The psychoimmunoendocrine network and tumor immunology. *Behavioral Medicine Abstracts, 6*(1), 1–4.

45. Goleman, D. (1985). Opioids and denial: Two mechanisms for bypassing pain. *Advances, 2*(3), pp. 35–45.

46. Mandenoff, A., Fumeron, F., & Apfelbaum, M., & Margules, D.L. (1982). Endogenous opiates and energy balance. *Science, 215* (4539), 1536–1537.

47. Martinez, J.L. (1985, August). Enkephalins: Hormonal modulators of learning and memory. Paper presented at the meeting of the American Psychological Association, Los Angeles.

48. Davis, J. (1984). *Endorphins*. Garden City, NY: Dial.

49. Carr, D.B., Bullen, B.A., Skrinar, G.S., Arnold, M.A., Rosenblatt, M., Beitins, I.Z., Martin, J.B., McArthur, J.W. (1981). Physical conditioning facilitates the exercise-induced secretion of beta-endorphin and beta-lipotropin in women. *New England Journal of Medicine, 305*(10), 560–563; Bortz, W.M., Angwin, P., & Mefford, I.N. (1981). Catecholamines, dopamine, and endorphin levels during extreme exercise. *New England Journal of Medicine*, 305(10), 466–467.

50. Levine, J. (Speaker). (1982). *Pain, placebos and endorphins* (Series on

the Healing Brain Cassette Recording). Los Altos, CA: Institute for the Study of Human Knowledge.

51. Goldstein, A. (1980). Thrills in response to music and other stimuli. *Physiological Psychology, 8*(1), 126–129; See also Ornstein, R., & Thompson, R.F. (1984). *The amazing brain.* Boston: Houghton Mifflin.

52. Jones, E.G. (1983, March). *The structure of the cerebral cortex.* Presentation at a seminar on the Frontiers of Research in the Neurosciences, Cornell University Medical College, New York.

53. Marx, J.L. (1985). "Anxiety peptide" found in brain. *Science, 227* (4689), 934.

CHAPTER 6. HOW TIES THAT BIND BENEFIT OUR HEALTH

1. Sobel, D.S. (Speaker). (1982). *Medical self-care* (Series on the Healing Brain Cassette Recording No. 16). Los Altos, CA: Institute for the Study of Human Knowledge. A physician, Sobel is chief of preventive medicine of the Kaiser-Permanente Medical Group in San Jose and Oakland, CA. Sobel is also medical director of the ISHK.

2. Minkler, M. (Speaker). (1984). *Social networks & health* (Series on the Healing Brain Cassette Recording No. T5–7). Los Altos, CA: Institute for the Study of Human Knowledge. Minkler is a specialist in health behavior and health education at the University of California School of Public Health, Berkeley.

3. Larson, B. (1984). *There's a lot more to health than not being sick.* Waco, TX: Word Books. Larson, who has observed in his ministry that social support seems to protect people against illness, is senior pastor of University Presbyterian Church in Seattle. He is the author of 14 books and is a former Visiting Fellow at Princeton Theological Seminary.

4. Holmes, T.H. (1956). Multidiscipline studies of tuberculosis. In P. Sparer (Ed)., *Personality, stress and tuberculosis* (pp. 65–151). New York: International Universities Press.

5. Tillmann, W.A., & Hobbs, C.E. (1949). The accident-prone automobile driver: A study of the psychiatric and social background. *American Journal of Psychiatry, 106,* 321–331; Dunham, J.H. (1961). Social structures and mental disorders: Competing hypotheses of explanation. *Milbank Memorial Fund Quarterly. 39,* 259.

6. Bovard, E.W. (1959). The effects of social stimuli on the response to stress. *Psychological Review, 66,* 269.

7. Marmot, M.G. (1983). Stress, social support and cultural variations in heart disease. *Journal of Psychosomatic Research, 27*(5), 377–384.

8. Boyce, W.T., Schaefer, C., & Uitti, C. (1985). Permanence and change: Psychosocial factors in the outcome of adolescent pregnancy. *Social Science and Medicine, 21*(11), 1279–1287.

9. Berkman, L.F., & Syme, S.L. (1979). Social networks, host resistance, and mortality: A nine-year follow-up study of Alameda County residents. *American Journal of Epidemiology, 109*(2), 186–204.

10. Reynolds, P., & Kaplan, G.A. (1986, March). *Social connections and cancer: A prospective study of Alameda County residents.* Paper presented at the annual meeting of the Society of Behavioral Medicine, San Francisco.

11. House, J.S., & Wells, J.A. (1978). Occupation stress, social support, and health. In A. McLean, G. Black, & M. Colligan (Eds.), *Reducing occupational stress: Proceedings of a conference* (NIOSH Publication 78–140, pp. 8–29). Washington: U.S. Dept. of Health, Education and Welfare; Holt, R.R. (1982). Occupation stress. In L. Goldberger & S. Breznitz (Eds.), *Handbook of stress.* New York: Free Press.

12. Comstock. G.W., & Partridge, K.B. (1972). Church attendance and health. *Journal of Chronic Diseases, 25*, 665–672; Graham, T.W., Kaplan, B.H., Cornoni-Huntley, J.C., James, S.A., Becker, C., Hames, C.G., & Heyden, S. (1978). Frequency of church attendance and blood pressure elevation. *Journal of Behavioral Medicine, 1*(l), 37–43.

13. Watts, R.J., Milburn, N.G., Brown, D.R., & Gary, L.E. (1985, November). *Epidemiological research on blacks and depression: A sociocultural perspective.* Paper presented at the annual meeting of the American Public Health Association, Washington, DC.

14. Bruhn, J.G. (1965). An epidemiological study of myocardial infarctions in an Italian-American community. *Journal of Chronic Diseases, 18*, 353–365; Bruhn, J.G., Chandler, B., Miller, C., Wolf, S., & Lynn, T.N. (1966). Social aspects of coronary heart disease in two adjacent, ethnically different communities. *American Journal of Public Health, 56*(9), 1493–1506.

15. Medalie, J.H., & Goldbourt, U. (1976). Angina pectoris among 10,000 men, II: Psychosocial and other risk factors. *American Journal of Medicine, 60*, 910–921.

16. Burg, M.M., Blumenthal, J.A., Barefoot, J.C., Williams, R.B., & Haney, T.L. (1986, March). *Social support as a buffer against the development of coronary artery disease.* Paper presented at the annual meeting of the Society of Behavioral Medicine, San Francisco.

17. Syme, L. (Speaker). (1982). *People need people.* (Series on the Healing Brain Cassette Recording No. 12). Los Altos, CA: Institute for the Study of Human Knowledge.

18. Doi, L.T. (1974). Amae: A key concept for understanding Japanese personality structure. In T.S. Lebra & W.P. Lebra (Eds.), *Japanese culture and behavior* (pp. 145–154). Honolulu: University Press of Hawaii.

19. Nuckolls, K.B., Cassel, J., & Kaplan, B.H. (1972). Psychosocial assets, life crises and the prognosis of pregnancy. *American Journal of Epidemiology, 95*(5), 431–441.

20. Sosa, R., Kennell, J., Klaus, M., Robertson, S., & Urrutia, J. (1980). The effect of a supportive companion on perinatal problems, length

349

of labor and mother-infant interaction. *New England Journal of Medicine, 303*(11), 597–600.

21. Gore, S. (1978). The effect of social support in moderating the health consequences of unemployment. *Journal of Health and Social Behavior, 19*, 157–165.

22. de Araujo, G., van Arsdel, P.P., Holmes, T.H., & Dudley, D.L. (1973). Life change, coping ability and chronic intrinsic asthma. *Journal of Psychosomatic Research, 17*, 359–363.

23. Kiecolt-Glaser, J., Glaser, R., Williger, D., Messick, G., Sheppard, S., Ricker, D., & Romisher, S.C. (1984, May). *The enhancement of immune competence by relaxation and social contact.* Paper presented at the annual meeting of the Society of Behavioral Medicine, Philadelphia.

24. Kemeny, M. (1984, August). *Immunological predictors of recurrence in Herpes Simplex II.* Paper presented at the annual meeting of the American Psychological Association, Toronto.

25. Jemmott, J.B. III (1985, March). *Psychoneuroimmunology: Basic principles and experimental advances.* Presentation at the meeting of the Society of Behavioral Medicine, New Orleans.

26. Kiecolt-Glaser, J. (1986, March). *Clinical psychoneuroimmunology in health and disease: Effects of marital quality and disruption.* Paper presented at the annual meeting of the Society of Behavioral Medicine, San Francisco.

27. Thomas, P.D., Goodwin, J.M., & Goodwin, J.S. (1985). Effect of social support on stress-related changes in cholesterol level, uric acid level, and immune function in an elderly sample. *American Journal of Psychiatry, 142*(6), 735–737.

28. Sobel, D.S. (Speaker). (1984). *Social networks & health* (Series on the Healing Brain Cassette Recording Number T5–7). Los Altos, CA: Institute for the Study of Human Knowledge.

29. Messeni, P. (1984, June). *Panel on pets as social support.* Meeting of the Pacific division of the American Association for the Advancement of Science, San Francisco.

30. Antonovsky, A. (1979). *Health, stress and coping.* San Francisco: Jossey-Bass; Antonovsky, A. (Speaker). (1983). *Who stays healthy under stress?* (Series on the Healing Brain Cassette Recording No. T534). Los Altos, CA: Institute for the Study of Human Knowledge.

31. Maddi, S.R., & Kobasa, S.C. (1984). *The hardy executive: Health under stress.* Homewood, IL: Dow Jones-Irwin.

32. Ibid., p. 23.

33. Kobasa, S., & Puccett, M.C. (1983). Personality and social resources in stress resistance. *Journal of Personality and Social Psychology, 45*(4), 839–850.

34. Lefcourt, H. (1984, August). *Locus of control and social support: Interactive moderators of stress.* Paper presented at the annual meeting of the American Psychological Association, Toronto.

35. Revenson, T.A., Wollman, C.A., & Felton, B.J. (1983). Social sup-

ports as stress buffers for adult cancer patients. *Psychosomatic Medicine, 45*(4), p. 329.

36. Ibid.

37. Joffres, M., Reed, D.M., & Nomura, A.M.Y. (1985). Psychosocial processes and cancer incidence among Japanese men in Hawaii. *American Journal of Epidemiology, 121*(4), 488–500.

38. Patterson, J.K., Stern, M.P., Haffner, S.M., & Hazuda, H.P. (1986, March). *Social support and cardiovascular risk factors in Mexican Americans and non-Hispanic whites.* Poster presentation at the annual meeting of the Society of Behavioral Medicine, San Francisco.

39. Mancia, G., Grassi, G., Pomidossi, G., Gregorini, L., Bertinieri, G., Parati, G., Ferrari, A., & Zanchetti, A. (1983). Effects of blood pressure measurement by the doctor on a patient's blood pressure and heart rate. *Lancet, 2*(8352), 695–698.

40. Jarvinen, K.A.J. (1955). Can ward rounds be a danger to patients with myocardial infarction? *British Medical Journal, 1*, 318–320.

41. Klein, R.F., Kliner, V.A., Zipes, D.P., Troyer, W.G., & Wallace, A.G. (1968). Transfer from a coronary care unit. *Archives of Internal Medicine, 122*, 104–108.

42. Skinner, J.E., Lie, J.T., & Entman, M.L. (1975). Modification of ventricular fibrillation latency following coronary artery occlusion in the conscious pig: The effects of psychologic stress and beta-adrenergic blockade. *Circulation, 51*(4), 656–667.

43. Henry, J.P., & Stephens, P.M. (1977). *Stress, health, and the social environment.* New York: Springer-Verlag.

44. Haenzel, W., Loveland, D.B., & Sirkin, M.G. (1962). Lung-cancer mortality as related to residence and smoking histories. *Journal of the National Cancer Institute, 28*, 947–1001.

CHAPTER 7. TAKING CHARGE
AND LIVING LONGER

1. Nathan, R., as quoted by Maness, B. (1985, November). Staying fit: Physician, heal thyself. *The Continental*, p. 11. Nathan, coauthor of *Stress management: A comprehensive guide to wellness,* is an associate professor of psychiatry at the Louisiana State University Medical Center in Shreveport.

2. Langer, E.J. (1983). *The psychology of control.* Beverly Hills, CA: Sage, p. 14. Langer is a professor of psychology at Harvard and a member of the division on aging of the Faculty of Medicine. As a doctoral student at Yale, she began research on the power of control as a belief.

3. Langer, E.J., & Rodin, J. (1976). The effects of choice and enhanced personal responsibility for the age: A field experiment in an institutional setting. *Journal of Personality and Social Psychology, 34*, 191–198.

4. Rodin, J. (1979). Managing the stress of aging: The role of control and coping. In S. Levine & U. Holger (Eds.), *Coping and health* (pp. 171–202). New York: Plenum.

5. Johnson, J.H., & Sarason, I.G. (1978). Life stress, depression and anxiety: Internal-external control as a moderator variable. *Journal of Psychosomatic Research, 22*, 205–208.

6. Igou, J.F., & Caracci, K. (1985, November). *The relationship between locus of control and depression in institutionalized elderly.* Presentation at the meeting of the American Public Health Association, Washington, DC.

7. Thompson, S.C. (1981). Will it hurt less if I can control it? A complex answer to a simple question. *Psychological Bulletin, 90*(1), 89–101.

8. Bandura, A. (1986, March). *Perceived self-efficacy and health functioning.* Paper presented at the annual meeting of the Society of Behavioral Medicine, San Francisco.

9. Aldrich, C.K., & Mendkoff, E. (1963). Relocation of the aged and disabled: A mortality study. *Journal of American Geriatrics Society, 11*(3), 285–194.

10. Mumford, E., Schlesinger, H.J., & Glass, G.V. (1982). The effects of psychological intervention on recovery from surgery and heart attacks: An analysis of the literature. *American Journal of Public Health, 72*(2), 141–151.

11. Wallace, L.M. (1984). Psychological preparation as a method of reducing the stress of surgery. *Journal of Human Stress, 10*(2), 62–77.

12. Egbert, L.D., Battit, G.E., Welch, C.E., & Bartlett, M.K. (1964). Reduction of post operative pain by encouragement and instruction of patients. *New England Journal of Medicine, 270* (16), 825–827.

13. Cromwell, R.I., Butterfield, E.C., Brayfield, F.M., & Curry, J.J. (1977). *Acute myocardial infarction: Reaction and recovery.* St. Louis: Mosby.

14. Bartlett, E.E. (1984, July/August). Studies demonstrate patient education reduces hospital stay. *Human Aspects of Anesthesia*, pp. 1, 6, 7.

15. Mumford, Schlesinger, & Glass, 1982, p. 144.

16. Antonovsky, A. (Speaker). (1984). *Who stays healthy under stress?* (Series on the Healing Brain Cassette Recording No. T534). Los Altos, CA: Institute for the Study of Human Knowledge; Krantz, D.S. (1980). Cognitive processes and recovery from heart attack: A review and theoretical analysis. *Journal of Human Stress, 6*(3), 27–38.

17. Meichenbaum, D. (1983, March). *Cognitive behavior modification: Theory and techniques.* CBM seminar, Houston.

18. Pennebaker, J.W., Burnam, M.A., Schaeffer, M.A., & Harper, D.C. (1977). Lack of control as a determinant of perceived physical symptoms. *Journal of Personality and Social Psychology, 35*(3), 167–174.

19. Glass, D.C., & Singer, J.E. (1972). *Urban stress.* New York: Academic Press.

20. Cassell, J. (1973). The relation of the urban environment to health: Implications for prevention. *Mount Sinai Journal of Medicine, 40*, 539–550.

21. Stokols, D. (1972). On the distinction between density and crowding. *Psychological Review, 79*(3), 275–277.

22. Freedman, J.L., Heshka, S., & Levy, A. (1975). Population density and pathology: Is there a relationship? *Journal of Experimental Social Psychology, 11*, 539–552.

23. Saegert, S. (1973). Crowding: Cognitive overload and behavioral constraint. In W. Preiser (Ed.), *Proceedings of the Environmental Design Research Association* (vol. 2). Strouthberg, PA: Dowden, Hutchinson & Rose.

24. Wicker, A.W., Kirmeyer, S.L., Hanson, L., & Alexander, D. (1976). Effects of manning level on subjective experiences, performance, and verbal interaction in groups. *Organizational Behavior and Human Performance, 17*, 251–274.

25. Langer, E.J., & Saegert, S. (1977). Crowding and cognitive control. *Journal of Personality and Social Psychology, 35*(3), 175–182.

26. Baum, A., Singer, J.E., & Baum, C.S. (1981). Stress and the environment. *Journal of Social Issues, 37*(1), 4–35.

27. Lundberg, U. (1976). Urban community: Crowdedness and catecholamine secretion. *Journal of Human Stress, 2*, 26–32.

CHAPTER 8. OUR INFLUENCE OVER INFECTIONS

1. Maier, S., & Laudenslager, M. (1985, August). Stress and health: Exploring the links. *Psychology Today*, p. 46. Maier is a professor of psychology at the University of Colorado at Boulder and Laudenslager is an assistant research psychologist at the University of Denver and assistant clinical professor of psychiatry at the University of Colorado Health Sciences Center.

2. Solomon, G.F. (1985). The emerging field of psychoneuroimmunology with a special note on AIDS. *Advances, 2*(1), p. 8. Solomon, who hung a "psychoimmunology" sign on his door long before anyone knew what it meant, is now a professor of psychiatry at UCLA and adjunct professor of psychiatry at the University of California, San Francisco.

3. Growald, E.R. (1985). Health and wholeness: The mind-body mystery. *Advances, 2*(4), p. 7. Eileen Growald is president of the Institute for the Advancement of Health in New York, which sponsored the first national workshop on "The Psychosocial Aspects of AIDS."

4. Jacobs, M.A., Spilken, A., & Norman, M. (1969). Relationship of life change, maladaptive aggression, and upper respiratory infection in male college students. *Psychosomatic Medicine, 31* (1), 31–44.

5. Kasl, S.V., Evans, A.S., & Niederman, J.C. (1979). Psychosocial risk factors in the development of infectious mononucleosis. *Psychosomatic Medicine, 41*(6), 445–466.

6. Mason, J.W., Buescher, E.L., Belfer, M.L., Artenstein, M.S., Mougey, E.H. (1979). Prospective study of corticosteroid and catecholamine

levels in relation to viral respiratory illness. *Journal of Human Stress, 5*(3), 18–28.

7. Gruchow, H.W. (1979). Catecholamine activity and infectious disease episodes. *Journal of Human Stress, 5*(3), 11–17.

8. Dubos, R. (1965). *Man adapting.* New Haven: Yale University Press.

9. Schneck, J.M. (1947). The psychological component in a case of herpes simplex. *Psychosomatic Medicine, 9*(1), 62–64.

10. Blank, H., & Brody, M. (1950). Recurrent herpes simplex: A psychiatric and laboratory study. *Psychosomatic Medicine, 12*(4), 254–260.

11. Luborsky, L., Brightman, V.J., & Katcher, A.H. (1976). Herpes simplex virus and moods: A longitudinal study. *Journal of Psychosomatic Research, 20,* 543–548.

12. Verbrugge, L.M. (1985). Triggers of symptoms and health care. *Social Science and Medicine, 20*(9), 855–876.

13. Glaser, R., Kiecolt-Glaser, J., George, J.M., Speicher, C.E., & Holliday, J.E. (1984, May). *Stress, loneliness and herpes virus lat*ency. Presentation at the annual meeting of the Society of Behavioral Medicine, Philadelphia.

14. Kemeny, M. (1984, August). *Psychological and immunological predictions of recurrence in Herpes Simplex II.* Paper presented at the annual meeting of the American Psychological Association, Toronto.

15. Kemeny, M. (1985, August). *Stress and psychosocial factors predicting immunity and genital herpes recurrence.* Paper presented at the annual meeting of the American Psychological Association, Los Angeles; Kemeny, M. (1986, March). *Clinical psychoneuroimmunology in genital herpes recurrence.* Paper presented at the annual meeting of the Society of Behavioral Medicine, San Francisco.

16. Solomon, G.F. (Speaker). (1982). *Emotions, stress and immunity* (Healing Brain Series Cassette Recording No. 5). Los Altos, CA: Institute for the Study of Human Knowledge.

17. Cohen-Cole, S., Cogen, R., Stevens, A., Kirk, K., Gaitan, E., Hain, J., & Freeman, A. (1981). Psychosocial, endocrine, and immune factors in acute necrotizing ulcerative gingivitis ("Trenchmouth") [Abstract]. *Psychosomatic Medicine, 43*(1), 91.

18. Morse, D.R., Schacterle, G.R., Furst, M.L, Goldberg, J., Greenspan, B., Swiecinski, D., & Susek, J. (1982). The effect of stress and meditation on salivary protein and bacteria: A review and pilot study. *Journal of Human Stress, 8*(4), 31–39.

19. Kiecolt-Glaser, J.K., Glaser, R., Strain, E.C., Stout, J.C., Tarr, K.L., Holliday, J.E., & Speider, C.E. (1986). Modulation of cellular immunity in medical students. *Journal of Behavioral Medicine, 9*(1), 5–21.

20. Ibid., p. 19.

21. Jemmott, J.B., & Locke, S.E. (1984). Psychosocial factors, immunologic mediation, and human susceptibility to infectious diseases: How much do we know? *Psychological Bulletin, 95*(1), 78–108.

22. Borysenko, J. (1985, March). *Psychoneuroimmunology: Basic principles and experimental advances*. Paper presented at the annual meeting of the Society of Behavioral Medicine, New Orleans.

23. Locke, S.E.. Hurst, M.W., Heisel, S.J., Kraus, L., & Williams, M. (1979, March). *The influence of stress and other psychosocial factors on human immunity*. Presentation at the meeting of the American Psychosomatic Society, Dallas.

24. Schleifer, S.J., Keller, S.E., Camerino, M., Thornton, J.C., & Stein, M. (1983). Suppression of lymphocyte stimulation following bereavement. *Journal of American Medical Association, 250* (3), 374–377.

25. Jemmott, J.B., Borysenko, M., Chapman, R., Borysenko, J.Z., McClelland, D., Meyer, D., & Benson, H. (1983). Academic stress, power motivation, and decrease in secretion rate of salivary immunoglobulin. *Lancet, 1*(8339), 1400–1402; Upole, V.K., Appel, M.A. Holroyd, K.A., Gorkin, L., Stauder, L.J., & Saab, P.G. (1983, March). *Stress and psychological vulnerability to physical illness*. Paper presented at the annual meeting of the Society of Behavioral Medicine, Baltimore.

26. Bunney, W., Shapiro, A., Ader, R., Davis, J., Herd, A., Kopin, I.J., Krieger, D., Matthysse, S., Stunkard, A., Weissman, M., & Wyatt, R.J. (1982). Panel report on stress and illness. In G.R. Elliott & C. Eisdorfer (Eds.), *Stress and human health.* (pp. 257–337). New York: Springer.

27. Wolf, S. (1963). A new view of disease. *Journal of the American Medical Association, 184*(2), 143–144.

28. Ibid., p. 143.

29. Selye, S. (1976). *The stress of life*. New York: McGraw-Hill, p. 301.

30. Dubos, R.J. (1951). Biological and social aspects of tuberculosis. *Bulletin of the New York Academy of Medicine, 27*, 351–369.

31. Jenkins, C.D. (1979). Psychosocial modifiers of response to stress. *Journal of Human Stress, 5*(4), p. 3.

32. Selye, H. (1956). Recent progress in stress research, with reference to tuberculosis. In P.J. Sparer (Ed.), *Personality, stress and tuberculosis* (pp. 45–64). New York: International Universities Press.

33. Holmes, T.H. (1956). Multidiscipline studies of tuberculosis. In Sparer, pp. 65–151.

34. Cluff, L.E., Canter, A., & Imboden, J.B. (1966). Asian influenza: Infection, disease, and psychological factors. *Archives of Internal Medicine, 117*, 159–164.

35. Imboden, J.B., Canter, A., & Cluff, L.E. (1961). Convalescence from influenza. *Archives of Internal Medicine, 108*, 393–399.

36. Temoshok, L. (1986, March). *Clinical psychoneuroimmunology in AIDS*. Paper presented at the annual meeting of the Society of Behavioral Medicine, San Francisco.

37. Spivak, S.L., & Wormser, G.P. (1985). How common is HTLV-III infection in the United States? *New England Journal of Medicine, 313*(21), 1352.

38. Temoshok, L. (1985, March). *AIDS: Current research in behavioral medicine*. Symposium presentation at the meeting of the Society of Behavioral Medicine, New Orleans.

39. Fettner, A.G., & Check, W.A. (1984). *The truth about AIDS*. New York: Holt, Rinehart and Winston.

40. Spivak & Wormser, 1985; AIDS virus: Infection up? (1985, Nov. 23). *Science News*, p. 325.

41. Goedert, J.J., Biggar, R.J., Weiss, S.H., Eyster, M.E., Melbye, M., Wilson, S., Ginzburg, H.M., Grossman, R.J., DiGioia, R.A., Sanchez, W.C., Giron, J.A., Ebbesen, P., Gallo, R.C., & Blattner, W.A. Three-year incidence of AIDS in five cohorts of HTLV-III-infected risk group members. *Science, 231*(4741), 992–995.

42. Mandel, J.S. (1985, March). *AIDS: Current research in behavioral medicine*. Symposium presentation at the meeting of the Society of Behavior Medicine, New Orleans.

43. Silberner, J. (1985, April 27). AIDS: Disease, research efforts advance. *Science News*, pp. 260–261.

44. Brown, N.M. (1984). AIDS' blood-borne calling card. *Research/ Penn State, 5*(2), pp. 3–5; Gardner, M. (1984, November). *Molecular biology of suspect agents*. Presentation at the annual meeting of the American Public Health Association, Anaheim, CA.

45. Cesario, T. (1984, November). *Clinical aspects of AIDS*. Presentation at the annual meeting of the American Public Health Association, Anaheim, CA.

46. Geschwind, N., as quoted in Fettner & Check, 1984, p. 58.

47. Laurence, J. (1985). The immune system in AIDS. *Scientific American, 253*(6), pp. 84–93.

48. Ho, D.D., Rota, T.R., Schooley, R.T., Kaplan, J.C., Allan, J.D., Groopman, J.E., Resnick, L., Felsenstein, D., Andrews, C.A., & Hirsch, M.S. (1985). Isolation of HTLV-III from cerebrospinal fluid and neural tissues of patients with neurologic syndromes related to the acquired immunodeficiency syndrome. *New England Journal of Medicine, 313*(24), 1493–1497.

49. Bahnson, C.B. (1984, August). *Psychological aspects of AIDS*. Symposium summary at the annual meeting of the American Psychological Association, Toronto, Canada.

50. Mandel, J. (1983, August). *Kaposi's sarcoma patients: Psychosocial parameters*. Presentation at the annual meeting of the American Psychological Association, Anaheim, CA.

51. Mandel, J., March 1985, personal communication.

52. Coates, T.J. (1986, March). *A prospective sero-epidemiological study of AIDS in homosexual men residing in San Francisco*. Paper presented at the annual meeting of the Society of Behavioral Medicine, San Francisco.

53. Popovic, M., Sarngadharin, M.G., Read, E., & Gallo, R.C. (1984). Detection, isolation and continuous production of cytopathic retrovirus (HTLV-III) from patients with AIDS and pre-AIDS. *Science*,

224(4648), 497–50; Associated Press. (1984, April 24). Probable cause of AIDS found. *Houston Chronicle*, p. 10, section 1.

54. Vilmer, E., Ropuzioux, C., Brun, F.V., Fischer, A., Chermann, J.-C., Barre-Sinoussi, F., Gazengel, C., Dauguet, C., Manigne, P., Griscelli, C., & Montagnier, L. (1984). Isolation of new lymphotropic retrovirus from two siblings with haemophilia B, one with AIDS. *Lancet*, *1*(8380), 753–757.

55. Marx, J.L. (1985). A virus by any other name.... *Science, 227* (4693), 1449–1451.

56. Tross, S., & Holland, J. (1985, March). *AIDS: Current research in behavioral medicine.* Symposium presentation at the annual meeting of the Society of Behavioral Medicine, New Orleans.

57. Hoofnagle, J.H. (1981). Seriologic markers of hepatitis B virus infection. *Annual Review of Medicine, 32*, 1–11.

58. Coates, T.J. (1985, March). *AIDS: Current research in behavioral medicine.* Symposium presentation at the annual meeting of the Society of Behavioral Medicine, New Orleans.

59. Levy, J.A., & Ziegler, J.L. (1983). Acquired immunodeficiency syndrome is an opportunistic infection and Kaposi's sarcoma results from secondary immune stimulation. *Lancet, 2*(8341), 78–80.

60. Kalyanaraman, V.S., Cabradilla, C.D., Getchell, J.P., Narayanan, R., Braff, E.H., Chermann, J.-C., Barre-Sinoussi, F., Montagnier, L., Spira, T.J., Kaplan, J., Fishbein, D., Jaffe, H.W., Curran, J.W., & Francis, D.P. (1984). Antibodies to the core protein of lymphadenopathy-associated virus (LAV) in patients with AIDS. *Science, 225*(4659), 321–323.

61. Zaia, J., as quoted by Mathews, C. (1986, January). Seeking "cofactors" of AIDS. City of Hope *President's Newsletter*, pp. 3–4.

62. Haverkos, H. (1984, November). *Epidemiology of AIDS.* Presentation at the annual meeting of the American Public Health Association, Anaheim, CA.

63. Talal, M.A. (1983). A clinician and a scientist looks at acquired immune deficiency syndrome, AIDS: A validation of immunology's theoretical foundation. *Immunology Today, 4*(Suppl.), 180–183.

64. Raeburn, P., Associated Press. (1985, May 23). Mining the mystery of Legionnaire's disease. Boulder *Daily Camera*, p. 1B.

65. Centers for Disease Control. (1985, June 14). Legionellosis—Staffordshire, England, and Wayne County, Michigan. *Morbidity and Mortality Weekly Report*, pp. 344, 349–350.

66. Weiner, H. (1977). *Psychobiology and human disease.* New York: Elsevier-North Holland.

67. Ibid., p. xi.

68. Friedman, S.B., & Glasgow, L.A. (1966). Psychologic factors and resistance to infectious disease. *Pediatric Clinics of North America, 13*, 315–355.

69. Engel, G.L. (1977). The need for a new medical model: A challenge for biomedicine. *Science, 196*(4286), 129–136; Gordon, J.S., & Fadi-

man, J. (1984). Toward an integral medicine. In J.S. Gordon, D.T. Jaffe & D.E. Bresler (Eds.), *Mind, body, and health* (pp. 3–13). New York: Human Sciences Press.

70. Knowles, J.H. (1977). The responsibility of the individual. In J.H. Knowles (Ed.), *Doing better and feeling worse* (pp. 57–80). New York: Norton; Public Health Service. (1979). *Healthy people: The Surgeon General's report on health promotion and disease prevention* (DHEW Publication No. 79–55071). Washington, DC: Government Printing Office.

CHAPTER 9. DISSATISFACTION AND ILLNESS

1. Maultsby, M.C. Jr. (1975). *Help yourself to happiness*. New York: Institute of Rational Living, p. 1. A psychiatrist at the University of Kentucky College of Medicine, Maultsby's specialty is rational behavior therapy. He does research on the effects of RBT on psychosomatic disease.

2. Larson, B. (1984). *There's a lot more to health than not being sick*. Waco, TX: Word Books, p. 123. For more on Larson, see Note 3 in the references for Chapter 6.

3. Verbrugge, L.M. (1982). Work satisfaction and physical health. *Journal of Community Health*, 7(4), 162–283.

4. Rose, R.M., Jenkins, C.D., & Hurst, M.W. (1978). *Air traffic controller health change study: A prospective investigation of physical, psychological and work-related changes* (Contract No. DOT-FA737WA-3211). Boston: Boston University School of Medicine.

5. Hinkle, L.E., & Wolff, H.G. (1957). Health and the social environment: Experimental investigations. In A.H. Leighton, J.A. Clausen & R.N. Wilson (Eds.). *Explorations in social psychiatry* (pp. 105–132). New York: Basic Books.

6. Snell, W.E. Jr. (1985). *The masculine role as a moderator of stress-distress relationships*. Paper presented at the meeting of the Southwestern Psychological Association, Austin, TX.

7. O'Neil, J.M. (1981). Male sex role conflicts, sexism, and masculinity: Psychological implications for men, women, and the counseling psychologist. *The Counseling Psychologist*, 9, 61–80.

8. Pepitone-Arreola-Rockwell, F., Somner, B., Sassenrath, E.N., Rozee-Koker, P., & Stringer-Moore, D. Stress and health in working women. *Journal of Human Stress*, 7(4), 19–26.

9. Hazuda, H. (1984, March). *Women's employment status and their risks for chronic disease*. Colloquium presentation, University of Texas School of Public Health, Houston.

10. See Linthicum, L. (1985, May 24). Women and "macho stress." *Houston Post*, p. 1J.

11. Wheeler, A.P., Lee, E.S., & Loe, H.D. (1983). Employment, sense of well-being, and use of professional services among women. *American Journal of Public Health, 73*(8), 908–911.

12. Waldron, I.,& Herold, J. (1984, May). *Employment, attitudes toward employment, and women's health.* Presentation at the annual meeting of the Society of Behavioral Medicine, Philadelphia.

13. Pietromonaco, P.R., Manis, J., & Frohart-Lane, K. (1984, August). *Psychological consequences of multiple social roles.* Paper presented at the annual meeting of the American Psychological Association, Toronto.

14. Duncan, D., & Whitney. R.J. (1985, November). *Retirement, work and volunteering: Effects on mental well-being.* Presentation at the annual meeting of the American Public Health Association, Washington, DC.

15. Colligan, M.J., & Murphy, L.R. (1979). Mass psychogenic illness in organizations: An overview. *Journal of Occupational Psychology, 52,* 77–90.

16. Baker, D. (1983, November). *Stress and the stuffy building syndrome.* Paper presented at the annual meeting of the American Public Health Association, Dallas.

17. Pasick, R.J. (1985, November). *Job complexity, worker control and health.* Paper presented at the annual meeting of the American Public Health Association, Washington, DC.

18. Karasek, R.A., Theorell, T.G.T., Schwartz, J., Pieper, C., & Alfredson, L. (1982). Job, psychological factors and coronary heart disease. *Advances in Cardiology, 29,* 62–67.

19. Haynes, S.G. (1984). Type A behavior, employment status, and coronary heart disease in women. *Behavioral Medicine Update, 6*(4), 11–15.

20. Ibid, p. 13.

21. Palmore, E. (1969). Predicting longevity: A follow-up controlling for age. *Gerontologist, 9,* 247–250; Special Task Force to the Secretary of Health, Education and Welfare (1973). *Work in America.* Cambridge: MIT Press.

22. Liljefors, I., & Rahe, R.H. (1970). An identical twin study of psychosocial factors in coronary heart disease in Sweden. *Psychosomatic Medicine, 32,* 523–542.

23. Theorell, T., & Rahe, R.H. (1972). Behavior and life satisfaction characteristics of Swedish subjects with myocardial infarction. *Journal of Chronic Diseases, 25,* 139–147.

24. Sales, S.M., House, J. (1971). Job dissatisfaction as a possible risk factor in coronary heart disease. *Journal of Chronic Diseases, 23,* 861–873.

25. Bruhn, J.G., Paredes, A., Adsett, C.A., & Wolf, S. (1974). Psychological predictors of sudden death in MI. *Journal of Psychosomatic Research, 18,* 187–191.

26. Eaton, J.W., & Weil, R.J. (1955). *Culture and mental disorders.* New York: Free Press of Glencoe.

27. Neff, J.A., & Husaini, B.A. (1984, November). *Urbanicity, race, and psychological distress*. Paper presented at the annual meeting of the American Public Health Association, Anaheim, CA.

28. Frankenhaeuser, M., Lundberg, U., & Forsman, L. (1980). Note on arousing Type A persons by depriving them of work. *Journal of Psychosomatic Research, 24*, 45–47.

29. Robinson, E.A. (1965). Richard Cory. In Zabel, M.D. (Ed.), *Selected poems of Edwin Arlington Robinson*. New York: Macmillan, p. 10. (Originally published 1897).

30. Schneider, M. (1975). The quality of life in large American cities: Objective and subjective social indicators. *Social Indicators Research, 1*, 495–509.

31. Ibid., p. 505.

32. Liu, B. (1973). *The quality of life in the United States: 1970*. Kansas City, MO: Midwest Research Institute.

33. Greeley, A.M. (1981, January). The state of the nation's happiness. *Psychology Today*, pp. 14–16.

34. Ibid., p. 16.

CHAPTER 10. WHAT WISHING TO DIE DOES

1. Frankl, V.E. (1962). *Man's search for meaning*. Boston: Beacon Press, p. 75. Frankl, an existential psychotherapist who wrote of his experiences in a concentration camp, developed logotherapy, designed to help people find meaning in life.

2. Bartrop, R.W., Luckhurst, E., Lazarus, L., Kiloh, L.G., & Penny, R. (1977). Depressed lymphocyte function after bereavement. *Lancet, 1*(8016), 834–836.

3. Schleifer, S.J., Keller, S.E., Camerino, M., Thornton, J.C., & Stein, M. (1983). Suppression of lymphocyte stimulation following bereavement. *Journal of the American Medical Association, 250*(3), 374–377.

4. Linn, B.S., Linn, M.W., & Jensen, M.D. (1982). Degree of depression and immune responsiveness [Abstract]. *Psychosomatic Medicine, 44*(1), 128–129.

5. Kiecolt-Glaser, J.K., Garner, W., Speicher, C., Penn, G., Holliday, J., & Glaser, R. (1984). Psychosocial modifiers of immunocompetence in medical students. *Psychosomatic Medicine, 46*(1), 7–14.

6. Helsing, K.J., Szklo, M., & Comstock, G.W. (1981). Factors associated with mortality after widowhood. *American Journal of Public Health, 71*(8), 802–809.

7. Young, M., Benjamin, B., & Wallis, C. (1963). The mortality of widowers. *Lancet, 2*(7305), 454–456.

8. Rees, W.D., & Lutkins, S.G. (1967). Mortality of bereavement. *British Medical Journal, 4*(5570), 13–16.

9. Levy, S.M. (1983, August). *Emotional expression and survival in breast*

cancer patients: Immunological correlates. Paper presented at the meeting of the American Psychological Association, Anaheim, CA.

10. Frankenhaeuser, M. (1979). Psychobiological aspects of life stress. In S. Levine & U. Holger (Eds.), *Coping and health* (pp. 203–223). New York: Plenum.

11. Borysenko, J.Z. (1982). Behavioral-physiological factors in the development and management of cancer. *General Hospital Psychiatry, 4,* 69–74.

12. Laudenslager, M., Ryan, S.M., Drugan, R.C., Hyson, R.L., & Maier, S.F. (1983). Coping and immunosuppression: Inescapable but not escapable shock suppresses lymphocyte proliferation. *Science, 221*(4610), 568–570.

13. Ibid., p. 568.

14. Maier, S., Laudenslager, M., & Ryan, S. (1985). Stressor controllability, immune function, and endogenous opiates. In J. Overmeier & S. Brush (Eds.), *Affect, conditioning, and cognition: Essays on the determinants of behavior* (pp. 183–201). Hillsdale, NJ: Erlbaum.

15. Ahluwalia, P., Zacharko, R.M., & Anisman, H. (1985, October). *Dopamine variations associated with acute and chronic stressors.* Presentation at the annual meeting of the Society for Neuroscience, Dallas.

16. Coe, C.L., Rosenberg, L.T., & Levine, S. (1983, August). *Endocrine and immune responses to maternal loss in nonhuman primates.* Paper presented at the meeting of the American Psychological Association, Anaheim, CA.

17. Wolf, S. (1967). The end of the rope: The role of the brain in cardiac death. *Canadian Medical Association Journal, 97,* 1022–1025.

18. Lynch, J.J. (1977). *The broken heart: The medical consequences of loneliness.* New York: Basic Books.

19. Engel, G.L. (1970). The "medical model" in psychiatry. *Canadian Psychiatric Association Journal, 15*(6), 527–538; Engel, G.L. (1971). Sudden and rapid death during psychological stress. *Annals of Internal Medicine, 74,* 771–782.

20. Associated Press (1983, August 26). *Houston Post,* p. 26A.

21. Wilson, I.C., & Reece, J.C. (1964). Simultaneous death in schizophrenic twins. *Archives of General Psychiatry, 11,* 377–384.

22. Engel, G.L. (1968). A life setting conducive to illness: The giving up-given up complex. *Bulletin of the Menninger Clinic, 32,* 358.

23. Greene, W.A., Goldstein, S., & Moss, A.J. (1972). Psychosocial aspects of sudden death. *Archives of Internal Medicine, 129,* 725–731.

24. Engel, G. (1977, November). Emotional stress and sudden death. *Psychology Today,* p. 114.

25. Walters, M. (1944). Psychic death: Report of a possible case. *Archives of Neurology and Psychiatry, 52*(1), 84–85.

26. Bauer, J. (1957). Sudden, unexpected death. *Postgraduate Medicine, 22*(4), A34–A44.

27. Weisman, A.D., & Hackett, T.P. (1961). Predilection to death. *Psychosomatic Medicine, 23*(3), 232–256.

28. Cannon, W.B. (1942). "Voodoo" death. *American* Anthropologist, *44*(2), 169–181.

29. Mathis, J.L. (1964). A sophisticated version of voodoo death. *Psychosomatic Medicine, 26,* 104.

30. Cannon, 1942, p. 176.

31. Ibid., p. 179.

32. Ibid., p. 180.

33. Finney, J.M.T. (1934). Discussion of papers on shock. *Annals of Surgery, 100,* 746.

34. Miller, T.R. (1977). Psychophysiologic aspects of cancer. *Cancer, 39,* p. 414.

35. Richter, C.P. (1957). On the phenomenon of sudden death in animals and man. *Psychosomatic Medicine, 19*(3), 191–198.

36. Ibid., p. 196.

37. Ibid., p. 197.

38. National Institutes of Health. *Proceedings of the Forum on Coronary Prone Behavior* (DHEW Publication No. 78–1451). Bethesda, MD: NIH, p. 162.

39. Corley, K.C., Mauck, H.P., & Shiel, F. O'M. (1975). Cardiac responses associated with "yoked chair" shock avoidance in squirrel monkeys. *Psychophysiology, 12,* 439–444.

40. Phillips, D.P., & Feldman, K.A. (1973). A dip in deaths before ceremonial occasions: Some new relationships between social integration and mortality. *American Sociological Review, 38,* 678–696.

41. Ibid., p. 678.

42. Ibid., p. 679.

43. Wolf, S. (1976). Protective social forces that counterbalance stress. *Journal of the South Carolina Medical Association, 72*(2), 57–59.

44. Wolf, 1967, p. 1024.

45. Bettelheim, B. (1943). Individual and mass behavior in extreme situations. *Journal of Abnormal and Social Psychology, 38,* 417–452.

46. Dimsdale, J.E. (1974). The coping behavior of Nazi concentration camp survivors. *American Journal of Psychiatry, 131*(7), p. 795.

47. Frankl, 1962.

48. Achterberg, J., Matthews-Simonton, S., & Simonton, O.C. (1977). Psychology of the exceptional cancer patient: A description of patients who outlive life expectancies. *Psychotherapy: Theory, Research and Practice, 41,* 416–422.

CHAPTER 11. GETTING SICK WHEN WE DO

1. Engel, G. (1968). A life setting conducive to illness: The giving up-given up complex. *Bulletin of the Menninger Clinic, 32,* p. 356. Engel, a longtime professor of psychiatry and professor of medicine at the

University of Rochester Medical Center, New York, pioneered the biopsychosocial model of disease, contending that the traditional medical model fails to account for the psychological and social factors that contribute to illness.

2. Siegel, B.S. (1986). *Love, medicine & miracles.* New York: Harper & Row, p. 108. For more on Siegel, a New Haven surgeon, see Chapter 13 references.

3. Engel, 1968, 355–365.

4. Schmale, A.H. (1972). Giving up as a final common pathway to changes in health. *Advances in Psychosomatic Medicine, 8,* 20–40.

5. Engel, G.L. (1955). Studies of ulcerative colitis. III: The nature of the psychologic processes. *American Journal of Medicine, 19,* p. 231.

6. Siegel, 1986.

7. Schmale, A.H., & Engel, G.L. (1967). The giving up-given up complex illustrated on film. *Archives of General Psychiatry, 17,* 135–145.

8. Mei-Tal, V., Meyerowitz, S., & Engel, G.L. (1970). The role of psychological process in a somatic disorder. *Psychosomatic Medicine, 32*(1), 67–86.

9. Schmale, A.H. (1958). Relationship of separation and depression to disease. *Psychosomatic Medicine, 20*(4), 259–277.

10. Greene, W.A. (1965). Disease response to life stress. *Journal of the American Medical Women's Association, 20*(2), 133–140.

11. Adamson, J.D., & Schmale, A.H. (1965). Object loss, giving up, and the onset of psychiatric disease. *Psychosomatic Medicine, 27*(6), p. 565.

12. Schmale & Engel, 1967, p. 138.

13. Ibid., p. 141.

14. Ibid., p. 142.

15. Mei-Tal, Meyerowitz, & Engel, 1970, p. 78.

16. Adamson & Schmale, 1965, p. 566.

17. Mei-Tal, Meyerowitz, & Engel, 1970, p. 80.

18. Schmale, 1958, p. 275.

19. Ibid., p. 274.

20. Engel, G.L., & Schmale, A.H. (1972). Conservation-withdrawal: A primary regulatory process for organismic homeostasis. Ciba Foundation Symposium 8, *Physiology, emotion & psychosomatic illness.* Amsterdam, Holland: Associated Scientific Publishers.

21. Engel, G.L., Reichsman, F., & Segal, H.L. (1956). A study of an infant with a gastric fistula. *Psychosomatic Medicine, 18*(5), 374–398.

22. Wolf, S. (1958). Cardiovascular reactions to symbolic stimuli. *Circulation, 28,* 287–292; Wolf, S. (1967). The end of the rope: The role of the brain in cardiac death. *Canadian Medical Association Journal, 97,* 1022–1025.

23. Hess, W.R. (1957). *The functional organization of the diencephalon.* New York: Grune & Stratton; Gellhorn, E. (1967). *Principles of autonomic-somatic integrations.* Minneapolis: University of Minnesota Press; Engel & Schmale, 1972.

24. Jarvik, L.F., & Russell, D. (1979). Anxiety, aging and the third emergency reaction. *Journal of Gerontology, 34*(2), 197–200.

25. Engel, G.L. (1970). Sudden death and the "medical model" in psychiatry. *Canadian Psychiatric Association Journal, 15*(6), 527–538.

26. Saul, L.J. (1966). Sudden death at impasse. *Psychoanalytic Forum, 1*, 88–89.

27. Greene, W.A., Goldstein, S., & Moss, A.J. (1972). Psychosocial aspects of sudden death. *Archives of Internal Medicine, 129*, 725–731.

28. Chesney, M.A., & Rosenman, R.H. (1983). Specificity in stress models: Examples drawn from Type A behaviour. In C.L. Cooper (Ed.), *Stress research* (pp. 21–34). Chichester, Eng.: Wiley.

29. Henry, J.P., & Stephens, P.M. (1977). *Stress, health, and the social environment: A sociobiologic approach to medicine.* New York: Springer-Verlag.

30. Price, V.A. (1982). *Type A behavior pattern: A model for research and practice.* New York: Academic Press.

31. Levy, S.M. (1985). Behavior as a biological response modifier: The psychoimmunoendocrine network and tumor immunology. *Behavioral Medicine Abstracts, 6*(1), 1–4.

32. Wolff, H.G. (1950). Life stress and bodily disease—A formulation. *Proceedings of the Association for Research in Nervous and Mental Diseases, 29*, 1059–1094.

33. Adsett, C.A., Schottstaedt, W.W., & Wolf, S.G. (1958). Changes in coronary blood flow and other hemodynamic indicators induced by stressful interviews. *Psychosomatic Medicine, 24*, 331–336; Wolf, S., 1958.

34. Hinkle, L.E., & Wolf, S. (1952). A summary of experimental evidence relating life stress to diabetes mellitus. *Journal of Mount Sinai Hospital, 19*(4), 537–570.

35. Wolff, H.G. (1947). Protective reaction patterns and disease. *Annals of Internal Medicine, 27*, 944–969.

36. Wolf, S., & Goodell, H. (1976). *Behavioral science in clinical medicine.* Springfield, IL: Charles C Thomas.

37. Utkin, I.A. (1960). *Theoretical and practical questions of experimental medicine and biology in monkeys.* New York: Pergamon.

38. Weiner, H., Thaler, M., Reiser, M.F., & Mirsky, I. (1957). Etiology of duodenal ulcer. *Psychosomatic Medicine, 19*(1), 1–10.

39. Grant, J.M. (1959). Studies in celiac disease. I: The interrelationship between gliadin, psychological factors and symptom formation. *Psychosomatic Medicine, 21*, 431–432.

40. Bursten, B. (1962). Psychological state and sputum eosinophilia. *Psychosomatic Medicine, 24*(6), 529–534.

41. Parens, H., McConville, B.J., & Kaplan, S.M. (1966). The prediction of illness from the response to separation. *Psychosomatic Medicine, 28*(2), 162–176.

CHAPTER 12. FROM FEELING HELPLESS TO GOING WITH THE FLOW

1. Gallagher, W. (1986, May). The dark affliction of mind and body. *Discover*, p. 73.

2. Eliot, R.S., as quoted by Wallis, C., Mehrtens, R., & Thompson, D. (1983, June 6). Stress: Can we cope? *Time*, p. 48. Eliot, director of the National Center of Preventive and Stress Medicine at St. Luke's Heart Lung Center in Phoenix, was formerly a professor of cardiology at the University of Nebraska. In his book *Is It Worth Dying For* (coauthored with D.L. Breo; Bantam Books, New York, 1984), Eliot takes the position that "most of the time you can't fight and you can't flee, but you can learn to flow" (p. 225).

3. Eliot, R.S. (1986, July). *Cognitive and behavioral stress management considerations*. Presentation at a conference on Stress and the Heart of the American College of Cardiology, Jackson Hole, Wyoming.

4. Seligman, M.E.P. (1986, March). *Helplessness and explanatory style: Risk factors for depression and disease*. Paper presented at the annual meeting of the Society of Behavioral Medicine, San Francisco.

5. Peterson, C., & Seligman, M.E.P. (1984). Causal explanations as a risk factor for depression: Theory and evidence. *Psychological Review*, *91*(3), 347–374.

6. Seligman, M.E.P., & Maier, S.F. (1967). Failure to escape traumatic shock. *Journal of Experimental Psychology*, *74*, 1–9; Overmier, J.B., & Seligman, M.E.P. (1967). Effects of inescapable shock upon subsequent escape and avoidance learning. *Journal of Comparative and Physiological Psychology*, *63*, 28–33.

7. Maier, S.F., & Seligman, M.E.P. (1976). Learned helplessness: Theory and evidence. *Journal of Experimental Psychology: General*, *105*, 3–46.

8. Abramson, L.Y., Seligman, M.E.P., & Teasdale, J.D. (1978). Learned helplessness in humans: Critique and reformulation. *Journal of Abnormal Psychology*, *87*(1), 49–74.

9. Miller, S.M., & Seligman, M.E.P. (1982). The reformulated model of helplessness and depression: Evidence and theory. In R.W.J. Neufeld (Ed.), *Psychological stress and psychopathology* (pp. 149–179). New York: McGraw-Hill.

10. Dweck, C.S. (1975). The role of expectations and attributions in the alleviation of learned helplessness. *Journal of Personality and Social Psychology*, *31*(4), 674–685.

11. Bulman, R.J., & Wortman, C.B. (1977). Attributions of blame and coping in the "real world:" Severe accident victims react to their lot. *Journal of Personality and Social Psychology*, *35*, 351–363.

12. Timko, C., & Janoff-Bulman, R. (1985). Attributions, vulnerability, and psychological adjustment: The case of breast cancer. *Health Psychology*, *4*(6), 521–544.

13. Rodin, J. (1979). Managing the stress of aging: The role of control and coping. In S. Levine & U. Holger (Eds.), *Coping and health* (pp. 171–202). New York: Plenum.

14. Lefcourt, H.M. (1973). The function of illusions of control and freedom. *American Psychologist, 28*, 417–425.

15. Langer, E.J., & Rodin, J. (1976). The effects of choice and enhanced personality for the aged: A field experience in an institutional setting. *Journal of Personality and Social Psychology, 34*, 91–98.

16. Brown, G.W., Harris, T., & Copeland, J.R. (1977). Depression and loss. *British Journal of Psychiatry, 130*, 1–18.

17. Locke, S.E., Hurst, M.W., Heisel, J.S., Kraus, L., & Williams, R.M. (1979). *Life change stress and human natural killer cell activity.* (Research report). Boston: Department of Biological Sciences and Psychosomatic Medicine, Division of Psychiatry, Boston University School of Medicine.

18. Shekelle, R.B., Raynor, W.J., Ostfeld, A.M., Garron, D.C., Bieliauskas, L.A., Liu, S.C., Maliza, C., & Paul, O. (1981). Psychological depression and 17-year risk of death from cancer. *Psychosomatic Medicine, 43*(2), 117–125; Levy, S.M., Herberman, R.B., Maluish, A.M., Schlien, B., & Lippman, M. (1985). Prognostic risk assessment in primary breast cancer by behavioral and immunological parameters. *Health Psychologist, 4*(2), 99–113.

19. Peterson, C. (1982). Learned helplessness and health psychology. *Health Psychology, 1*(2), 153–168.

20. Weiss, J.M., Glazer, H.I., Pohorecky, L.A., Bailey, W.H., & Schneider, L.H. (1979). Coping behavior and stress-induced behavioral depression: Studies of the role of brain catecholamines. In R.A. Depue (Ed.), *The psychology of the depressive disorders* (pp. 125–160). New York: Academic Press.

21. Gallagher, 1986, pp. 66–76.

22. Ahluwalia, P., Zacharko, R.M., & Anisman, H. (1985, October). *Dopamine variations associated with acute and chronic stressors.* Presentation at the annual meeting of the Society of Neuroscience, Dallas.

23. Siever, L.J., & Davis, K.L. (1985). Overview: Toward a dysregulation hypothesis of depression. *American Journal of Psychiatry, 142*(9), 1017–1031.

24. Akiskal, H.S., & McKinney, W.T. (1975). Overview of recent research in depression. *Archives of General Psychiatry, 32*, 285–305.

25. Träskman, L., Asberg, M., Bertilsson, L., & Sjöstrand, L. (1981). Monoamine metabolites in CSF and suicidal behavior. *Archives of General Psychiatry, 38*, 631–636; Ballenger, J.C., Goodwin, F.K., Major, L.F., & Brown, G.L. (1979). Alcohol and central serotonin metabolism in man. *Archives of General Psychiatry, 224*–227; Murphy, D.L., Campbell, I. & Costa, J.L. (1978). Current status of the indoleamine hypothesis of the affective disorders. In M.A. Lipton, A. DiMascio & K.F. Killam (Eds.), *Psychopharmacology: A generation of progress* (pp. 1235–1247). New York: Raven Press.

26. Rosenthal, N.E., Davenport, Y., Cowdry, R.W., Webster, M.H., & Goodwin, F.K. (1980). Monoamine metabolites in cerebrospinal fluid of depressive subgroups. *Psychiatry Research, 2,* 113–119.

27. Fischette, C.T., Biegon, A., & McEwen, B.S. (1983). Sex differences in Serotonin 1 receptor binding in rat brain. *Science, 222*(4621), 333–335.

28. Nadi, N.S., Nurnberger, J.I., & Gershon, E.S. (1984). Muscarinic cholinergic receptors on skin fibroblasts in familial affective disorder. *New England Journal of Medicine, 311*(4), 225–230.

29. Murphy, Campbell, & Costa, 1978; Levine, J. (Speaker). (1981). *Pain, placebos and endorphins* (Series on the Healing Brain Cassette Recording No. 6). Los Altos, CA: Institute for the Advancement of Human Knowledge.

30. Wender, P.H., & Klein, D.F. (1981). *Mind, mood & medicine: A guide to the new biopsychiatry.* New York: Meridian.

31. Rush, A.J., Beck, A.T., Kovacs, M., Weissenburger, J., & Hollon, S.D. (1982). Comparison of the effects of cognitive therapy and pharmacotherapy on hopelessness and self-concept. *American Journal of Psychiatry, 139*(7), 862–866.

32. Bower, B. (1986, May 24). Treating depression: Can we talk? *Science News,* p. 324.

33. Paul, S., as quoted by Gallagher, W. (1986, May). The dark affliction of mind and body. *Discover,* p. 76.

34. Burns, D. (1980). *Feeling good: The new mood therapy.* New York: William Morrow.

35. Carroll, B.J. (1972). Control of plasma cortisol levels in depression: Studies with the dexamethasone suppression test. In B. Davies, B.J. Carroll & R. Mowbray (Eds.), *Depressive illness: Some research studies* (pp. 87–148). Springfield, IL: Charles C Thomas.

36. Callen, K.E. (1983). Mental and emotional aspects of long-distance running. *Psychosomatics, 24,* 133–151.

37. Hayden, R.M. (1984, August). *Physical fitness and mental health: Causal connection or simply correlation.* Paper presented at the annual meeting of the American Psychological Association, Toronto.

38. Wurtman, R.J. (1982). Nutrients that modify brain function. *Scientific American, 246*(4), pp. 50–59.

39. Sabelli, H.C., Fawcett, J., Gusovsky, F., Javaid, J., Edwards, J., & Jeffriess, H. (1983). Urinary phenyl acetate: A diagnostic test for depression? *Science, 220*(4602), 1187–1188.

40. Kolata, G.B. (1981). Clinical trial of psychotherapies is under way. *Science, 212*(4493), 432–433.

41. Neufeld, R.W., & Mothersill, K.J. (1980). Stress as an irritant of psychopathology. In I.G. Sarason & C.D. Spielberger (Eds.), *Stress and anxiety* (Vol. 7, p. 43). Washington: Hemisphere.

42. McClelland, D.C. (1976). Sources of stress in the drive for power. In G. Serban (Ed.), *Psychopathology of human adaptation* (pp. 247–270). New York: Plenum.

43. Burchfield, S.R., Hamilton, K.L., & Banks, K.L. Affiliative needs, interpersonal stress and symptomatology. *Journal of Human Stress, 8*(1), 5–9.

44. McClelland, D.C., Floor, E., Davidson, R.J., & Saron, C. (1980). Stressed power motivation, sympathetic activation, immune function, and illness. *Journal of Human Stress, 6*(2), 11–19.

45. McClelland, D.C., Ross, G., & Patel, V. (1985). The effect of an academic examination on salivary norepinephrine and immunoglobulin levels. *Journal of Human Stress, 11*(2), 52–59.

46. Jemmott, J.B. III, Borysenko, J.Z., Borysenko, M., McClelland, D.C., Chapman, R., Meyer, D., & Benson, H. (1983). Academic stress, power motivation, and decrease in secretion rate of salivary secretory immunoglobulin A. *Lancet, 1*(8339), 1400–1402.

47. Ellis, A. (1973). Rational-emotive therapy. In R. Corsini (Ed.), *Current psychotherapies* (pp. 167–206). Itasca, IL: Peacock.

48. Suls, J., & Mullen, B. (1981). Life events, perceived control and illness: The role of uncertainty. *Journal of Human Stress, 7*(2), 30–34.

49. Niebuhr, R., as quoted by Suls & Mullen, ibid., p. 30.

CHAPTER 13. LOVE OPTIMISM AND HEALING

1. Mack, R. (1984). Occasional notes: Lessons from living with cancer. *New England Journal of Medicine, 311*(25), pp. 1642–1643. Mack, a "hard-driving" 50–year-old surgeon at Swedish Hospital Medical Center in Seattle, was operated on for lung cancer in April 1979. He continued to be active at his hospital and was elected chief of the medical staff while he reset personal priorities and brought more love, joy and satisfaction into his life. Robert Mack died in his sleep in December 1985, listening to the imagery tapes he used for relaxation.

2. Siegel, B.S. (1986). *Love, medicine, & miracles.* New York: Harper & Row, p. 181. A pediatric and general surgeon in New Haven, Connecticut, Siegel is an assistant clinical professor of surgery at Yale Medical School.

3. King Solomon. Proverbs, 17:22. *The Bible: Revised Standard Version.* New York: American Bible Society, 1971.

4. Sobel, D.S. (Speaker). (1984). *Mind-made health: The placebo effect and the intrinsic healing systems of the body* (Series on the Healing Brain Cassette Recording No. T530). Los Altos, CA: Institute for the Study of Human Knowledge.

5. McClelland, D.C. (1985, March). *Motivation and immune function in health and disease.* Paper presented at the meeting of the Society of Behavioral Medicine, New Orleans.

6. Borysenko, J.Z. (1985). Healing motives: An interview with David C. McClelland. *Advances, 2*(2), pp. 29–41.

7. Ibid., p. 36.

8. McClelland, D.C., Alexander, C., & Marks, E. (1982). The need for power, stress, immune function, and illness among male prisoners. *Journal of Abnormal Psychology*, *91*(1), 61–70.

9. Siegel, 1986.

10. Borysenko, 1985, p. 38.

11. Siegel, 1986, p. 186.

12. Minkler, M. (Speaker). (1983). *Social networks and health: People need people* (Series on the Healing Brain Cassette Recording No. T57). Los Altos, CA: Institute for Study of Human Knowledge; Angier, N. (1983, August). Four-legged therapists. *Discover*, pp. 86–89.

13. Horn, J., & Meer, J. (1984, August). The pleasure of their company. *Psychology Today*, pp. 52–57; Dolan, M. (1980, April 10). Home Rx—wet nose, soft fur, and wagging tail. *Nursing Times, 76*, p. 628; Kidd, A.H., & Feldman, B.M. (1981). Pet ownership and self-perceptions of older people. *Psychological Reports, 48*, 867–875.

14. Rodin, J. (1979). Managing the stress of aging: The role of control and coping. In S. Levine & U. Holger (Eds.), *Coping and health* (pp. 171–202). New York: Plenum.

15. Nerem, R.M., Levesque, M.J., & Cornhill, J.F. (1980). Social environment as a factor in diet-induced atherosclerosis. *Science, 208*(4452), 1475–1476.

16. Whitcher, S.J., & Fisher, J.D. (1979). Multidimensional reaction to therapeutic touch in a hospital setting. *Journal of Personality and Social Psychology, 37*(1), 87–96.

17. Glaser, R., Kiecolt-Glaser, J., George, J.M., Speicher, C.E., & Holliday, J.E. (1984, May). *Stress, loneliness, and herpesvirus latency*. Paper presented at the meeting of the Society of Behavioral Medicine, Philadelphia.

18. Diamond, M.C. (1976). Anatomical brain changes induced by environment. In L. Petrinovich & J.L. McGaugh (Eds.), *Knowing, thinking, and believing* (pp. 215–241). New York: Plenum; Diamond, M.C., Connor, J.R., Orenberg, E.K., Bissell, M., Yost, M., & Krueger, A. (1980). Environmental influences on serotonin and cyclic nucleotides in rat cerebral cortex. *Science, 210*(4470), 652–654; Diamond, M. (Speaker). (1983). *How the brain grows in response to experience* (Series on the Healing Brain Cassette Recording No. T55). Los Altos, CA: Institute for the Study of Human Knowledge.

19. Hopson, J.L. (1984, November). PT conversation with Marian Diamond: A love affair with the brain. *Psychology Today*, p. 70.

20. Rosch, P.J. (1986). *Stress, Type A behavior and coronary heart disease: What's the bottom line?* Manuscript submitted for publication.

21. Selye, H. (1976). *The stress of life* (rev. ed.). New York: McGraw-Hill.

22. Dubos, R. (Speaker). (1981). *Self-healing* (Healing Brain Series Cassette Recording No. 15). Los Altos, CA: Institute for the Study of Human Knowledge.

23. Kandel, E.R., & Schwartz, J.H. (1982). Molecular biology of learning: Modulation of transmitter release. *Science, 218*(4571), 433–443.

24. Lavigne, M. (1983, December). The secret mind of the brain. *Columbia Magazine*, pp. 12–17.

25. Maslow, A. (1971). *The farther reaches of human nature*. New York: Viking.

26. Ulrich, R.S. (1981). Natural versus urban scenes: Some psychophysiological effects. *Environment and Behavior, 13*(5), 523–556; Ulrich, R.S. (1979). Visual landscapes and psychological well-being. *Landscape Research, 4*, 17–23.

27. Ulrich, R.S. (1984). View through a window may influence recovery from surgery. *Science, 224*(4647), 420–421.

28. O'Regan, B. (1985, March). Positive emotions: The emerging science of feelings. Report on a conference on "How might positive emotions affect physical health?" (pp. 5–6, 15–18). New York: Institute for the Advancement of Health.

29. Zajonc, R.B. (1985). Emotion and facial efference: A theory reclaimed. *Science, 228*(4695), 15–21.

30. Siegman, A.W., & Feldstein, S. (1985, March). *The relationship of expressive vocal behavior and severity of coronary artery disease*. Paper presented at the meeting of the Society of Behavioral Medicine, New Orleans.

31. Williams, R. (1985, March). *Approaches to alteration of Type A behavior pattern*. Discussion presented at the meeting of the Society of Behavioral Medicine, New Orleans.

32. Langer, E.J., Janis, I.L., & Wolfer, J.A. (1975). Reduction of psychological stress in surgical patients. *Journal of Experimental Social Psychology, 11*, 155–165.

33. Eastman, P. (1985, July 23). How to live a long life: Psychological vs. physiological aspects of growing old. *Houston Post*, pp. 5B, 8B.

34. Ibid., p. 8B.

35. Gottschalk, L.A. (1985). Hope and other deterrents to illness. *American Journal of Psychotherapy, 39*(4), 515–524.

36. Gottschalk, L.A. (1979). *The content analysis of verbal behavior: Further studies*. New York: Spectrum; Locke, S.E., & Colligan, D. (1986, March). Mind cures. *Omni*, pp. 51–54, 112–114.

37. Scheier, M.F., & Carver, C.S. (1985). Optimism, coping, and health: Assessment and implications of generalized outcome expectancies. *Health Psychology, 4*(3), 219–247.

38. Mossey, J.A., & Shapiro, E. (1982). Self-rated health: A predictor of mortality among the elderly. *American Journal of Public Health, 72*(8), 800–808.

39. Kaplan, G.A., & Camacho, T. (1983). Perceived health and mortality: A nine-year follow-up of the Human Population Laboratory cohort. *American Journal of Epidemiology, 117*(3), 292–304.

40. Vaillant, G.E. (1979). Natural history of male psychologic health: Effects of mental health on physical health. *New England Journal of Medicine, 301*(23), 1249–1254.

41. Kobasa, S.C., Maddi, S.R., & Courington, S. (1981). Personality and constitution as mediators in the stress-illness relationship. *Journal of Health and Social Behavior, 22,* 368–378.

42. Mason, R.C., Clark, G., Reeves, R.B., & Wagner, S.B. (1969). Acceptance and healing. *Journal of Religion and Health, 8,* 123–142.

43. Drake, R., as quoted in *Brain/Mind Bulletin* (1984, November 19). Power of beliefs, optimism tied to hemispheres, p. 1.

44. Palmore, E. (1969). Predicting longevity: A follow-up controlling for age. *Gerontologist, 9,* 247–250.

45. Hinkle, L.E. (1961). Ecological observations of the relation of physical illness, mental illness, and the social environment. *Psychosomatic Medicine, 23*(4), 289–296.

46. Kiecolt-Glaser, J. (1986, March). *Clinical psychoneuroimmunology in health and disease: Effects of marital quality and disruption.* Paper presented at the annual meeting of the Society of Behavioral Medicine, San Francisco.

47. Medalie, J.H., & Goldbourt, U. (1976). Angina pectoris among 10,000 men, II: Psychosocial and other risk factors. *American Journal of Medicine, 60,* 910–921.

48. Shaver, P., & Freedman, J. (1976, Aug. 26). Your pursuit of happiness. *Psychology Today,* pp. 29, 75.

49. Ibid., pp. 29–32, 75.

50. Larson, B. (1984). *There's a lot more to health than not being sick.* Waco, TX: Word Books.

51. Ibid., p. 123.

52. Zuckerman, D.M., Kasl, S.V., & Ostfeld, A.M. (1984). Psychosocial predictors of mortality among the elderly poor. *American Journal of Epidemiology, 119*(3), 410–423.

53. Peale, N.V. (1952). *The power of positive thinking.* Englewood Cliffs, NJ: Prentice-Hall; Peale (1961). *The tough-minded optimist.* Englewood Cliffs: Prentice-Hall;

54. Schuller, R.H. (1983). *Tough times never last but tough people do.* Nashville, TN: Thomas Nelson; Schuller (1977). *Daily power thoughts.* Old Tappan, NJ: Spire Books.

55. Brooks, C.H. (1922). *The practice of autosuggestion by the methods of Émile Coué* (rev. ed.). New York: Dodd, Mead.

56. Cousins, N. (1976). Anatomy of an illness (as perceived by the patient). *New England Journal of Medicine, 295*(26), 1458–1463.

57. Cousins, N. (1983). *The healing heart.* New York: Norton.

58. Cousins, N. (1979). *Anatomy of an illness as perceived by the patient.* New York: Norton.

59. Martin, R.A., & Lefcourt, H.M. (1983). Sense of humor as a moderator of the relation between stressors and moods. *Journal of Personality and Social Psychology, 45*(6), 1313–1324.

60. Dillon, K.M., Minchoff, B., & Baker, K.H. (1985-86). Positive emo-

tional states and enhancement of the immune system. *International Journal of Psychiatry in Medicine, 15*(1), 13–18.

61. Levi, L. (1965). The urinary output of adrenalin and noradrenalin during pleasant and unpleasant emotional states. *Psychosomatic Medicine, 27*, 80–85.

62. Laughing toward longevity. (1985, June). *University of California, Berkeley Wellness Letter*, p. 1.

63. Fry, W.F. Jr., & Stoft, P.E. (1971). Mirth and oxygen saturation levels of peripheral blood. *Psychotherapy and Psychosomatics, 19*, 76–84.

64. Freud, S. (1959). Humour. In J. Strachey (Ed.), *Collected papers of Sigmund Freud* (Vol. 5, p. 217). New York: Basic Books.

65. Koestler, A. (1964). *The act of creation*. London: Hutchinson; O'Connell, W.E. (1976). Freudian humour: The eupsychia of everyday life. In A.J. Chapman & H. Foot (Eds.), *Humour and laughter: Theory, research, and applications* (pp. 313–329). London: Wiley.

66. Moody, R.A. Jr. (1978). *Laugh after laugh: The healing power of humor*. Jacksonville, FL: Headwaters Press.

CHAPTER 14. WHAT FAITH DOES
FOR PATIENTS AND DOCTORS

1. Blau, J.N. (1985). Clinician and placebo [Letter to editor]. *Lancet, 1*(8424), p. 344. Blau, on the staff of the National Hospital for Nervous Diseases in London, explained he had become "supersaturated by the denigrating remarks about doctors helping patients other than through tablets." He said he was wrong about the anesthetist having no need for eliciting placebo responses. "He visits patients the night before an operation and, if he gains rapport, confidence and trust, knows that he will give less anaesthetic the next day."

2. Schweitzer, A., as quoted in introduction to Norman Cousins' invited address, *New dimensions in healing*, at the annual meeting of the American Psychological Association, August 1985, Los Angeles. A medical missionary, theologian and organist who attracted worldwide attention for developing medical facilities in Gabon (then in French Equatorial Africa), Schweitzer won the Nobel Peace Prize in 1952.

3. Achterberg, J. (1985). *Imagery in healing: Shamanism and modern medicine*. Boston: New Science Library, p. 85.

4. Beecher, H.K. (1955). The powerful placebo. *Journal of the American Medical Association, 159*(17), 1602–1606; Benson, H., & Epstein, M.D. (1975). The placebo effect: A neglected asset in the care of patients. *JAMA, 232*(12), 1225–1227; Brody, H. (1977). *Placebos and the philosophy of medicine*. Chicago: University of Chicago Press; Wolf, S. (1959). The pharmacology of placebos. *Pharmacological Reviews, 11*, 689–704.

5. Agras, W.S., Chesney, M.A., Ader, R., Jacobs, R.G., & Hovell, M. (1986, March). *The enigmatic placebo response: Lessons from hypertension*

research. Symposium presented at the annual meeting of the Society of Behavioral Medicine, San Francisco.

6. Frank, J.D. (1973). Persuasion and healing (rev. ed.). Baltimore: Johns Hopkins University Press.

7. Wolf, S., 1959, p. 689.

8. Cousins, N. (1981). *Human options*. New York: Norton, pp. 19–20.

9. Shapiro, A.K. (1959). The placebo effect in the history of medical treatment: Implications for psychiatry. *American Journal of Psychiatry, 116*, 298–304.

10. Weil, A. (1983). *Health and healing*. Boston: Houghton Mifflin.

11. Achterberg, 1985.

12. Lipkin, M. (1984). Suggestion and healing. *Perspectives in Biology and Medicine, 28*(1), 121–126.

13. Modell, W. (1955). *The relief of symptoms*. Philadelphia: Saunders.

14. Goodwin, J.S., Goodwin, J.M., & Vogel, A.V. (1979). Knowledge and use of placebos by house officers and nurses. *Annals of Internal Medicine, 91*, 106–110.

15. Frank, J.D. (1975). The faith that heals. *Johns Hopkins Medical Journal, 137*, 127–131.

16. Gowdey, C.W. (1983). A guide to the pharmacology of placebos. *Canadian Medical Association Journal, 128*, 921–925.

17. Pepper, O.H.P. (1945). A note on the placebo. *American Journal of Pharmacy, 117*, 409–412.

18. Frank, J.D. (1975). Psychotherapy of bodily disease. *Psychotherapy and Psychosomatics, 26*(4), 192–202.

19. Adler, H.M., & Hammett, V.B.O. (1973). The doctor-patient relationship revisited: An analysis of the placebo effect. *Annals of Internal Medicine, 78*, 595–598.

20. Perry, S.W. III, & Heidrich, G. (1981). Placebo response: Myth and matter. *American Journal of Nursing, 81*(4), 720–725.

21. Shapiro, 1959, p. 300.

22. Beck, F.M. (1977). Placebos in dentistry: Their profound potential effects. *Journal of the American Dental Association, 95*, 1122–1136.

23. Weil, 1983, p. 265.

24. Benson, H., & McCallie, D.P. (1979). Angina pectoris and the placebo effect. *New England Journal of Medicine, 300*(25), 1424–1429.

25. Diamond, E.G., Kittle, C.F., & Crockett, J.E. (1958). Evaluation of internal mammary artery ligation and sham procedure in angina pectoris. *Circulation, 18*, 712–713; Cobb, L.A., Thomas, G.I., Dillard, D.H., Merendino, K.A., & Bruce, R.A. (1959). An evaluation of internal-mammary-artery ligation by a double-blind technic. *New England Journal of Medicine, 260*(2), 1115–1118.

26. Benson & McCallie, 1979, p. 1426.

27. Frank, 1975, p. 192; National Cooperative Study Group (1976). Un-

stable angina pectoris: To compare medical and surgical therapy. *American Journal of Cardiology, 37*, 896–902.

28. Thomsen, J., Bretlau, P., Tos, M., & Johnsen, N.J. (1981). Placebo effect in surgery for Ménière's disease. *Archives of Otolaryngology, 107*, 271–277.

29. Thomsen, Bretlau, Tos, & Johnsen (1983). Placebo effect in surgery for Ménière's disease: Three-year follow-up. *Otolaryngology-Head and Neck Surgery, 91*, p. 183.

30. Gliedman, L.H., Gantt, W.H., & Teitelbaum, H.A. (1957). Some implications of conditioned reflex studies for placebo research. *American Journal of Psychiatry, 113*, 1102–1107.

31. Beecher, H.K. (1956). Relationship of significance of wound to pain experienced. *Journal of the American Medical Association, 161*(17), 1609–1613.

32. Wolf, 1959.

33. Blackwell, B., Bloomfield, S.S., & Buncher, C.R. (1972). Demonstration to medical students of placebo responses and non-drug factors. *Lancet, 1*(7763), 1279–1282.

34. Rehder, H. (1955). Wunderheilungen: Ein experiment. *Hippokrates, 26*, 577–580.

35. Beecher, M.M. (1986, Jan. 8). 3 cardiologists report prayers for their patients are "answered." *Medical Tribune*, pp. 3, 15.

36. Beecher, 1986, quoting Kennel and Merriman, p. 15.

37. Ader, R., & Cohen, N. (1982). Behaviorally-conditioned immuno-suppression and murine systemic lupus erythematosus. *Science, 215*(4539), 1534–1536.

38. Smith, G.R., & McDaniel, S.M. (1983). Psychologically mediated effect on the delayed hypersensitivity reaction to tuberculin in humans. *Psychosomatic Medicine, 45*(1), 65–70.

CHAPTER 15. EFFECT OF ATTITUDES
ON DRUGS AND RECOVERY

1. Eddy, M.B. (1875). *Science and health*. New York: Harper & Row, p. 155. Mary Baker Eddy, who died in 1910, was the founder of Christian Science.

2. Mendelsohn, R.S. (1979). *Confessions of a medical heretic*. New York: Warner Books, pp. 192–193. Mendelsohn is an associate professor of preventive medicine and community health at the University of Illinois School of Medicine.

3. Weil, A. (1983). *Health and healing*. Boston: Houghton Mifflin.

4. Brody, H. (1977). *Placebos and the philosophy of medicine*. Chicago: University of Chicago Press.

5. Sobel, D.S. (Speaker). (1982). *The placebo effect* (Series on the Healing Brain Cassette Recording No. 7). Los Altos, CA: Institute for the Study of Human Knowledge.

6. Ross, M., & Olson, J.M. (1981). An expectancy-attribution model of the effects of placebos. *Psychological Review, 88*(5), 408– 437.

7. Salomon, K., & Hart, R. (1978). Pitfalls and prospects in clinical research on antianxiety drugs: benzodiazepines and placebos—a research review. *Journal of Clinical Psychiatry, 39*, 823–831.

8. Shapiro, A.K., Struening, E.L., Shapiro, E., & Milcarek, B.I. (1983). Diazepam: How much better than placebo? *Journal of Psychosomatic Research, 17*(1), 51–73.

9. Wolf, S. (1959). The pharmacology of placebos. *Pharmacological Reviews, 11*, 689–704.

10. Ibid., p. 698.

11. Walker, S.H. (1953). Ineffectiveness of aureomycin in primary atypical pneumonia: A controlled study of 212 cases. *American Journal of Medicine, 15*, 593–602.

12. Brown, M.G., & Riseman, J.E.F. (1937). The comparative value of purine derivatives in the treatment of angina pectoris. *Journal of the American Medical Association, 109*(4), 256–258.

13. Evans, W., & Hoyle, C. (1933). The comparative value of drugs used in the continuous treatment of angina pectoris. *Quarterly Journal of Medicine, 2*, 311–338; LeRoy, G.V. (1941). The effectiveness of the xanthine drugs in the treatment of angina pectoris. I. Aminophylline. *Journal of the American Medical Association, 116*(10), 921–925.

14. Vogelsang, A., & Shute, E.V. (1946). Effect of vitamin E in coronary heart disease. I. The anginal syndrome. *Medical Records, 160*, 91–96.

15. Toone, W.M. (1973). Effects of vitamin E: Good and bad. *New England Journal of Medicine, 289*(18), 979–980.

16. Anderson, T.W. (1974). Vitamin E in angina pectoris. *Canadian Medical Association Journal, 110*, 401–406; Gillilan, R.E., Mondell, B., & Warbasse, J.R. (1977). Quantitative evaluation of vitamin E in the treatment of angina pectoris. *American Heart Journal, 93*, 444–449.

17. Benson, H., & McCallie, D.P. (1979). Angina pectoris and the placebo effect. *New England Journal of Medicine, 300*(25), p. 1426.

18. Weil, 1983, p. 220.

19. Ibid., p. 221.

20. Roberts, R., Croft, C., Gold, H.K., Hartwell, T.D., Jaffe, A.S., Muller, J.E., Mullin, S.M., Parker, C., Passamani, E.R., Poole, W.K., Raabe, D.S. Jr., Rude, R.E., Stone, P.H., Turi, Z.G., Sobel, B.E., Willerson, J.T., Braunwald, E., & the MILIS Study Group. (1984). Effect of propranolol on myocardial-infarct size in a randomized blinded multicenter trial. *New England Journal of Medicine, 311*(4), 218–225.

21. Klopfer, B. (1957). Psychological variables in human cancer. *Journal of Projective Techniques, 21*, 331–340.

22. Gardner, M. (1984, August). Cruel deception in the Philippines. *Discover*, p. 8.

23. Simonton, O.C., & Simonton, S.S. (1975). Belief systems and management of the emotional aspects of malignancy. *Journal of Transpersonal Psychology, 7*(1), p. 32.

24. Cousins, N., as quoted in *The Magazine* of the *Houston Post*, February 10, 1985, p. 4; Cousins, N. (1985, August). *New dimensions in healing.* Paper presented at the meeting of the American Psychological Association, Los Angeles.

25. Mendelsohn, 1979, p. 193.

26. Bennett, H.L., & Davis, H.S. (1984). Non-verbal response to intra-operative conservation. *Anesthesia and Analgesia, 63*, 185.

27. Bennett, H.L. (1984, July/August). Can intraoperative conversation affect patients' nervous systems? *Human Aspects of Anesthesia*, pp. 1,3.

28. Lown, B. (1983). Introduction. In N. Cousins, *The healing heart* (pp. 11–28). New York: Norton.

29. King Solomon. Proverbs 18:21. *The Holy Bible: New International Version.* Grand Rapids, MI: Zondervan, 1978, p. 698.

30. Penick, S.B., & Fisher, S. (1965). Drug-set interaction: Psychological and physiological effects of epinephrine under differential expectations. *Psychosomatic Medicine, 27*(2), 177–182.

31. Penick, S.B., & Hinkle, L.E. (1964). The effect of expectation on response to phenmetrazine. *Psychosomatic Medicine, 26*(4), 369– 373.

32. Agra, W.W., Horne, M., & Taylor, C.B. (1982). Expectation and blood-pressure-lowering effects of relaxation. *Psychosomatic Medicine, 44*, 389– 393.

33. Moore, D.S. (1985). *Statistics: Concepts and controversies* (2nd ed.). New York: Freeman.

34. Pihl, R.O. (1980). Stress, cognitive style and drug abuse. *Stress, 1*(2), 5–10.

35. Carlin, A.S., Bakker, C.P., Halpern, L., & Post, R.D. (1972). Social facilitation of marihuana intoxication: Impact of social set and pharmacologic activity. *Journal of Abnormal Psychology, 80*, 132–140.

36. Weil, A.T., Zinberg, N.E., & Nelsen, J.M. (1968). Clinical and psychological effects of marihuana in man. *Science, 162*(3859), 1234– 1242.

37. Phil, R.O., Segal, Z., & Shea, D. (1978). Negative expectancy as a mediating variable in marihuana intoxication. *Journal of Clinical Psychology, 34*(4), 978–982.

38. Marlatt, G.A., & Rohsenow, D.J. (1980). Cognitive processes in alcohol use: Expectancy and the balanced placebo design. In N.K. Mello (Ed.), *Advances in substance abuse* (Vol. 1). Greenwich, CT: JAI Press; Marlatt & Rohsenow. (1981, December). The think-drink effect. *Psychology Today*, pp. 60–69, 93.

39. Brown, S.A. (1984, August). *Tension reduction and social interaction: Alcohol versus expectancy effects.* Poster presented at the meeting of the American Psychological Association, Toronto.

40. Dinnerstein, A.J., & Halm, J. (1970). Modification of placebo effects by means of drugs: Effects of aspirin and placebos on self-rated moods. *Journal of Abnormal Psychology, 75*(3), 308–314.

41. Brody, H. (1977). *Placebos and the philosophy of medicine.* Chicago: University of Chicago Press; Weil, 1983.

42. Evans, F.J. (1974, April). The power of a sugar pill. *Psychology Today*, pp. 55–59; Evans. (1981). The placebo response in pain control. *Psychopharmacology Bulletin, 17*(2), 72–79.

43. Lowinger, P., & Dobie, S. (1969). What makes the placebo work? *Archives of General Psychiatry, 20*, 84–88.

44. Frank, J.D. (1974). *Persuasion and healing: A comparative study of psychotherapy* (rev. ed.). New York: Schocken Books.

45. Bok, S. (1974). The ethics of giving placebos. *Scientific American, 231*(5), p. 18.

46. Melmon, K.L., & Morrelli, H.F., *Clinical pharmacology*, as quoted by Bok, 1974, p. 18.

47. Holman, H.R. (1976). The "excellence" deception in medicine. *Hospital Practice, 11*(4), pp. 11, 18, 21.

48. Dubos, R. (1979). Introduction. In N. Cousins, *Anatomy of an illness* (pp. 11–23). New York: Norton.

49. Mason, R.C., Clark, G., Reeves, R.B., & Wagner, S.B. (1969). Acceptance and healing. *Journal of Religion and Health, 8*, 123–142.

50. Ibid., p. 140.

51. Beecher, H.K. (1955). The powerful placebo. *Journal of American Medical Association, 159*(17), 1602–1606.

52. Wolf, S. (1959). The pharmacology of placebos. *Pharmacological Reviews, 11*, 689–704.

53. Perry, S.W. III, & Heidrich, G. (1981). Placebo response: Myth and matter. *American Journal of Nursing, 81*(4), 720–725.

54. Cousins, N. (1983). *The healing heart*. New York: Norton.

55. Goodwin, J.S., Goodwin, J.M., & Vogel, A.V. (1979). Knowledge and use of placebos by house officers and nurses. *Annals of Internal Medicine, 91*, 106–110.

56. Ibid., p. 108.

57. Brody, 1977; Weil, 1983.

58. Weil, 1983, p. 210.

59. Benson, H., & Epstein, M.D. (1975). The placebo effect: A neglected asset in the care of patients. *Journal of the American Medical Association, 232*(12), 1225–1227.

60. Evans, F.J. (1974). The placebo response in pain reduction. In J.J. Bonica (Ed.), *Advances in neurology* (Vol. 4). New York: Raven Press.

61. Ross, M., & Olson, J.M. (1982). Placebo effects in medical research and practice. In J.R. Eiser (Ed.), *Social psychology and behavioral medicine* (pp. 441–458). Chichester, England: Wiley.

62. Weil, 1983, p. 217.

63. Prioleau, L., Murdock, M., & Brody, N. (1983). An analysis of psychotherapy versus placebo studies. *Behavioral and brain sciences, 6*(2), 275–310.

64. Brody, 1977; London, P., & Engstrom, D. (1982, September/October). Mind over pain. *American Health*, pp. 62–67.

377

65. Park, L.C., & Covi, L. (1965). Nonblind placebo trial. *Archives of General Psychiatry, 12*, 336–345.

66. Agras, W.S., Chesney, M.A., Ader, R., Jacob, R.G., & Hovell, M. (1986, March). *The enigmatic placebo response: Lessons from hypertension research.* Symposium at the annual meeting of the Society of Behavioral Medicine, San Francisco.

CHAPTER 16. TURNING ON OUR SELF-HEALER

1. Joy, W.B. (1979). *Joy's way.* Los Angeles: J.P. Tarcher, p. 129. An internist specializing in lung and heart diseases, Joy left the practice of orthodox medicine at age 34 to lecture and write on "the transformational process."

2. Eliot, R.S. (1986, July). *Cognitive and behavioral stress management considerations.* Presentation at a conference on Stress and the Heart of the American College of Cardiology, Jackson Hole, Wyoming.

3. Anderson, E.A., Moyers, J.R., & Johnson, A.K. (1985, March). *Psychological preparation for cardiac surgery, recovery, and acute postoperative hypertension.* Paper presented at the meeting of the Society of Behavioral Medicine, New Orleans.

4. Langer, E.J., Janis, I.L., & Wolfer, J.A. (1975). Reduction of psychological stress in surgical patients. *Journal of Experimental Social Psychology, 11*, 155–165.

5. Melamed, B.G., & Siegel, L.J. (1975). Reduction of anxiety in children facing hospitalization and surgery by use of filmed modeling. *Journal of Consulting and Clinical Psychology, 43*, 511–521.

6. Wallace, L.M. (1984). Psychological preparation as a method of reducing the stress of surgery. *Journal of Human Stress, 10*(2), 62–77.

7. Gravelle, K. (1985). Can a feeling of capability reduce arthritis pain? *Advances, 2*(3), pp. 8–13.

8. Bandura, A. (1986, March). *Perceived self-efficacy and health functioning.* Paper presented at the annual meeting of the Society of Behavioral Medicine, San Francisco.

9. London, P., & Engstrom, D. (1982, September/October). Mind over pain. *American Health*, pp. 62–67.

10. London & Engstrom, 1982, p. 67.

11. Bowers, K.S., & Kelly, P. (1979). Stress, disease, psychotherapy, and hypnosis. *Journal of Abnormal Psychology, 88*(5), 490–505.

12. Black, S. (1969). *Mind and body.* London: William Kimber.

13. Collison, D.A. (1975). Which asthmatic patients should be treated by hypnotherapy. *Medical Journal of Australia, 1*, 776–781.

14. Cedercreutz, C. (1978). Hypnotic treatment of 100 cases of migraine. In F.H. Frankel & H.S. Zamansky (Eds.), *Hypnosis at its bicentennial* (pp. 255–259). New York: Plenum.

15. Mason, A.A. (1952). A case of congenital Ichthyosiform Erythrodermia of Brocq treated by hypnosis. *British Medical Journal, 2*, 422–423.

16. Barber, T.X. (1984). Changing "unchangeable" bodily processes by (hypnotic) suggestions: A new look at hypnosis, cognitions, imagining, and the mind-body problem. In A.A. Sheikh (Ed.), *Imagination and healing* (pp. 69–127). Farmingdale, NY: Baywood.

17. Black, S., Humphrey, J.H., & Niven, J.S. (1963). Inhibition of Mantoux reaction by direct suggestion under hypnosis. *British Medical Journal, 1*, 1649–1652.

18. Hall, H.R. (1982-83). Hypnosis and the immune system: A review with implications for cancer and the psychology of healing. *Journal of Clinical Hypnosis, 25*(2-3), 92–103.

19. Sachar, E.J., Fishman, J.R., & Mason, J.W. (1965). Influences of the hypnotic trance on plasma 17-hydroxycorticosteroid concentration. *Psychosomatic Medicine, 27*, 330–341.

20. Drutz, D.J., & Mills, J. (1982). Immunity and infection. In D.P. Stites, J.D. Stobo, H.H. Fudenberg, & J.V. Wells (Eds.). *Basic & clinical immunology* (pp. 209–232). Los Altos, CA: Lange.

21. Thomas, L. (1979). *The medusa and the snail.* New York: Viking, p. 81.

22. Siegel, B.S. (1986). *Love, medicine & miracles.* New York: Harper & Row.

23. Nash, M., & Baker, E. (1984, February). Trance encounters: Susceptibility to hypnosis. *Psychology Today*, pp. 72–73.

24. Bentler, P.M., O'Hara, J.W., & Krasner, L. (1963). Hypnosis and placebo. *Psychological Reports, 12*, 153–154.

25. Bowers & Kelly, 1979, p. 500.

26. Green, E., & Green, A. (1975). *Beyond biofeedback.* New York: Delta.

27. Achterberg, J. (1985). *Imagery in healing: Shamanism and modern medicine.* Boston: New Science Library.

28. Schwartz, G.E. (1984). Psychophysiology of imagery and healing: A systems perspective. In A.A. Sheikh (Ed.), *Imagination and healing* (pp. 35–50). Farmingdale, NY: Baywood.

29. Ley, R.G., & Freeman, R.J. (1984). Imagery, cerebral laterality, and the healing process. In A.A. Sheikh (Ed.), *Imagination and healing* (pp. 51–67). Farmingdale, NY: Baywood.

30. Achterberg, J., Lawlis, G.F., Simonton, O.C., & Simonton, S. (1977). Psychological factors and blood chemistries as disease outcome predictors for cancer patients. *Multivariate Experimental Clinical Research, 3*, 107–122.

31. Levine, J. (Speaker). (1981). *Pain, placebos and endorphins* (Series on the Healing Brain Cassette Recording No. 6). Los Altos, CA: Institute for the Advancement of Human Knowledge.

32. Fields, H.L. (1984). Neurophysiology of pain and pain modulation. *American Journal of Medicine, 77*(3A), 2–8.

33. Levine, J.D., Gordon, N.C., & Fields, H.L. (1978). The mechanisms of placebo analgesia. *Lancet, 2*(8091), 654–657.

34. Goldstein, A., & Grevert, P. (1978). Placebo analgesia, endorphins, and naloxone. *Lancet, 2*(8204/5), 1385.

35. Fields, H.L., & Levine, J.D. (1981). Biology of placebo analgesia. *American Journal of Medicine, 70*(4), 745–746; Grunbaum, A. (1981). The placebo concept. *Behavioral Research and Therapy, 19*, 157–167.

36. Friedman, R. (1986). Nature's link between pleasure and pain. *Stanford Medicine, 3*(3), pp. 29–32.

37. Rosch, P.J. (1986). *Stress, Type A behavior and coronary heart disease: What's the bottom line?* Manuscript submitted for publication.

38. Benson, H., with Klipper, M.Z. (1975). *The relaxation response.* New York: William Morrow.

39. Eliot, R.S. (1986, July). *The importance of measuring psychosocial stress.* Presentation at a conference on Stress and the Heart of the American College of Cardiology, Jackson Hole, Wyoming.

40. Rodin, J. (1979). Managing the stress of aging: The role of control and coping. In S. Levine & U. Holger (Eds.), *Coping and health* (pp. 171–202). New York: Plenum.

41. Cousins, N. (1979). *The anatomy of an illness.* New York: Norton.

42. Meichenbaum, D., & Jerembko, M.E. (Eds.). (1983). *Stress reduction and prevention.* New York: Plenum.

43. Cousins, 1979, p. 56.

44. Eliot, R.S. (Speaker). (1985). *The importance of clarifying your values and developing positive self-talks* (Series on "It's Not Worth Dying For" Cassette Recording No. 2A). Paradise Valley, AZ: Health Research Associates.

St. Martin's Press: a passage from *Joy's Way*, by W. Brugh Joy, copyright © 1979 by W. Brugh Joy, Jeremy P. Tarcher, Inc.

Science Digest: a brief excerpt from "Lunching to Win!" by Andrew C. Revkin, quoted from *Science Digest*, copyright © 1985 by the Hearst Corporation. All rights reserved.

Scientific American: a short segment from "The Ethics of Giving Placebos," by Sissela Bok, vol. 231, 1974.

Scribner's: a stanza from "Richard Cory," a poem by Edwin Arlington Robinson now in the public domain. Original publisher was Charles Scribner's Sons, 1897.

Shambhala: a few lines from *Imagery in Healing: Shamanism and Modern Medicine*, by Jeanne Achterberg, copyright © 1985. Reprinted by arrangement with Shambhala Publications, Inc., Boston.

Wiley: a brief excerpt from "Specificity in Stress Models: Examples Drawn from Type A Behaviour," by Margaret A. Chesney and Ray H. Rosenman, in C.L. Cooper, ed., *Stress Research*, copyright 1984, John Wiley & Sons, Ltd.

Word Books: a sentence from *The Be-Happy Attitudes*, by Robert H. Schuller, copyright © 1985 by Robert H. Schuller. Used by permission of Word Books, Publisher, Waco, Texas.

Word Books: two excerpts from *There's A Lot More to Health Than Not Being Sick* by Bruce Larson, copyright © 1981, 1984. Used by permission of Word Books, Publisher, Waco, Texas.

Finally, I wish most of all to acknowledge Joan Stoliar, whose time and talent, knowledge and experience have played a vital part in making this book a reality.

Index

and hopelessness, 237
and natural killer cells, 231
good and bad, 230, 235
of cause, 229
of the elderly, 236
Aureomycin, 289
Australia, 189
Autoimmunities, 76, 285
Autonomic nervous system, 90,
192, 218, 294, 319, 324
Autoradiography, 98
Awfulizing, 60, 101
(*see also* "Catastrophizing")

B-cells, 75
and bereavement, 188
and stress hormones, 250
depressed by faulty coping, 75, 159
(*see also* Leukocytes and
Lymphocytes)
Bacteria, 29, 35, 77, 86, 188
activated by negative moods, 38,
157
(*see also* Germs and Microbes)
Baltimore, 163
Bantu natives, 44
Barbiturate, 102
Baseball Hall of Fame, 230
Beaber, Rex Julian, 51
Beauty, 262, 326
Beck, Aaron, 244
Bedouins, 44
Beecher, Henry, 281
Behavior, 30, 246
and brain, 100
and cancer, 22, 236
and illness, 20, 62, 80, 171
influenced by suggestion, 276
"Behavioral sinks," 50
Beliefs
and control, 61, 144, 309
and health, 23, 287
and illness, 13, 53, 143, 154
and "needs," 154
as key to placebos, 275
as key to self-healing systems,
287, 313
in self-efficacy, 144, 312

Ben Gurion University, 136
Bennett, Henry, 294
Benson, Herbert, 290
Benzodiazepines, 123
Bereavement
and impaired immunity, 188
and mortality rates, 189
Beta-blockers, 290–291, 306
Beta-endorphins, 117–119, 121
(*see also* Endorphins)
Beth Israel Hospital, 290
Bettelheim, Bruno, 205
Binge eating, 108, 117
Biofeedback
and enhancing immunity, 321
and warming hands, 319
Biogenic amines, 100, 104
Biological mechanism, 17, 91
Biological psychology, 13
Biology, 16
Biopsychosocial concept, 28, 31
Blood-brain barrier, 114
Blood flow, 52, 316, 319
Blood glucose, 80, 93, 222, 296
Blood pressure, 54, 78, 93, 218
after bypass surgery, 309
and caring effect, 258
and pets, 136
and placebo response, 280,
282–283, 298, 307
and power needs, 249
effects of expectations on, 296
effects of imagery on, 319
in presence of physician, 138–
139
lowering of, 110, 136, 280
monitoring of, 307
Blood test, 165
Blood vessels, 78
Body
relationship with mind, 13–14,
16–17, 19, 188, 256
system of checks and balances,
324
Borysenko, Joan, 159
Boston, 146, 249
Boston University School of Medicine, 36
Bourne, Peter, 73
Boyce, Thomas, 62, 129

and giving up, 221
and influence on serotonin, 242
decrease after relaxation, 158
elevation of, 102, 158, 246
Coué, Émile, 268
Courage, 187, 252, 309
Cousins, Norman, 269, 271, 293, 326
Crime, 42, 50
Criticism, 211, 249
Crowding, 148–149
Cultural lag, 48
Cures, 31, 274, 317–318, 322
Curse, 198–199
Cyclophosphamide, 285
Cynicism, 16, 53, 78, 267
Cystic fibrosis, 29
Cytomegalovirus, 169

Darvon, 291, 306
DBI peptide, 123
Deafness, 279
Death
　apprehension of, 200
　frightened to, 199
　from cancer, 21, 206
　from giving up, 201, 206
　from grief, 194, 207
　postponement of, 23, 191
　predilection to, 197
　rates, 42–43, 189–190, 239
　sudden, 193–194
　voodoo, 198–199
Deceit, 277, 307
Dendrites, 99, 259
Denmark
　surgical study, 279
Dental caries, 158
Dental students, 250
Deoxyribonucleic acid (DNA)
　recombinant, 21
　repair system, 19, 79
Depression, 97, 195, 247
　and brain chemistry, 100–101, 244, 245
　and catecholamines, 91, 100, 247
　and causal attributions, 230

and clinical trials, 244, 247
and cognitive distortions, 245
and diet, 107, 115, 247
and external control, 143–144
and genital herpes, 157
and lack of support, 239
and learned helplessness, 231
and lower NK cell activity, 74, 239
and neurotransmitters, 88, 100, 102, 243, 246–247
and physical exercise, 246–247
effect on T-cells, 157
in combat units, 73
in women vs. men, 239, 242
modes of therapy for, 243–244, 246
preceding sudden death, 195, 220
Desipramine, 100
Despair, 207, 240
Detached retina, 301
Diabetes, 46, 92, 159, 222, 224
Diagnosis, 15–16, 103, 241, 284
Diamond, Marian, 259
Diarrhea, 220, 223
Diastolic blood pressure, 139
　(see also Blood pressure)
Diazepam (see Valium)
Diet, 107
　and cancer, 22
　and depression, 112, 115
　pills, 296
　(see also Nutrition)
Dimsdale, Joel, 70
Disregulation
　of central nervous system, 13
　of hypothalamus-pituitary-adrenal system, 101–102
　of neurotransmitters, 88, 101, 115, 241, 246
Dissatisfaction
　and more symptoms, 176
　at work, 178–179, 181
　in life, 181
Dissociation, 318
Dizziness, 179, 279, 298, 303
DNA (see Deoxyribonucleic acid)
Doom-and-gloom, 185, 320
　(see also "Catastrophizing")

Widowed, 137, 188–190, 196
Wilson, Ian, 194
Wives
  and support, 131–134, 137
Wolf, Stewart, 33, 68, 182, 204,
  222–224, 281
Wolff, Harold, 222
Women
  and death, 39
  and expected effects of alcohol,
    298
  and pregnancy, 133
  and psychological hardiness, 60
  reaction to carbohydrates and
    proteins, 109
  recovery from surgery, 258, 311
Words
  effect on physiological pro-
    cesses, 315

Work stress, 176
  and illness, 178–180
  and physical factors, 180
  and women, 177–178
Working women, 176–178
  Mexican-American, 177
World War II, 281
Wurtman, Judith, 116
Wurtman, Richard, 108, 110, 111,
  113

Yale-New Haven Hospital, 310
Yale Medical School, 36
Yale University, 154
Yom Kippur, 71, 203

About the Author

BLAIR JUSTICE, Ph.D., Rice University, was an award-winning medical writer and science editor for metropolitan newspapers before becoming a psychologist. He teaches courses on the biopsychosocial bases of mental and physical health and on stress, coping, and illness at the University of Texas Health Science Center in Houston, where he is a professor of psychology in the School of Public Health. The author of more than 50 journal articles and chapters and three books, Dr. Justice is a life member of the National Association of Science Writers and belongs to the Society of Behavioral Medicine.